THE
ITINERANT
COACH

THE
ITINERANT
COACH

THE FOOTBALLING LIFE AND TIMES OF
STEVE DARBY

ANTONY SUTTON

FAIRPLAY
PUBLISHING

First published in 2021 by Fair Play Publishing
PO Box 4101, Balgowlah Heights, NSW 2093, Australia
www.fairplaypublishing.com.au

ISBN: 978-1-925914-25-2
ISBN: 978-1-925914-26-0 (ePub)

Cover design by Nada Orlic
Interior by Leslie Priestley

All inquiries should be made to the Publisher via
sales@fairplaypublishing.com.au

A catalogue record of this book is available from the
National Library of Australia.

NATIONAL
LIBRARY
OF AUSTRALIA

CONTENTS

Preface

I have coached in World Cup games and in cup finals in front of 100,000 fans, but the only time I got that tightening feeling in my stomach again was when I was being a dad, watching my daughter play in a school cup final on a pitch in Hanoi, Vietnam. A corner came across; she volleyed the ball and left-footed it into the net for the winning goal.

I watched as she ran towards her mates, screaming, and I got that feeling again. The love of the game mattered right then: not the money or the glory, but the love of the game. I hope I never lose it.

People who read this book will understand that feeling.

Steve

Part I: Home

1. The Learning Years – Anfield Road, Liverpool

Outside the Shankly Gates
I heard a Kopite calling:
Shankly they have taken you away
But you left a great eleven
Before you went to heaven
Now it's glory round the Fields of Anfield Road

— **'The Fields of Anfield Road', Liverpool Supporters.**

Steve Darby was born into a working-class family on Tancred Road in Liverpool. His mother was a housewife, a 1950s woman of bonhomie, Liverpool born and bred who had grown up in Everton, as had his father. His dad was a docker, as was his dad's dad before him, and it was expected that Steve would follow in the family tradition. But it wasn't regular work; every morning, his father would leave home and head down to the docks, hoping to be singled out for work that day. If there was none, he would return home with nothing.

During the Second World War, Liverpool held the dubious distinction of being the second-most bombed city in the United Kingdom after London, with nearly 4,000 lives lost and whole neighbourhoods destroyed. From 1940 onwards, the German Luftwaffe spent almost 18 months visiting hell on the docks that hugged both sides of the River Mersey as they sought to obliterate Britain's vital sea lanes used for trade with the United States. While the docks were the main strategic targets, residential and commercial districts suffered widespread damage. Even after the war ended in 1945, a generation of children would have to find their own amusement amid the debris and the rubble outside their front doors.

By the mid-1950s, the city was changing. Slowly but surely, memories of the war were receding as the city's bomb damage was replaced by new buildings, and people began to look to the future. Children who had grown up fearing the bombs whistling down nightly were now teenagers interested in clothes, music and football. Nobody knew it then, of course, but within the relatively short period of a few years, Liverpool would become the world centre of football and music.

If you were born and raised in the shadow of Liverpool Football Club's famous Kop terrace in the 1950s and 1960s, just as the great Bill Shankly was laying the groundwork for a super club which would dominate Europe, chances were slim you would like to grow up as a train driver.

All Steve ever wanted to be was a footballer. From an early age, he would inhale the aroma of match day—the Woodbines and the pipe tobacco. The match day program odours may not be as popular as they once were, but the smells have stayed with him to this day.

Much of the area around Anfield retains the same 1950s buildings, though tarmac roads have replaced the old cobbled streets where Steve used to play. In those days, outside toilets were the norm, and bath time was a weekly event, whether or not it was needed. There were still patches of open land, bomb sites from the war that had yet to be built upon, and, in the absence of any organised recreational facilities, an adventure playground for local kids who soon learnt scraped knees and bruises were just a part of growing up.

Five days after Steve was born, he would have seen thousands of people walking past his house in a ritual that would soon become familiar. Liverpool, then in the old Division Two (what we now call the championship), were hosting the top-of-the-table Blackburn Rovers.

It wasn't a bad Liverpool team. Far from it. Scottish striker Billy Liddell had joined the club in 1938 as a 16-year-old but was showing no sign of slowing down. He went on to score 30 goals that season, with the local newspaper, the *Liverpool Echo*, gushing about how 'inspirational' he was. Alongside Liddell was Essex boy, John Evans, and between them, they plundered 59 goals in what was, truth be told, one of Liverpool's worst-ever seasons.

Ronnie Moran and Geoff Twentyman were two other stalwarts of that

Liverpool team, and both went on to play immense roles in the club and the legacy that Shankly inevitably built. Moran went on to be a coach, and even caretaker manager, in the 1990s. Twentyman had previously played under Shankly at Carlisle before signing for Liverpool, but he left Merseyside shortly before the arrival of his former boss. Clearly Shankly had seen something he liked in his former player as he invited him to return in 1967 as a scout, later unearthing players such as Ian Rush and Phil Neal.

Liverpool beat the Blackburn Rovers 4–1 that day, with Liddell and Evans each scoring a brace, which means scoring two goals in one game. Liddell also missed a penalty. At that time, Steve would have been cradled in his mother's arms in the living room of their small terraced house, listening to the roars of the crowd each time Liverpool scored. Who knows? Perhaps after the game, he would have seen supporters heading down his street on their way to Walton Lane to catch a bus home in a jubilant mood.

The world was a lot smaller in those post-war years. Britain may have had an empire that covered much of the globe, but the sun was slowly setting as colonies and territories sought and gained independence. Young people would go to a local school and expect to find a job for life either in manufacturing or industry, often following in the footsteps of their parents and grandparents. In 1955, unemployment was at 215,000, or just one per cent of the workforce. People didn't think about travelling far for work, especially in a city like Liverpool, which was built around docks that were the hub of the empire.

Growing up in this environment was fun for Steve. The close-knit environment made for a close-knit social life. Everyone knew their neighbours, where they worked and what they did. The cobbled streets were free of traffic, and Steve grew up playing with his mates among the narrow lanes and alleyways. The lack of any entertainment meant the kids had to improvise by creating their own amusement. Fun meant hanging out with your neighbours, and everyone would look after everyone.

In 1960, Steve took his first steps out into the big wide world when he started at the local primary school. He would open the front door of his small house every day, which he moved to when he was five; he would turn right down Hayfield Street, left on to Burnand Street and an immediate right on to Back Rockfield Road. He would walk along to the end, past the corner with Baltic Street, which had been bombed during the war, and he would stare up at Liverpool FC's main stand. He would walk along the main stand, turn right on to Anfield Road, past the Anfield Road End, which he would touch twice a day, past the famous Arkles pub and on to Anfield Road Primary School, a journey of just over a mile.

'I loved school. I could play football there! I would play in the morning before classes started. I would play at breaktime, and I would play at lunchtime. I enjoyed studying, and I enjoyed learning new things, but mostly I enjoyed playing football!'

As Steve embarked on his first commute to school, within the walls of Anfield and out at the training ground at Melwood, Bill Shankly was into his second season as manager and slowly building the nucleus of a team that would earn promotion to Division One with players like Roger Hunt, Ian Callaghan and Gerry Byrne making their marks. At the same time, five young Liverpool lads were starting out on a series of gigs in Hamburg, Germany, that would be the launch pad for a brand of music which would shake the world.

After school, Steve would return home and straight away be back on the streets playing football.

'We didn't have the money for a real leather ball. I don't even think you could buy them. We would just use a tennis ball as everyone did. Sometimes we would have a bigger, plastic ball, but usually we had to make do with a tennis ball. In the summer, we would play cricket, but my cricket never took off. Cobbled streets weren't the best place to learn that particular game.'

One of those dates only remembered by a special breed of kid, the football-daft kid, was March 10, 1962. No one special was born on that day. There was no earth-shattering event in the world of politics. However, the date is etched indelibly in Steve Darby's mind because it was the first time he went to see his beloved Liverpool play.

It is easy to imagine the seven-year-old lad, wrapped up against the chill, running eagerly down the road to Anfield, perhaps holding on to his father's hand, the familiar aromas already having a special meaning. It was a short walk, of course, but match day would have made it longer, having to dodge in between the other supporters, pass the cigarette sellers and walk by the hotdog stands, smoke rising from the grills.

The moment when a young lad first passes through a creaky old turnstile and makes his way out into the stands, or on to the terrace, is one of those glorious moments in his childhood journey. These days, of course, with camera phones, proud dads are quick to post images of Junior's awe the first time he sees the pitch he read and heard so much about.

It was hardly surprising how taken Steve was by the vivid colours laid out before him like a carpet. The pitch at Anfield in the 1960s bore no resemblance to the snooker table finish we can see today. In March, it certainly wouldn't have been a uniform verdant, but Steve's world was one of grey streets, grey houses and grey clothes. Colours were for posh folks, not little urchins living in a gritty, inner-city neighbourhood.

In Denis Mitchell's seminal look at urban life in the 1950s, *Morning in the Streets*, a woman from nearby Bootle recalls a first trip to the countryside with her description: 'We went to Shrewsbury yesterday with the Bootle Evening Townswomen Guild, and oh, the countryside was magnificent. It was every shade of green ... I didn't know there were so many shades of green.'

Steve stood on a milk crate next to his dad on the Kop for 90 minutes, waiting for the game to begin, drinking in the colours, the smell and the atmosphere. Before television came along and rewrote the rules, English football matches used to kick off at 3.00 p.m. on a Saturday afternoon to allow the working men time to pop in at the stadium after clocking off and on their way home to the pubs or their families.

Green double-decker buses would pour out workers from the docks and factories on Anfield Road, and fans would pay their money at the gate and take their favourite spots on the terraces, waiting for their mates to catch up on the latest gossip. As the terrace filled, Steve and his dad would get hemmed in and choke on the smell of cigarette smoke and sweat, but the excited child only had eyes for the field.

Liverpool were still in Division Two at the time, and going into this game, they were five points clear of second-placed Leyton Orient, while opponent Derby County was nestled comfortably mid-table. The Reds had been in imperious form with big wins over Norwich City, Brighton & Hove Albion and Middlesbrough, with Roger Hunt hitting nine goals in his previous six games. The goal frenzy acted as a magnet at the turnstiles as Liverpool's biggest crowd since the middle of October looked forward to the game.

It wasn't only a young local lad who was eagerly anticipating the game. Liverpool's fine form had attracted interest from the Scottish national team who sent someone to look at defender Ron Yeats and striker Ian St John ahead of an international game with England that was to take place a few weeks later. As it happened it was two Englishmen who caught the eyes of fans, as Roger Hunt and Jimmy Meila each grabbed a couple of goals. Liverpool went on to win the game 4–1 and earned promotion at the end of the season. In Steve Darby, they had a new supporter for life.

The following season, Steve went to his first away game. It was August, and Liverpool was playing against the Blackburn Rovers. Without a car, they travelled by bus and saw their heroes lose 1–0. It wasn't enough to put Steve off, and soon he and his father were going to see Liverpool one week and Everton the next, crossing Anfield Road and cutting through Stanley Park, down the gentle slope and past the small lake to see the Toffees.

Match days took on a routine of sorts with Steve finding his first part-time job. 'Nobody in our street had a car, so the location was perfect for people who were wealthy enough to afford one. There were no car parks in the area like there are now, and there were no parking restrictions, so people could park anywhere they wanted, including right in front of our house. My mates and I, all budding entrepreneurs, soon saw we had something valuable, so we would approach these people on match day and tell them how dangerous this area was, but we would watch out for their cars for a few pennies. Then, once we'd got enough money, we would head off to the match!'

Six weeks after that trip to Blackburn, a little piece of history was made. The Beatles, who were between eight and 15 years older than Steve, released their first single in October 1962, a day before Liverpool entertained the Bolton Wanderers. While much is made of the band and the Mersey Sound that spawned the likes of Gerry and the Pacemakers and Cilla Black, the whole scene passed Steve by.

Without any internet and with a black-and-white TV showing a couple of channels, there weren't many ways for Steve and his mates to keep up with events outside of their own Stanley Park universe, even if they had wanted to. Millions of young girls around the world learned to scream on demand at Paul McCartney's mischievous smile or a shake of his foppish hair, but Steve remained doggedly determined to emulate his own hero, Gordon Banks. Even when his mother mentioned in passing that she was working with Cilla Black close to the Cavern, Steve's thoughts were elsewhere.

Steve's universe grew even bigger later in the 1962/63 season as he and his father followed the Reds all the way to Yorkshire. Liverpool's league form may have been inconsistent as they tried to adapt to life in the top flight, but they had no such troubles in the FA Cup, dispatching Wrexham, Burnley (after a replay), Arsenal and West Ham United before being drawn against Leicester City in the semi-final.

This was in the days when the FA Cup was still a major trophy, and the local newspaper, *Liverpool Echo*, cashed in with a colourful front page showing Bill Stevenson, Ron Yeats, Ian St John, Jimmy Meila, Roger Hunt and Ronnie Moran captured in a variety of action poses, set against a backdrop of a hand-drawn Anfield. With Everton winning the Division One title, there was the newly promoted Liverpool with their own tilt at glory, and Steve didn't want to miss out.

Liverpool, roared on by the thousands of Koppites who had crossed the Pennines to Sheffield Wednesday's Hillsborough, lost the game 1–0, and Bill Shankly wasn't happy.

'A travesty of a result. The most one-sided game I have ever seen. Even the Leicester supporters were too stunned to cheer.'

Steve, also disappointed, returned home on the bus. But he was also in awe. Leicester City's goalkeeper that day, the man who was given a lot of the credit for Leicester's surprise victory, was Gordon Banks. Liverpool reportedly had 34 efforts on goal, yet the newly capped England goalie performed heroically between the sticks, later describing it as his best-ever performance. Losing an FA Cup semi-final is never nice, the old adage being you never remember the losers, but for Steve, seeing the impressive Banks was one of those moments that would stay with him forever. He wanted to be a goalkeeper.

Liverpool's season petered out after the loss. They went on to lose four of the last six games of the season and sat by mutely while Everton paraded the title. While the red half of Merseyside pondered what might have been, Steve found renewed impetus.

'My dad would take me over to Stanley Park. We would put a couple of jumpers on the ground, and he would take shots at me. Often I would be sent scurrying after the ball, but I did make some saves as well, and he would say things like "Well done" or "Good save". Mum was less happy when I would come home covered in dog shit! We didn't have a washing machine, and she had to wash everything by hand!'

As well as playing football at school or in Stanley Park, Steve would often head round to his mate's house and have a kick-around there. Paul Bennett lived at 23 Anfield Road, all of a three-minute walk, and for many years, the two of them would be inseparable as they went through school together sharing in many adventures and misdeeds along the way.

Paul's house had a long, narrow garden behind it, and the pair would throw jumpers on the grass, and Steve would live out his Banksian fantasies while his mate took aim. When it rained, they would play inside; Paul's father had a full-size snooker table, 'a rarity in Liverpool in those days', and they would commandeer the smooth surface for the Subbuteo matches. While Steve's house no longer remains, Paul's does and is now known as the Anfield Hotel with its own website describing itself as 'redeveloped from a rundown listed building into a quality boutique hotel with a reputation for great customer service', catering to the large number of overseas Liverpool fans making a pilgrimage to see their favourite team.

Steve's football obsession was clear in those early years, but it was no different for millions of other kids around the world who loved the game. Steve's obsession, though, was married to an attention to detail that would serve him well in his future career. He was always studious. He describes himself as a sponge, and even though he is quite blasé about his academic efforts, his preparation and eye for detail were taken out of the classroom and into his obsession. In those rare moments when he wasn't to be found in and around Stanley Park kicking a ball, he would be in his room making copious notes and throwing dice.

Steve was into fantasy football long before it became a big business, and the legacy of those solitary moments exist to this day in his voluminous archive. In an old exercise book are the results of a season's worth of football, played out behind a closed door. Eight teams made up the North, Midland and South Leagues, and each page has the matches, results and league tables smartly written down with straight lines, ruled in to add effect. Results were decided on a roll of the dice; there were no clean sheets for this budding keeper to take pride in, and after the regular season was over, the top two in each league went into a play-off before Liverpool—who else—was crowned champion after beating Chelsea in the final, 5–1! And that's just one notebook! Every time his father would buy a new shirt, Steve would grab the cardboard support and start a new season. He also did the same for cricket.

In that uniquely Liverpudlian way, Steve wasn't too upset that Everton had won the league. Not only had he been to most of their home games, but their one-time striker, Dave Hickson, was his father's favourite player, so much so that Steve's middle name was Dave.

Fifty-five years later, as I was researching this book with Steve, we took shelter from a downpour in Arkles, a famous pub right outside Anfield. Steve removed his Thai jacket to reveal a grey Everton polo shirt. The rivalry, nay, bitter hatred, that can be found in cities like London, Birmingham and Sheffield seems to have no place in Liverpool. As we supped our drinks, I asked him what was with the Everton shirt. 'It's all football to me.' One can sense, in Liverpool, at least, that he wasn't alone with that way of thinking.

Meanwhile, his football education, both on and off the field, continued. Liverpool won the Division One title in 1963/64, and with that success, qualification for the relatively new European Cup. After beating KR (Iceland), Anderlecht (Belgium) and Cologne (then West Germany), the Liverpool players found themselves in the semi-final drawn against the holder and Italian giant Inter Milan.

Steve wouldn't be needing his trusty old milk crate for this particular game as, for the first time in his life, he found himself in the seats along with his dad. 'I'd never thought of sitting at a football match before. It wasn't for us. It was for the rich people.'

Liverpool won the game 3-1 with an early goal from Hunt, taking advantage of plenty of space in the penalty area to volley home Ian Callaghan from a delightfully worked-free kick, both scoring in front of the Kop. Inter had pulled one back in between the first two strikes, but Liverpool and their adoring public were in fine form, and when St John scrambled home from close range in the second half, the Kop serenaded the visitors with a chant of 'Go back to Italy'. Unfortunately, Liverpool were to lose the second leg in Milan eight days later 3-0, but Steve and the rest of the Kop didn't have long to wait for more glory.

Having defeated Leeds United in the FA Cup final a few weeks before the Inter games, Liverpool had guaranteed another pop at European success, this time in the European Cup Winners Cup. Again, Liverpool reached the semi-finals, having overcome Juventus, Standard Liege and Honved before being drawn against Celtic. The team lost the first leg at Parkhead 1-0 a week earlier but was confident of overturning that slim deficit in front of the fans.

Two goals in six minutes of the second half, made by Tommy Smith and Geoff Strong, proved that the fans' confidence was not misplaced. Then, in the last minute, came controversy. With seconds remaining, Celtic's Bobby Lennox had the ball in the back of the net. The thousands of Celtic fans who had made the journey south from Scotland and east from Ireland erupted in a tidal wave of green and white in the Anfield Road end, convinced that Lennox's strike would be enough to send the Hoops through to the final.

However, the Belgian referee had other ideas and whistled for offside. The Celtic fans erupted in fury, throwing so many bottles on the pitch that one journalist called it 'the stupid savagery of the Glasgow thug whose reaction to defeat is violence', and the play had to be held up for several minutes while dozens of police cleared the goalmouth area. Amid all this chaos was Steve, unable to make his way on to his beloved Kop.

'It was the first time I'd been scared at football. I'd never seen anything like it. I never knew people could behave like that.'

He may have been shaken by his experiences on the terraces, but in no way was he stirred from his passion for football. At school, he was in the middle of a special project, and at home resting on the mantelpiece were some tickets for more football matches, for later in the summer England was to host the World Cup, with three games taking place just down the road at Everton's Goodison Park.

World Cups used to be quite easy events to catch, especially if you lived close to one of the stadiums that were being used. There was none of this online registration, ordering and balloting that fans have to endure these days. Steve knew nothing of the behind-the-scenes politics then, but would find out in later life!

An 11-year-old Steve was unaware, of course. All he knew was there would be more football to play, more football to watch and more football to talk about with his mates. Underpinning this enthusiasm was the thrill of getting to see the likes of Pele and Garrincha, literally in his own backyard. Who needed a big wide world when the world came to him?

Unperturbed by any commercially driven hype or seasonal face-painting nationalism, Steve's father would have headed to Goodison Park to purchase a block of four tickets for himself and his son, handing over his hard-earned cash from the docks, walking back up the hill to wait as match tickets would not be available until April. It was perhaps a long wait, but then 1965/66 was a pretty remarkable season on Merseyside, with Liverpool crowned Division One champions and Everton lifting the FA Cup after beating Sheffield Wednesday 3–2 in the final. There was also still the morning, breaktime and lunchtime kick-arounds to be enjoyed at Anfield Road School, while the teachers embraced football fever by providing a project to keep young minds academically challenged in such heady times. The World Cup just down the road was the perfect way to end the season for the football-daft Steve, although he was a bit peeved with the academic project he was asked to work on. 'I sadly drew Bulgaria in the project, but I produced dozens of pages and still remember Asparoukhov and Yakimov!'

On July 12, Steve was a bundle of nervous energy as he waited for his mother to get ready. The long, balmy days of summer would have made the walk through Stanley Park delightful as Steve raced to keep up with his mum, one hand holding tightly to his trusty milk crate. Their tickets for the Park End had arrived in good time, and Steve was determined to secure as good a place as possible on the terracing behind the goal, but with his father not yet finished at the docks, they waited around the turnstiles until a kindly gentleman offered to take the lad on to the terrace, leaving his mother to retrace her steps back home. Steve rushed to his favourite spot, and soon enough his father turned up, knowing exactly where to find him without the need for GPS or instant messaging.

In the days before colour TV and social media (however did we cope?), an individual's fame or notoriety was passed on by the printed word or grainy black-and-white film. So, despite having never seen either Pele or Garrincha in the flesh, Steve and his father, as two keen football fans, were more than aware of the duo's abilities.

While the game was no classic, Bulgaria's aggressive tactics ensured Brazil's silky skills were bottled up; the supporters saw enough to know they were witnessing two special players, and it was appropriate that both put their names on the scoresheet with free kicks in each half. For Steve, it was a magical moment as he was standing behind the goal where Garrincha's curler beat the wall and the keeper, the budding young keeper on a milk crate showing little sympathy for a fellow member of the goalkeepers' union as he marvelled at Garrincha's technique with a dead ball. 'I still remember, to this day, watching the ball bend around the wall. I had never seen that before.' The next day, he was on Stanley Park with his pals, playing at being Garrincha and failing miserably.

Back home after the game, the precious yellow match ticket tucked away in his slowly expanding scrap book, Steve relived the game in his mind. While he drooled over the glimpses of step-overs and trickery he had seen on the pitch, when it came to a kick-around with his mates over the next couple of days, he was back between the jumpers.

It was still only July, and in football terms 1966 had already been pretty special. On the 15th, fans and writers were left seeking yet more flowery adjectives as Hungary, arguably the best team in the world in the early 1950s, even beating England twice, came up against Brazil, the reigning champions, in what was to be quite a special game.

After the battering Pele had taken at the hands of the Bulgarians, coach Vincente Feola dropped the number ten, but it still wasn't a bad team that lined up in the famous yellow shirts with Gilmar, Gerson, Tostao, Jairzinho and Garrincha in the starting line-up. The Hungarians were no pushovers with the likes of Ferenc Bene, Florian Albert and Janos Farkas. Much of the support inside Goodison was for the Hungary team, perhaps the underdogs, with Albert receiving a lot of acclaim, but they didn't need any extra support, running out 3-1 as the winners. 'I still remember the Hungarian goal, Albert wide to Bene, who crossed for Farkas, who volleyed home. Still the best goal I have ever seen.' Years later in Bahrain, Steve had his team try to replicate the move on the sandy training ground but gave up, disheartened, when the guy playing Bene got his feet mixed up and fell over in some camel shit.

Drooling, Steve walked back up the slope in Stanley Park replaying the goal in his mind, headed upstairs in his home and added the purple match ticket to his scrapbook. Defeat in the third group stage game at Goodison against Portugal by 3-1 meant Brazil's hopes of winning a third straight World Cup were dashed, leaving the team to dejectedly troop off field and back to their hotel. Any disappointment the fans may have felt at seeing the Brazilians exit the World Cup were soon forgotten, though, as they feasted their eyes on another exceptional talent—Eusebio. He scored twice against Brazil, setting up a quarter final tie against North Korea who had surprisingly defeated Italy 1-0 at Ayresome Park!

It may be the ultimate in football, but not all games live up to star billing, and very few are remembered through the years. People do remember Portugal versus North Korea whether or not they were there. Especially they remember Pak Do Ik.

Steve's father had ordered semi-final tickets as well. According to the initial draw, the winner of the Portuguese tie would have played at Goodison, and as the fates would have it, they would have come up against England! FIFA had other ideas though. They decided England versus Portugal was the more attractive semi-final, and therefore, it needed to be seen by more people. It was then switched to Wembley, leaving Goodison to host West Germany versus

Soviet Union instead. Many Scousers stayed away; the crowd of 38,000 people was the smallest seen at Goodison during the World Cup, but Steve would have been there if he could. What budding goalkeeper would not want to see the great Lev Yashin up close? His father had other ideas, though, and for the first time in his life, Steve headed to London for the semi-final and some sightseeing!

Steve's mother had also joined father and son for the trip to London, and as they took in the sights, they found themselves following in the footsteps of more football greats. Argentina had lost to England 1-0 in the quarter final, a game best remembered for the antics of the Argentine team and their captain, Antonio Rattin. While visiting Buckingham Palace, who should the Darby family bump into but Rattin and some of his teammates? It wasn't just that football felt bound to come to Steve's own backyard. When he finally ventured beyond his own postcode, he still rubbed shoulders with football!

Sadly, Steve's father was unable to get tickets for the World Cup final itself, so much like the rest of the country, they were glued to a TV to enjoy the moment. It was a wondrous end to a wondrous summer.

In the football world, years are defined by seasons, and for Steve, surely nothing could match 1965/66. In a way, the end of the World Cup brought the curtain down on the first part of the budding goalkeeper's life. His comfortable existence—walking to school and walking to football—had come to an end. Steve had fully embraced school and a tatty bit of brown card lists his achievements in those early years—winning the city football championships, the Jack Sharp Shield and the Hall Cain Shield, representing the Liverpool Chess team, as well as being captain of the cricket team, house captain, school prefect and junior chess champion.

But he had outgrown Anfield Road School and was now forced to travel further afield for his education. He wasn't daunted by this new universe he was about to enter. A new school meant new friends, and, he was sure, more chances to play football!

2. The Leaving of Liverpool

In between all the football and the World Cup, Steve also went through the rigours of the 11+, an exam that essentially decided a child's future at the time. If you passed, you had the opportunity to study at the grammar schools and were considered to be a cut above the secondary modern or technical schools, which absorbed those whose talents didn't extend to exam preparation at such a young age. In brief, the 11+ was designed to test a young learner's ability to problem solve using verbal and non-verbal reasoning. It was controversial and later abolished, though fortunately for Steve, his desire for knowledge saw him pass the exam, and along with a dozen of his classmates at Anfield Road, he was entered into the grammar school stream. This was a big deal for the docker's son, and his parents were as proud as punch as they dressed their young lad and sent him on his way to the bus stop for his first day at the new school.

Along with his mate, Paul Bennett, Steve was sent to Collegiate, an imposing classical building with a long history and a strange curriculum. There was Latin, ancient Greek, masters with mortars and gowns, and, allegedly, the cane to beat recalcitrant students into line! This was all somewhat foreign for a scally who had grown up in the shadow of the Kop, but for all its traditions and foreign languages, there was football to be played, and Steve just carried on as before.

Collegiate was on Shaw Street and while it was only a short bus ride away for Steve and Paul, it was like entering a whole new world. It was built in the 1840s after concerned local bigwigs felt their city needed 'to establish an institution in Liverpool for the general instruction of all classes combining scientific and commercial with sound religious knowledge' to cater for the estimated 25,000 children who didn't attend any type of school at all, leaving them illiterate and ill-equipped to take part in the ongoing Industrial Revolution. Harvey Lonsdale Elmes was selected from almost 30 applicants to design the building; Elmes was already well known in the city thanks to his efforts with St George's Hall, which was on its way to becoming one of the finest buildings in the city.

Latin and Greek exposed Steve to language learning for the first time, and it was an experience that was to hold him in good stead in years to come. Latin, the language of the Romans of yore and scientists of today, was taught by one of those wonderfully eccentric masters we have seen so often portrayed in nostalgic 1950s films such as *Goodbye Mr Chips*.

Norman Gain, nicknamed Nippy Jim, used to read *Jeeves* in English and *The Iliad* in Latin, an Alistair-Sim-type character who did everything with a swagger. Even his entrance into the classroom was achieved with an element of style with his long flowing gown, a man completely at ease in his environment and confident of his ability to tutor young minds in the finer aspects of a language he knew they would never use.

The students were less keen on the PE teacher. Taffy Edwards was a dour individual, passionate but not particularly approachable. Except, of course, he and Steve got on like a house on fire. Perhaps the teacher could see something of himself in this precocious youth, someone hardworking, disciplined and, at times, single-minded. In that first year, Steve won the shotput with a new school record of 27 feet, 10 inches and the discus with a throw of 58 feet, 10 inches at the school sports day, while his mate, Paul, started the day off winning the pole vault.

Playing football remained Steve's first love and would take up most of his time. From 1969, when he was 14, he found himself going to Anfield or Goodison a lot less as playing the game increasingly took up his time on the weekends.

He would represent the school on Saturday mornings while he joined the Boy's Brigade, just so he could play on Saturday afternoons. It wouldn't be long before this agile teenager was between the sticks for a pub team on Sundays, mixing it with local rough lads whose idea of breakfast before a game was to top up on the previous night's alcohol intake.

It was tough. Football then was much more of a contact sport than it is now, and if you wanted to play, you needed to earn the right to play, and that meant imposing yourself physically and mentally. There would be head butts, shoulders and elbows flying around, and if you went down and stayed down, well, let's just say there wasn't a whole lot of sympathy from either your opponent or your teammates, or even the match officials. The trainer would come on with his bucket of ice-cold water and magic sponge, generic tracksuit pants tucked inside his socks, with Brylcreem hair, and he didn't do TLC. Most had been through the war; everyday life was a hardship for them. They weren't going to get all lovey dovey because some spotty teenager had lost a couple of teeth in a challenge. 'Just spit them out, lad, and get back out there.'

'I later got to play for Tuebrook Boys Club, which was in a great competition, and I had a dream come true when I played at Anfield. We won, and I kept a clean sheet in the Merseyside Boys Club Cup final against Norris Green who had Steve Coppell playing for them. Paul Bennett scored for us!'

Then, in 1971, he was called up by Liverpool Grammar Schools to play a friendly against a team visiting from Cologne. Steve was in the squad, alongside Steve Coppell, who later went on to play for Tranmere Rovers, Manchester United and England before moving into management, and his game was on October 21 at Prescot. Before this game, Steve was like any football-daft kid— just kick the ball, get stuck in, and it will be all right, was the attitude, and remains much the same on many parks around the country at weekends. But watching Cologne play was like watching a totally different ball game.

'I knew something was different. I just didn't know what, but it was fascinating watching the German lads play. Their passing, their movement, and the way they built from the back—it all got me thinking about football in another way. We never really thought about how to play the game; we just played. Cologne showed us how we should be thinking about football.'

At the time, he was an associated schoolboy with Tranmere Rovers across the River Mersey on the Wirral, and twice a week, Steve would take the bus from his new home in West Derby. He had all the mod cons: hot running water, an inside bathroom. He would take the proverbial ferry across the Mersey and board another bus to the Tranmere training ground to be put through his paces under the watchful eye of Alec Muir. The ferry still runs to this day but caters solely to a tourist trade that would have been unimaginable in the 1970s. Back then, there were a lot less cars on the road because most people were reliant upon public transport. Marine travel can have its drawbacks, though, and while tourists may enjoy criss-crossing the Mersey listening to Gerry and the Pacemakers, heavy fog would disrupt services for humble commuters as it did one night for Steve as he was heading home after training. Ferry services had been cancelled due to poor visibility, and with foghorns breaking through the mists that enveloped the river, the teenager was left at the dock in the spectral gloom waiting for the fog to lift. 'A taxi wasn't an option; I was quite a way from the nearest bus, and of course, I didn't have a mobile phone to call my parents and have them pick me up—not that we had a car!'

Football, which had been easy and fun for so long, soon showed its brutal nature to Steve when Muir sat him down and told him he wasn't going to make it, and he should consider the university option. 'Take it, son. You have a wonderful opportunity to make something of yourself. Most of these kids aren't going to make the grade here, and when they leave, they have nothing to fall back on. Stay at school.' It wasn't the news Steve wanted to hear, and little did he know he would, in later years, be cast in the role of Muir, but at that moment, he was devastated—until the Cologne game.

A month after playing against the Germans, it was evident Steve had been thinking deeply about football. Along with his mate, Paul Bennett, they set about analysing the performances of the Collegiate football teams for the November issue of *The Commentator*, the school newspaper. In a column entitled "Why Are the School's Football Teams Unsuccessful?" 16-year-old Steve tried to get to the bottom of the team's poor results, and it is worth quoting in full those early thoughts to see how much the Cologne game had influenced his thinking:

First of all, let us examine the 1st XI record up to half term:
Played 7: Won 1: Drawn 4: Lost 2: goals for 6, against 11
We see that the team has an inability to score goals while the defence is sound (except for the 0–5 thrashing by Prescot), and when we see that five of the six goals have been headers from corners, we begin to wonder if there is something wrong in the way the team plays.

We believe that from the first year all boys are taught to play the 'kick up the middle and chase after it' style of play whereas if they were taught how to play football and not how to kick the ball, the school teams would do better. At the moment the 1st XI play 'kick and rush' and, as the saying goes, this is kids' stuff.

The outlook for the Senior Shield does not look too good, but it is a well-known fact that a mediocre 1st XI side usually wins the shield and this is what we are hoping for. The outlook for the Junior Shield is also rather bleak since the Under-15 team has already been knocked out of the Martindale Cup by Highfield (2–4) but perhaps they can come up with a winning formation before Christmas.

It isn't too fanciful to picture Steve and Paul sitting together, perhaps in the octagonal building at school or perhaps over the snooker table at Paul's house, naming their Subbuteo players after their teammates and moving them round the green surface while discussing their individual merits and translating those home thoughts on paper. One thing, though, is clear. The disappointment that followed the rejection from Tranmere wasn't allowed to fester for long, and the determination with which he pursued different sports and the eye for detail that was evident in his fantasy football adventures were coalescing into a future career path that would take him far beyond the comfort of assorted Liverpool postcodes. But first, there was the tantalising possibility of a Darby heading to university. Not just any old university, but Oxford!

'It was never going to happen. My parents were thrilled about the idea of course, but I never gave it much thought. I knew I wasn't going there. I was made an offer, as they say, after an entrance exam. I needed three As in my A Levels, and there was no chance of that. I ended up with 4 A Levels but not any As in them!'

With typical thoroughness, Steve set about researching alternate colleges, including Loughborough, Alsager and Chester. Eventually, he hit upon the City of Leeds and Carnegie College on the other side of the Pennines, and with little fuss started his academic life in September 1973. Yes, there were lessons and lectures to attend and all that kind of stuff, but while he was training to be a PE teacher, Steve continued playing when he could. He joined the college team that had just been promoted to Division One of the Yorkshire League, which would see the college boys travel round tough mining villages in and around

Leeds and Sheffield. This was a time of industrial unrest across the country, with several nationwide strikes effectively grinding public services to a halt and the government introducing a three-day week to try and handle disruption in the energy sector. No doubt the arrival of these college boys on a Saturday afternoon would have been greeted with amusement from men who spent much of their lives underground.

It was to be a tough debut season in the top division for the college and of course for their rookie keeper. But then, Steve was used to the aches and pains that came from mixing it with proper bruisers who would regularly drink their age in pints, have a quick fag before kick-off, and proceed to kick lumps out of any fresh-faced, spotty young lad who crossed their path on the pitch. Some parents accompanied the team to one away game at Emley where the locals seemed to take great delight in taking the mickey out of one of the students. One lad's mother took great offence at the abuse being directed at her son, and when the ref blew the final whistle, she marched down the tunnel and whacked one of the Emley players with her umbrella! 'Emley was some place. I got battered there by a lad called Pamment, and after the game, someone poured a pint of beer over me!'

The team criss-crossed the county in their college minibus, marvelling at their opponents whose names seemed to bear little relation to reality— Mexborough, Worsborough Bridge Miners Welfare Athletic, Rawmarsh Welfare and Frecheville Community Association. The college boys finished 11th in that first season, and the following campaigns saw improvement as they consolidated themselves in Division One, even finishing fifth in the 1975/76 season.

Whatever battering Steve may have taken on the Saturday afternoon, Sundays would see him rise with the lark and carry his weary limbs back over the Pennines to Liverpool to enjoy family time—and yes, drop off his laundry— before lining up for his Sunday league side that even saw merit in paying his expenses for the weekly journey.

It was in his early days at Carnegie that Steve fell under the spell of another individual who would have a profound effect on him, not just through college but also in later years, and the bond they formed back in the 1970s has indeed lasted to the present day.

Merv Beck hails from Norwich; he even turned down the opportunity to sign for his local side, feeling the dressing room banter wasn't for him, so he pursued his passion in another direction. Such is the influence Beck has had on Steve that I felt it was worth making the trek north to meet the man face to face. After exchanging emails, I booked a train to Leeds, and, having arrived a few hours early, decided it would be a good idea to walk from the railway station in the city centre out to Headingley where we had arranged to meet. It was uphill all the way, and the driving showers that bit into my face just added to my discomfort, but all that was soon forgotten as Merv introduced himself to me in the hotel lobby. We found a quiet area and started talking.

Allen Wade remains relatively unknown. Hell, he even lacks a Wikipedia entry, but ask anyone involved in football coaching during the second half of the 20th century, and they will attest to the value and influence of Wade. Among his fellow alumni are Don Howe, Bobby Robson, Roy Hodgson, Dave Sexton, Dario Gradi and Bobby Houghton, a veritable who's who of coaching greats. And there's Merv Beck.

Beck fell under Wade's influence when they worked together at Loughborough College in the 1950s. In those days, many clubs saw coaches as necessary evils, not people to be trusted and invested in. Ambitious young men, frustrated by the old boys' network that dominated football club boardrooms, headed overseas to try their luck; the likes of Vic Buckingham and Jimmy Hogan are two of the best known, but while their influence on Johan Cruyff and Total Football remain fully appreciated overseas, they remain little known, even now, in their own backyard.

For the suits in England, a coach was seen as a guy who would get a team fit for the weekend, and, hopefully, win before ultimately getting the sack. The English felt that as they had invented the game, it wasn't necessary to think too much about the game. Get it forward, and hope some hulking great striker could force the ball over the line was about as far as tactics went, and it wasn't until Hungary embarrassed England at Wembley 6–3 in 1953 that people started to think otherwise.

That November night was a seminal moment for English football. Because England had invented and codified association football, there was a feeling, especially among the suits and boardrooms, that their game was superior to the rest of the world, and they used a near-perfect record of home internationals against foreign opposition, just a single defeat at home to the Republic of Ireland in 1949, as evidence to support their beliefs. So confident were they in their ability that they felt they didn't need to enter the first couple of World Cups; such extravagance was beneath them.

Not all football people shared the boardroom arrogance. Some coaches and managers over the years had been looking to break the mould of what Bernard Joy called 'power football, preferring brawn to brain, the bludgeon of the rapier'. The foreign teams looked down on the English attachment to 'long passes and hefty boots ... and the stress on stamina in training', while aiming their focus on 'subtlety, quickness and sharp thinking'.

That night versus Hungary, one man there who was impressed was Bobby Robson who later worked closely with Wade and went on to manage England and mentored his own conveyor belt of young coaches.

'We saw a style of play, a system of play that we had never seen before. None of these players meant anything to us. We didn't know about Puskas. All these fantastic players—they were men from Mars as far as we were concerned. They were coming to England. England had never been beaten at Wembley— this would be a 3-0, 4-0, maybe even 5-0 demolition of a small country that was just coming into European football. They called Puskas the "Galloping Major" because he was in the army—how could this guy serving for the Hungarian army come to Wembley and rifle us to defeat? But the way they played, their technical brilliance and expertise—our WM formation was kyboshed in 90 minutes of football. The game had a profound effect, not just on myself, but on all of us.'

Loughborough became a Petri dish of coaching, and its alumni an analogue LinkedIn as Wade built up a team of coaches to train the next generation of coaches in the finer points of the game, including the thoughtful young Merv. In some respects, Wade was positively revolutionary. The idea that possession determines everything rather went against the default mindset of getting the ball forward as quickly as possible and hoping for a knock down from the tall number nine. They also embraced football psychology, a science that has only recently become mainstream, but was being talked about and studied by Wade and Merv back in the 1960s.

By the early 1970s, Merv was teaching at Carnegie in Leeds, a sister college to Loughborough. He remained involved with Wade and once a year would help with FA coaching courses. He worked alongside the likes of Jimmy Armfield, and even a young Sven Goran Ericsson. He must have worked with hundreds, if not thousands, of students over his academic career. But he still recalls Steve.

'You can imagine over 25 years how many students I taught,' he started off, 'but Steve stood out. As a goalkeeper he wasn't big physically, but he was agile and brave. He worked hard on his technique.'

But so did many players. They weren't of the quality that sprang to mind when recalling the young Steve. 'He was always inquisitive; he always wanted to know more. Many students are happy to accept what they're being told, but not Steve. Everything was "What if ..." He would always be looking to push the envelope. He was like a sponge; he would listen, ask questions and then try to apply what he had learned on the field.'

If Cologne had shown Steve how football could be played, Merv was explaining how the German lads were able to do what they did, and, good sponge that he was, Steve absorbed it all. Merv, like Taffy before him, was cool, calm and confident. In the classroom, they would discuss the psychology behind defending a free kick or a corner. Steve would ask 'What if' and then they would put it into practice on the training pitch or match day in the Yorkshire League, where the nuances of defending were put to the test against tough miners who had little time for namby-pamby student types.

After graduating with an honours degree in education majoring in psychology, his first job in deepest Hampshire as a PE teacher was hardly on the frontline, not that it lasted all that long. Back at Carnegie, Merv had taken a phone call from Allen Wade who was looking for coaches to go to the Middle East, asking if Merv had any recommendations. The instructor picked up the phone. 'Would you be interested in coaching in Bahrain, Steve?'

The Bahrain Football Association had approached their English counterparts and sought help in developing football in their country. The island state in the Arabian Gulf had only gained independence from the UK in 1971, and thanks to the millions of gallons of oil that lay beneath its sands and waters, and the energy crisis that had hindered Steve's early days at college, it had money to burn on pet projects, football being one of them.

The FA approached Jack Mansell, which seemed a wise choice. Salford-born Mansell hadn't had the most illustrious of careers. He had made a couple of hundred appearances for Brighton and Hove Albion, Cardiff City and Portsmouth, but he had really come into his own when he hung up his boots and started coaching. His first appointment was with Blau Wit Amsterdam, and he was to spend five years in the Netherlands learning his trade. After a short stint in England with Rotherham United, Mansell was off to the United States where he worked with the Boston Beacons in the first North American Soccer League. Before being appointed to Bahrain, he added Reading and Galatasaray to his impressive portfolio and was now being asked to coach Bahrain's national team, as well as to mentor an eclectic group of eager young men who had little experience of coaching beyond the classroom and absolutely no idea what it would be like living in such a conservative country as Bahrain. From the muddy pitches of Liverpool and Yorkshire, Steve Darby was now being expected to convince experienced footballers he knew his stuff.

Little was known of the newly independent states of the Gulf in the middle of the 1970s, beyond the fact they had lots of money, but there was little time for any serious research. The first thing Steve needed to do was tell his employers he would be leaving in the New Year. 'Fortunately, they were very good about it. They knew I really wanted to get into football coaching, and they recognised this was a wonderful opportunity for me.'

Before packing his bags for his desert adventure, Steve returned to Liverpool to stay with his parents, and being the good Liverpool supporter, he took time out to head down to Melwood to catch the team training. The team built by Bill Shankly was at the peak of its powers and was the reigning European Cup holder, having defeated Bruges in the final the previous May. Shankly had retired in 1974 but had stayed in the city, and Steve was surprised to see him at the training ground getting some laps in on his own. Plucking up courage, the apprentice approached the master and introduced himself, saying he was about to start his own coaching career and asking him if there was any advice the great man could share.

Sweating from his exertions, the 65-year-old Scotsman was only too happy to help. 'First of all, make a cup of tea,' he started. 'Treat your body like a temple, and don't put bad oil in a Mercedes.' Let's say it wasn't a conversation—more a monologue—but Steve didn't care. He just sat there in awe of the great man, thrilled to pieces he was even talking to him.

And so it was in January 1978, the young man from Anfield found himself settling into a business class seat on Gulf Air on the apron at Heathrow. Looking out of the window, he knew he was ready for this challenge. It wasn't in a big-headed way; Darby didn't do ego, but he did it in the same calm, phlegmatic way with which he had faced previous challenges, be it in swimming, chess or, yes, football. He had been mentored by the best—Taffy Edwards, Alec Muir and Merv Beck via Jackie Charlton, and Howard Wilkinson—every step of the way, and now it was time to put all those lessons into action for himself. For Steve, it didn't matter whether it was Bahrain or Barcelona; it was something new, and he was determined to make the most of it. As far as he was concerned, Bahrain was an empty page. He knew nothing beyond the fact it was hot. Everything else he would pick up along the way, and anyway, he loved learning.

The flight passed without incident, and after landing in Bahrain, Steve was met at the airport and driven to a five-star hotel which would be his home for the next few days while something more permanent was found. 'I was a bit surprised to be given a car. I told them I had no licence, but they didn't seem to be put out too much. "We can arrange that," they told me, and of course they did. I was quite amazed by that. In England, everything you want requires you to jump through hoops and follow procedures and regulations, but here I'm getting a driving licence, just like that!'

An apartment was found a couple of miles west of the capital Manama in a town called Jidhafs. All the Western expats were congregated in compounds set apart from the local community. There was a small village nearby where local Bahrainis lived, but the expats weren't encouraged to go there, so instead, they replicated their own home environment behind the compound walls. Despite being a conservative state, Bahrain was more liberal when it came to alcohol and expats based in dry states like Kuwait or Saudi Arabia would often fly there for a weekend on the beer or spirits, excursions that still continue to this day.

Steve was given East Riffa to coach, while the other new coaches were spread round the other teams in the league. 'Training was a bit of a shock at first; the pitch was sand—nothing else—but we did a lot of ball work, which the players seemed to enjoy. Technically, they were very good, and I was helped in my efforts by a couple of the players who spoke some English, which made things easier, especially in those early days.'

Truth be told, being a coach in the desert wasn't the most arduous of tasks. It was a couple of hours a day at the most, plus the odd meeting with Mansell. There was plenty of free time, and that, combined with money to burn and freely available alcohol, has been the downfall of many an expat over the centuries. However, Steve was no drinker, but he was used to finding things to amuse himself when he had time to spare, so he decided that rather than sit by the pool with the others getting wasted, he would teach himself Arabic.

Of course he did, learning in his room for hours on end from a Berlitz phrase book and practising, with ever more confidence, on his players and the people around him. And of course, the more this enthusiastic young coach was able to converse with his players on their own terms, the more they trusted him, and the better they responded to his ideas on the sandy pitch ahead of match day. Yes, Steve was a foreigner on a good salary living in an exclusive compound, but his efforts to learn the local language and culture earned him respect and taught him valuable lessons for living abroad, lessons he would carry with him for the rest of his career.

As well as coaching East Riffa, Steve could look forward to assisting Mansell with one of the national teams. 'I learned a great deal from Jack Mansell who's an incredible coach. He sadly passed away in 2012. I lost track of him and never got a chance to thank him for his help.' It was while on international duty that he found himself in a dugout opposite one of the biggest names in world football. Don Revie had been a more-than-decent player in the early years after the Second World War, playing first for Leicester City and Hull City before making a name for himself as a deep lying centre forward with Manchester City, partly inspired by the Hungary game at Wembley. He ended his career at Leeds United and was, somewhat surprisingly, appointed player-manager at the Elland Road club in 1961 and for much of the decade, jockeyed with Liverpool for titles, honours and prestige. But while football fans beyond Anfield liked and respected Bill Shankly, Revie was never held in such high esteem outside of Leeds, in part for the alleged roughhouse tactics his team employed and their win-at-all-costs mentality. 'You get nowt for being second,' as he once said.

He stepped down as Leeds manager in 1974, just after securing United's second league title and took over as England manager, replacing World Cup winner Sir Alf Ramsey. But the homely methods that had worked so well in West Yorkshire didn't translate so well with players drawn from around the country, and England failed to qualify for the European Championships in 1976 and the World Cup two years later. Revie quit the England job in 1977 amid much controversy, announcing he would be taking the helm of the United Arab Emirates, pocketing a hefty salary that may have provided some compensation for the ten-year ban he got from the English Football Association (later overturned on appeal).

For football people who had grown up either winning trophies (Revie) or watching his favourite team win trophies (Darby), the World Military Cup may not be the most glamorous of competitions, but in the Gulf, serious local pride was at stake. Revie's UAE and Bahrain were forced to play a preliminary qualifier before going on to the qualifying rounds proper, and the first game in UAE saw the visitors come away with a 1-0 win, giving them a nice cushion for the second leg that was to be played at Isa Town Stadium. A Kalil Shwaer hat trick gave Bahrain a comfortable 3–0 victory and confirmed their place in the qualifying round.

Revie was magnanimous in defeat saying, 'I think it was a pretty fair result on the run of play,' before heaping praise on a player Steve rates highly enough to describe, to this day, as one of the best he has ever worked with. 'I thought the Bahrain keeper (Hamood Sultan) was magnificent. He did well in the first leg last week, but he surpassed even that performance this time.'

In the late 1970s, football hooliganism in England was probably at its peak, or nadir. Barely a week went by without sordid tales of fan violence being splashed across the sports pages, and TV channels delighted in showing graphic images of gangs of badly dressed, marauding youth battling each other or taking over high streets the length and breadth of the country. The rise of hooliganism had coincided with Steve spending less time on the terraces at Anfield or Goodison Park and more time playing on sparsely populated fields where any violence was more likely to come from the elbow of an unshaven centre forward, reeking of Watney's Pale Ale and a cheeky pre-match Rothman's.

Therefore, he was somewhat bemused to see visiting fans at a Bahrain versus UAE game.

'As rivalries go, it wasn't Manchester United versus Liverpool or Leeds United versus anyone, and given the setting, it was quite strange to see all these bearded gentlemen wearing *thobes* and *keffiyehs* throwing stuff onto the pitch and getting out of hand. The security personnel moved in and fired tear gas into them. They hadn't taken into account wind direction, though, and the gas blew away from the rioting fans into the rest of the stadium and me on the bench! Tear gas works, I found out. Your eyes burn, your throat burns, and I was throwing water onto my face to soothe the burning sensation.'

An indication of how much Steve had been accepted, not just as a coach but as a person, came a few weeks after the games against Revie in December 1978 during the Islamic month of Muharram, the second holiest month in the Muslim calendar. He had already been coaching the village team for a few weeks in his spare time which, of course, improved his Arabic skills, and he had become quite familiar in the area. Despite Bahrain's burgeoning wealth, the village was still quite traditional with as many donkeys on the street as cars, while malls were just a fantasy; all the while, people did their shopping at small hole-in-the-wall stores.

'I was invited to the village for the Muharram festival. It just wasn't done for a Westerner to do something like this; we lived in very different worlds, even though we were only a few minutes' drive away. Some players from the team invited me to join them for the celebrations, so they dressed me up in the traditional Arab costume—the long flowing *thobe*, or robe, and a headdress. I stood in the middle of the room looking like a modern-day Lawrence of Arabia, and they asked me to walk around a bit. As I did, they fell apart laughing. "Better you walk in between us; you walk like a foreigner!"'

'So, we walked around the village, the players surrounding me, but nobody really took any notice. It was fascinating seeing them parade through the village, beating their chests, self-flagellating with branches, and then using swords to injure themselves. It was intoxicating being caught up in all that, and yes, I felt very privileged to be allowed to watch. Unfortunately, or perhaps fortunately, this was in the days before we took selfies of everything; had we taken loads of photographs, we would have only drawn attention to ourselves, but nobody really seemed to mind me being there.'

While Steve was proving himself adept at being accepted by the local community, he was also actively involved in the local expat club. It has long been a maxim among Westerners that when they are working overseas, they form a club which brings them together after work and allows them to unwind away from the 'stresses' of their host community. Colonialists in India did it in the 18th century, and aid workers in Bangladesh continue to do it in the 21st. Bahrain was no different and had its very own Dilmun Club where members paid a membership fee which allowed access to the club's facilities, most importantly the swimming pool and the bar. Of course, the club also had a football team.

Some 30 years later, Steve would be working with the Thai national team alongside Bryan Robson and Peter Reid, both former England internationals. In March 1979, the hottest time of the year in the tropical country, Steve went to Thailand for the first time as part of the Dilmun Club's tour, and it seems to have been a roaring success with the team captain, Harry Boulton, saying, 'We shall definitely go back.'

The opening game of the tour saw them play Bangkok Sports Club on a pitch in the heart of the city, surrounded by a horse racing track which goes some way to explaining the crowd of 35,000 people. 'We got some support between races,' said Harry. Fat lot of good that support did them, as they lost 4–2.

Next up was a game played in front of a very different crowd as the lads journeyed north to Ban Chiang to play the local provincial side, and instead of playing in front of wildly cheering punters fuelled by easily available alcohol, in Udon Thani province the crowd consisted of saffron-clad monks from a local monastery. 'They were the best team we played,' said the captain, 'and we were lucky to win that one 1-0.' The tour ended in Pattaya where a last-minute defensive error saw the local Thai side equalise to make the final score 2-2.

Soon after the Thai tour, Steve returned to the UK to complete his coaching badges. He wasn't to return to Bahrain as the region was plunged into instability following the revolution in Iran on the other side of the Gulf. Like Iran, Bahrain had a mostly Shia population, though the rulers were Sunni, and there were fears the religious uprising could spread.

The Bahrain project was pulled and, following the FA course, Steve found himself with plenty of fresh experience and a growing number of contacts, yet temporarily out of work. It was one of those contacts who would introduce Steve to his next adventure.

Part II: The Australian Years

3. Tasmania

There is no better way of life in the world than that of the Australian. I firmly believe this. The grumbling, growling, cursing, profane, laughing, beer-drinking, abusive, loyal-to-his-mates Australian is one of the few free men left on this earth. He fears no one, crawls to no one, bludges on no one and acknowledges no master. Learn his way. **John O'Grady.**

Steve was on the sofa at his parents' home in West Derby when the phone rang. With Iran's instability threatening to ripple around the Gulf, there was no chance of a return to Bahrain anytime soon, so the coach was experiencing something all football coaches soon get familiar with—being out of work. The novelty of being back in England soon wore off, and there was a gut feeling within the Darby household that the new prime minister, Margaret Thatcher, was not going to be popular in their part of the north-west.

The phone call offered a way out. 'Tanzania? Great. I've never been to Africa, and it's in a fairly close time zone.'

Steve's love of learning at Collegiate and Anfield Road had unfortunately not extended as far as geography, hardly a surprise for a lad who had genuinely believed his postcode was the centre of the known universe. But he was happy to accept Tasmania, Australia's island state, rather than Tanzania, as a consolation prize.

It transpired that some of the coaches who were on the last course he had completed, his FA full badge, were from Tasmania, and they had returned to Australia with pockets full of names and phone numbers, as well as brimming with ideas of how they would propel the local sides to a promised land of titles and triumphs playing Total Football. When one of them heard of a vacancy a local club was struggling to fill, they remembered their mate, Steve, and recommended him for the job. The club, from Devonport on the north coast of the island, called Steve long distance and liked what they heard. In no time at all, Steve was packing his bags, saying goodbye to his parents and Britain's industrial strife, and heading to the other side of the globe, not knowing that Australia was to become his home for the best part of 20 years.

'I did my research. I rang a mate of mine, Keith Boden, who was a professional cricketer who had played in Australia, and he gave me the numbers of a couple of lads—great lads—who had played in Tasmania, and they all said, "Go. You'll love it."'

Very little was known about Australian football at the time, beyond the football pools during the English close season, when punters ranging from seasoned works-based syndicates, with their form books, to little old ladies trusting on grandchildren's dates of birth would try and select eight games, which would produce a score draw. It was hard enough in England with local knowledge, nigh on impossible for Australian state leagues about which no one knew a thing.

Steve got in touch with Eric Worthington who was the national head of coaching in Australia and was encouraged by the positive response he received. 'He said for me to get over because they needed fully qualified coaches.' Within a few weeks, Steve was walking around Sydney airport, looking and feeling very lost, when he was approached by a gentleman who introduced himself.

'Steve Darby?'

'Yes. That's me,' Steve replied. 'How the hell did you know who I was?'

'Only a stupid Pom would be wearing a suit and tie after getting off a long flight! I knew you were a football coach from the way you were dressed.'

And that was how Steve met Eric for the first time.

After a visit to Bondi Beach and a trip round Sydney, Steve stayed at Eric's house where he slept on a boat in the garden. The next morning, jet lag and all, Steve was thrown straight in the deep end when Eric told Steve he wanted to see him conduct a coaching session. It went well, and with an official seal of approval from the 'top man', it was time for Tassie (as Tasmania is affectionately referred to).

It's probably fair to say that very little was known about Australian football in Australia either. Depending on where you lived, Australians preferred rugby league, rugby union and Australian rules football. Australian soccer struggled against the more popular codes and cricket for any media coverage, as many locals struggled to identify with clubs like Sydney Croatia, Preston Macedonia or South Melbourne Hellas, clubs which were seen as insular and exclusive, rather than like the open and inclusive Balmain (league), Randwick (union) or Collingwood (AFL).

Steve was able to see this apathy first-hand as his plane touched down at Hobart Airport. 'G'day, mate,' called out the solitary photographer from the *Launceston Examiner* who was waiting on the runway. 'Can you juggle this ball down the steps, so I can get some photos?' Still feeling the effects of jet lag, Steve walked wearily down the steps, 'If I could do that, I would be in Madrid, not Hobart.'

Inside the terminal building, Steve was met by some Devonport officials and, picking up a local newspaper, settled back in the car for the drive north.

One of the stories in the paper hit Steve. In the football pages was Collingwood versus Carlton 98–76. *What a keeper I'll be here*, Steve thought. *I'll be brilliant.* This was news to the club officials who were convinced their new player-coach was a 'dynamic central midfield player'!

Tasmania then, as now, was Australia's smallest and least populated state. Devonport sits in the middle of the north coast overlooking the boisterous Bass Strait and, an overnight ferry away, Melbourne. The town itself has the third largest population on the island, after Hobart and Launceston, but with only about 30,000 people living in and around the town, it very much has the feel of a small, provincial town on a small, provincial island, lacking the glamour of Sydney. The core of the town was sandwiched between two rivers, the Don to the west and, appropriately for Steve, the Mersey to the east. To the south, a major freeway acted as an informal southern barrier, connecting the town with the state capital of Hobart, while to the north, a lighthouse on Mersey Bluff that was painted red and white had been built in the late 19th century to warn sailors of the hazardous waters.

'Devonport was quiet! No nightclubs—just the Aussie pubs. But there was something unique. As I was driving one day, I thought about what a huge sight screen it was at the cricket club! I was wrong; it was a drive-in. Something I had never seen before, and I loved it.'

In 1980, the Tasmanian State League boasted just ten teams: Burnie United, White Eagles (a club with links to the Polish community), Croatia Glenorchy (an eclectic mixture of a Croatian community forming a football club in a town named after a Scottish place), George Town United, Ulverstone (a town near

Devonport named after an English town in the Lake District), Devonport City, Rapid, Hobart Juventus, Launceston Juventus and Brighton Caledonia (who featured former Leeds United and England defender Jack Charlton's son, John, in the 1980 season). The previous season had seen Devonport City go winless in their last nine games, but they still managed to escape relegation by goal difference, while the reigning champions were Rapid, now known as Southern FC after a number of name changes.

Once Steve got used to the fact he was on the other side of the world and wouldn't be able to pop round to his mother's for a quick cup of tea, he settled in quickly. It helped that Tasmania was quite Anglo in scenery, place names and population, with towns like Ulverstone and Glenorchy providing clues as to the nature of the landscape.

For anyone taking up a new job in a strange location, it is ultimately the people you work for that can determine how successful you can be, and in Devonport, there could be no complaints.

'The club were fantastic, with wonderful people who did everything to help me settle in. All promises were kept and, as it is today, the club was the centre of the community, and it was a true community club catering for all levels of ability.' Steve went on to praise the committee that ran the football club for the first, and perhaps the last, time in his career. They 'were top class. Gordon Rimmer, Harold Pattison and Tony Mullet made sure everything I wanted to help bring the club forward was done.' He even found time to try another sport. 'I later grew to love Aussie rules and played a few games in the forward pocket!' Even now, 40 years on, Steve remains in touch with the club and many of his former players.

When it was time to get the balls, bibs and cones out, Steve was in for a bit of a surprise as it seemed the whole town had turned out to see their new coach. 'The first session was a bit of a shock as every player in the club turned out. So I had to "coach" more than 50 players! I remember all these little players, wearing strange woollen shirts with no sleeves ... Carlton, Collingwood and Hawthorn. Australian rules! I managed to get through that and then helped develop a system where I coached the first team three nights a week and the other teams once a week and, of course, played as player-coach at the weekend. When I wasn't coaching the lads, I was going around local schools doing coaching sessions.'

Despite almost being relegated the previous season, the ever 'glass half full' coach was impressed by some of the players he saw. 'There were some decent players, two Scottish lads, McKenna and McDonald, who could play. There were a number of tough Aussie lads, such as Frame, Best, Pizzerani, Ratsy, Stephen Rimmer and Gleeson, who not only battled hard, but had talent. There was also a young 15-year-old left back I gave his debut to—Kevin Smith—who, in hindsight, I should have sent to UK as he had so much talent. The youth team was talented, and I gave quite a few their chances. Abley, Meldrums and Rigby all went on to play for a decade for the club.'

The Rimmer lads were sons of committee member Gordon, but when Stephen was dropped, there was not a murmur from the boardroom. Gordon 'was a great bloke' and happy to let Steve do his job with the team and didn't take it as a personal affront when one of his sons wasn't felt to be up to the mark. This was only his second coaching gig; it would take Steve a few years to really appreciate Gordon's hands-off approach.

Before the season started, the town of Devonport hosted some world-class cricketers as a D.H. Robins XI player dropped in after a few games in New Zealand. As a big cricket fan, Steve thoroughly enjoyed the opportunity to meet some of his favourite players up close and personal. Derrick Harold Robins had played a couple of games for Warwickshire but found success in business and fame in the 1970s by taking cricket teams to apartheid South Africa, and his informal tours were a regular feature on the cricketing calendar.

'It was led by Henry Blofeld, who was, as you imagine, arrogant and colonial! The cricketers, though, were great lads. Bill Athey was a good player who had been on Middlesbrough's books, and David Bairstow could play. We won, but as we walked off, Chris Cowdrey (son of Colin) came up to me and said, "Well done, but now the real game begins." He put a few hundred pounds behind the bar and said, "Let's see who wins." A great challenge to the Devonport lads, but the Pommie bastards won! Though, being a naive drinker, I struggled for a few days after that night!'

The serious stuff started on April 5th with a local derby away to Ulverstone, 12 miles to the west. To reinforce the Anglo-Scottish impression, the team bus crossed the Forth River, drove through a town called Leith, and stopped off to allow the team captain to release his pigeons before arriving at Ulverstone's home ground, not too far the River Leven. Devonport City won 4–2, and their season was up and running.

A week later saw Devonport City play its first home game of the season, but disappointingly, the team was held 2–2 by Croatia Glenorchy. A first defeat followed 5–1 away to the reigning champions, Rapid, a team that would go on to retain its title in August, dropping just three points along the way. In the middle of May, a 1–1 draw at home to White Eagles saw Steve earn some nationwide column inches as Melbourne-based publication *Soccer Action* published a brief match report from the game. Under the misleading headline 'Devonport falls in a heap', the paper reports Devonport taking the lead in the first half through Pizzerani. In the second half, an 'excellent save' from Steve kept out a free kick, but though the keeper-coach was left 'stranded' for the equaliser, Devonport City held on for a draw in the face of incessant White Eagle pressure, thanks 'to Steve Darby who had a good game in (their) goal'.

The equaliser in that game had come from Nick Cook, a player Steve describes as a Gazza of Tasmania. 'Cooky is a bloke who everybody loved, a great player, and everybody had a story about him. We played against and together for six years and still keep in touch. In fact, I sent him a message 40 years to the day, reminding him of this goal he scored against me! On another occasion, after a big win, we decided to go to the casino in Hobart. I was dressed as an Arab in the full gear, and Cooky acted as my translator. He managed to convince a number of people I was a multi-millionaire Sheikh!'

A month later, Steve was again in the news as Devonport City ended Brighton Caledonia's unbeaten start to the season. Tommy McKenna scored the only goal of the game in the 32nd minute, but nerves were frayed in the second half when the visitors were awarded a penalty. Steve got a hand to Dickinson's spot kick and was able to save the rebound as well to secure the points. The team, however, struggled for consistency all season, going on to finish sixth in the ten-team league, with eight wins and eight defeats, with a 7–0 reverse away to George Town United (population 7,000), including six goals in 35 minutes, providing the low point in the season.

What Tasmanian football may have lacked in glamour, it more than made up for in physicality, and as 'a high-profile foreigner' the rookie goalkeeper-coach wasn't going to be given an easy ride by the local players looking to make a name for themselves.

'They battered me every game. I would come out for the ball in that crazy, head-first style that was common in the 1970s, and these opponents wouldn't back out of a challenge. There were sly digs, sledging of course; at times, I was convinced my name was Pommie Bastard, and more than once I was bundled into the back of the net, sometimes, even with the ball!'

But slogging it around Yorkshire in the back of a minibus, playing against teams of granite-hewn miners, had been just as valuable an education as anything in the classroom or on the training field, and the diminutive Steve gave as good as he got.

In May, Steve came up against a player with whom he would cross paths a few times later on in their careers, both in Australia and in Malaysia. Ken Worden was born in Preston, but after short spells with Burnley and his hometown side had moved to Australia in 1971 and had been in Tasmania for six years before ending up with the Hobart-based White Eagles. The Polish side also featured three brothers—Chris (18), Mark (17) and Andrew (15) Leszczynski—who went on to become regulars in the team for over a decade. Steve was to become very familiar with them later.

In early August, *Soccer Action* ran a front page story about a consortium of business people, football officials (many from Rapid) and a wool inspector putting together a bid to enter a Tasmanian team in the National Soccer League should the league be expanded as was being mooted at the time. The Tassie Tigers would be based in South Hobart using Rapid's ground and felt confident enough to predict an average gate of 3,000. Projected coach Ken Morton was said to have utilised his Manchester United contacts and asked former Scottish international Lou Macari to join the proposed club. Closer to home, Steve was among the players linked with Tassie Tigers, as were Peter Willis, Peter Saville, Eric Young, Peter Brine (formerly of Middlesbrough) and Ian Parker.

There was a glimmer of hope for the Tasmanian football community in the middle of September, when it was revealed that a Hobart-based TV channel would be broadcasting National League games from 1981, with *Soccer Action* proclaiming, 'The participation of a Hobart channel means it is almost certain that a Tasmanian team will be included in the (National League) next year.' While the story made good headlines for a while, neither Steve nor Ken Morton seemed impressed. Talking 40 years later, Steve doesn't recall the Macari link and remains unimpressed by the rumours or those names said to be behind the bid. 'Only two (of the consortium) were serious players. (Of the others) one was a barman and another, a captain in the Salvation Amy.'

As for Morton, he didn't bother sticking around to see whether the Tassie Tigers bid was successful. No sooner was the season over than he was heading to New South Wales and Wollongong City, another team with National League aspirations.

Even 40 years later, Tasmania is still struggling to build support for a team in the national league, now known as the A-League.

With the domestic season over, Devonport City still had a chance of glory in the Ampol Cup, but they came unstuck in the semi-finals against Rapid, who was after a domestic double. Despite starting well, it was Rapid who scored first, Ken Morton netting on 26 minutes. Steve's charges battled well, but two late goals ended any hopes the team had of glory, and Rapid could look forward to meeting Brighton Caledonia in the final. In the Cadbury Cup, a penalty save from Devonport's keeper-coach against Burnie United set up another semi-final, this time against Brighton Caledonia that they lost 5–0.

With the season over, it was time to take stock. As he was considering his next step, Steve was approached by *Soccer Action* and asked for his thoughts on Australia's potential opponents in the upcoming World Cup qualifiers, which were due to start in April 1981. The Australians, as ever, were confident they would qualify from their first-round group, where they were drawn with New Zealand, Fiji, Indonesia and Chinese Taipei, and without a ball kicked, they were already looking forward to the second round, where it was likely they would be drawn against teams from the Middle East. Having a foot in both camps, as it were, the paper asked Steve for his thoughts ahead of playing Gulf opposition.

'We saw Iraq in 1973 and Kuwait in 1977, but few of us know what they are like today,' said the paper in introducing the Tasmanian-based coach to its readers. 'One man who does is Steve Darby, player-coach of Devonport in Tasmania. Darby was assistant national coach of Bahrain from January 1978 until July last year (1980). During this time, he had the opportunity to study the Iraqis and the Kuwaitis as a number of top clubs from both countries visited Bahrain, and Darby himself played in Kuwait against club sides.'

The analytical skills Steve had developed with his old mate, Paul Bennett, while thinking about their teammates at Collegiate, were now married with the knowledge and experience of an international, professional coach, and Steve's column provided details not just about key players' strengths and weaknesses, but also cultural differences Australians could expect when they travelled to the region, from the food and dress to the influence of politics.

Unfortunately for the Australians, their optimism in the media was not matched by their efforts on the pitch, and they failed to get past the first round, leaving Steve's notes to lie forgotten in the paper's archives. Still, the article served to make more people around the country aware of this multilingual coach on the north coast of Tasmania, and a side panel on the page virtually issued a 'come and get me' plea with one of the paper's established writers saying Steve had the credentials to coach in the National League. It was a coaching equivalent of sticking a postcard in the newsagent titled, "Coach seeks New Opportunities".

Despite feeling at home in Devonport, Steve spent just the single season there. 'At the end of the season, I was approached by the president of Tasmanian Football, Vic Tuting, who, in conjunction with Eric Worthington, asked me to be state director of coaching on a three-year contract. Vic was Mr Tasmanian football. He had been involved with the football federation since 1937 and president since 1950, and it was difficult to imagine the game without him. On the condition I could carry on playing, I agreed and moved to the metropolis of Hobart. Within a week, I had been whisked off to New Zealand to qualify as a FIFA instructor for Oceania, the main lecturer being Sepp Blatter on football administration! Other coaches were Ivan Toplak and Heinz Marotzke. A good course, but very theoretical—not much on the grass!'

It's been said there is no room for sentimentality in football, and while Steve was grateful to Devonport City for providing him the opportunity to come and work in Australia and liked the people he had worked with, he jumped at the opportunity that was being offered by Worthington. Here he was, thousands of miles from home, with East Riffa and Devonport City on his CV, yet he was being offered perhaps the top coaching job in Tasmania, a few years shy of his 30th birthday.

Worthington, who had played for Queens Park Rangers and Watford after the war before going into teaching, had worked at Loughborough College in the 1960s where he was introduced to Allen Wade and Steve's old mentor, Merv Beck, so the fact he had approached the little known scouser wasn't really a surprise. Loughborough, in those days, was at the heart of an English coaching renaissance when ambitious young minds forensically analysed England's loss to Hungary a decade earlier and sought to drag the English game out of the technical wasteland it had inhabited since the 19th century and the graduates fanned out across the game in the years to come, slowly changing the way the game was studied, taught and played.

Unfortunately, Steve's appointment sucked him into a 'pommie mafia' debate that had haunted Australian football for a number of years. Sheffield-born Worthington, little known outside his own country, was appointed national director of coaching in 1973, and for a number of years after, there were accusations he favoured English coaches over others from the ethnically diverse Australian football ecosystem.

Journalist Michael Cockerill wrote an expansive piece about this so-called 'pommie mafia' in 1987, in which he put out in the public domain what many had been feeling privately for several years, that English coaches were being promoted ahead of other coaches, pointing to the fact that by 1987, 17 of 21 state appointments under Worthington, including Steve, had been English.

Worthington himself was nonplussed, admitting there was, indeed, a dominance of English coaches in the Australian setup, but it wasn't his fault. 'But you have to ask the question, "Who applied for these jobs?"' he said in the same story. 'To the best of my knowledge, only British coaches have applied. To me, it doesn't matter whether someone is English, Chinese or Australian, as long as the best man gets the job.'

It was an argument that was to rumble on for years, but for now, Steve's role was in Tasmania.

His season with Devonport had shown him there was little for footballers in the state beyond the league and the domestic cups. With the Tassie Tigers getting nowhere, some of the brightest stars in the Tasmanian firmament were able to move on. Morton's success at Rapid had seen him poached by newly promoted National Soccer League side Wollongong City, and he had taken three Tasmanian lads with him: sweeper Peter Willis (who had started his career with Leeds United), striker David Smith from Rapid and Robert Harrison who was Brighton Caledonia's goalkeeper. But they were the exceptions that proved the rule; Tasmanian football was off the beaten track, and a local player's career path would see a lad moving between the Hobart, Launceston and north coast clubs with little hope of moving beyond those limited horizons.

This isolation was best highlighted by the voice of Tasmanian football, Walter Pless, in an article he wrote in March 1981. Under a headline that screamed 'The Soccer Who?' Pless wrote, 'The fact that the Australian national soccer team, the Socceroos, has never played in Tasmania is a national disgrace.'

Steve had found a kindred spirit in Pless. Both were passionate about football, thought deeply about the game, and talked non-stop about it for hours on end. And they were not afraid to say what they felt. Although neither had made any ripples as players, they understood what it took to play the game and loved to share their knowledge and passion. At the same time, both were keen writers, and Pless's reputation as the go-to person for the island's football helped keep

Steve's name in the papers. Steve understood the sentiments when Walter wrote, 'A visit by the Socceroos is essential if soccer is to be promoted.' You can sense in those words the frustration Pless and other Tasmanian football people felt at being overlooked by the game across the Bass Strait. To this day, Australia has never played a full international in Tasmania.

While Steve would have been increasingly aware of this angst, as an outsider he would not have felt the disappointment so keenly. What he did sense, though, as a coach, was a challenge to try and do his bit by raising standards locally. 'I see the game basically as a triangle,' he told Pless in an interview soon after he was appointed.

'Kids form the base of this triangle, with State League players at the top. We must make the base very solid by getting more and more kids playing the game. Every person who coaches a primary or junior side should have attended a coaching course, so they at least have the fundamentals of the game behind them. I'd like to see more senior players get involved in coaching. We've got senior players with English experience, like Eric Young (Manchester United) and Peter Brine (Middlesbrough). There are other top-class players, like Tommy McKenna and Wolfgang Steutzel, who could help. I'm trying to get the top players to come back into the game at a coaching level.'

Steve saw his role as motivating the coaches, to give them new ideas they could pass on to the kids, and his aim was, within three years, for every school or junior side to have a coach who had attended a coaching course and for every State League club to have a coach who had passed internationally recognised courses.

Within weeks of taking up his new job, he 'conducted a preliminary coaching course, taken training sessions with clubs and appeared at two open forums on the subject of coaching'. And while he was passing on his knowledge and experiences, he was still soaking up ideas from his new home. State competition plays a big role in other Australian codes, not least the rugby league, where the State of Origin between New South Wales and Queensland is a major highlight of the season with sell-out crowds and large TV audiences watching the three-match series. When Steve had arrived in Australia in early 1980, there was a debate in football circles about introducing regular state-against-state competition, with South Australia coach, Edmund Kreft, saying a formal interstate competition could help bring more supporters to games. Steve saw resuscitating a statewide team as a way of encouraging players to look beyond the mundane ritual of heading north or south on Tasmania's Highway 1, and he set about trying to convince the clubs in the State League, as well as other states, of his seriousness.

However, Steve's position as director of coaching was nearly over before it even got started, if one news story was to be believed. In the second round of fixtures in the state league, Hobart Juventus met Launceston Juventus in what Brighton Caledonia coach, John Taylor, writing in *Soccer Action*, described as 'one of the most physical games of soccer seen in Tasmania'. Launceston won the game 2–1 after coach Ken Worden set the team up to play physically, but two sendings off and seven bookings blighted the game as a spectacle.

Nick Di Martino, described by Steve as 'an English style centre back, hard and uncompromising', played in the game for Hobart Juventus, and he recalls it as being a right feisty affair. 'The police were called as supporters jumped the fences to get involved. There were a number of arrests.'

A couple of weeks later, in his column, Taylor wrote Steve was at the game 'and was disgusted with the tactics employed by Launceston Juventus. Darby (sic) made his feelings public in the *Hobart Mercury*, and it seems he was hauled over the coals by Tasmanian Soccer Federation president Vic Tuting. I believe that Darby (sic) almost quit over the incident.' Darby, however, has little memory of this and refused to criticise the coaching methods.

'Yes, it disgusts me when I see coaches knocking each other,' he said, before citing the example of Ken Morton's move to Wollongong City. 'I hope that he does a great job. He does coach; he isn't just a motivator. He did a magnificent job in Tasmania. We used to sit and exchange ideas and talk about the game for hours. This should be done more often.'

A friendly game was arranged with Victoria Youth XI for May, and Steve selected a 'State of Origin' side that included one player from his old club, Devonport City, namely Chris Gleeson. Also featuring in the squad was a fellow Liverpudlian, Alastair Payne, who had been with Glenorchy Croatia since the late 1960s, and the highly rated 19-year-old Luciano Fabrizio (Hobart Juventus), who Steve described as 'a class act who could play anywhere even at a young age'.

The game was scheduled to be held on the same day and on the same pitch as a World Cup qualifier against Indonesia in Melbourne, which required consent from FIFA. Steve saw it as an opportunity to show off the local talent he was nurturing. 'Tasmania hasn't got the greatest name in soccer,' he said ahead of the game, 'but we're trying to change this. We have a totally professional attitude in terms of attitude and preparation, and we're not coming over just for the ride.'

With five of the squad travelling from the north of the island to Hobart to attend the weekly training, a round trip of some 450 kilometres, Steve was right to highlight the attitude in the squad. The Tasmanians won 2–0 with goals from Larry Nunn (Rapid) and Angelo Ambrosino (Australia Institute of Sport). A second game against a grandly named Rest of the World, actually made up of players from New Zealand and the United Kingdom, was played closer to home in Hobart, and the Tasmanians won 1–0. Games against the Australian Institute of Sport and Queensland were cancelled due to lack of funds, while the Victorian state federation didn't reply to requests for a game.

The Tasmanian State League finished in August, on a day of high drama in Hobart. Brighton Caledonia and Launceston Juventus went into the game neck and neck on 31 points, ten points clear of third-placed team Hobart Juventus, though Brighton had a slight advantage thanks to a superior goal difference. The pendulum was swinging towards Launceston Juventus as they led 2–1 with just three minutes remaining, when Brighton got a corner. Parker surprised everyone by crossing the ball to Charlton 30 yards out, and the English midfielder struck the sweetest of volleys to bring the scores level and secure the title for Brighton.

'Charlton was jubilant,' reported Walter Pless. 'It will, after all, probably be one of his greatest moments and the nearest he'll get to the feeling his father must have had when England won the World Cup in 1966.'

The next big event for Tasmanian football came in October, when National League runner-up South Melbourne Hellas came to town to play a Tassie All Stars in South Hobart. Unable to draw upon players from the northern clubs due to time restraints, Steve was only able to schedule a single training session ahead of the game.

Then, as now, South Melbourne Hellas were one of the biggest names in Australian football, having won the Victorian State League seven times and the Dockerty Cup twice. The team also featured Alun Evans, a striker Steve was familiar with from his days standing on the Kop in the late 1960s. In a country where football was under the radar at the best of times, South Melbourne was the nearest thing to box office, and getting the team to come to Tasmania was a major coup for Darby. Such was the excitement around the game that it was even recorded. Walter Pless recalls a camera filming the game 'from the back of a ute parked on the grass'. He should know; he was one of the commentators!

An early goal from Ian Parker, whose cross from the byline swung into the far corner of the goal, gave the home team the lead. Bruce Ward made it 2–0 with 11 minutes remaining, and although South Melbourne Hellas did have the ball in the net with eight minutes remaining through Vince Bannon, it was disallowed, and the Tasmanians hung on for a famous victory.

Steve was naturally elated after the game, telling the media, 'I'm very proud of every player. They showed a professional approach. What more have we got to prove?' his last comment being a reference to a Tasmanian side in the National Soccer League.

Immediately after the friendly, Steve headed to Sydney to attend an International Coach's Convention and the 1981 FIFA World Youth Cup, along with journalist Walter Pless, who was also a coach, and Ulverstone coach, Wolfgang Stuetzel. The convention featured presentations from the likes of former England coach, Walter Winterbottom, and Qatar under-21 coach, Evaristo, a former Brazilian international. The presence of Winterbottom would no doubt have intrigued Steve; he, too, had studied at Carnegie College in Leeds. Winterbottom is in the record books as England's longest-serving manager, starting in September 1946 and not relinquishing the role until 1962, when he was replaced by Alf Ramsey; perhaps his biggest achievement was convincing the football association that future managers should be the ones selecting the players to wear the Three Lions, not a selection committee, which was the standard practice.

The Tassie trio of Steve, Walter and Wolfgang were staying in the same hotel as the Qatar team, which had upset the odds by reaching the final of the World Youth Cup, beating Brazil in the quarter finals and defeating England in the semi-final at the Sydney Cricket Ground, in a game marred by crowd violence. Their reward was to face West Germany at the same venue.

Even in the 1980s, the Qatar team was doing everything first class, with their own private jumbo jet parked up at Sydney airport as proof of their riches. Pless recalls 'the players would go on massive shopping sprees in the city, returning with all manner of goods that later sometimes occupied the hotel corridors'. Sadly, all their bling counted for nothing on the day of the final, when the heavens opened. Pless was having breakfast when the Qatar players trooped in. 'The look on the faces of the Qatar players said it all. It was one of dejection. They had rarely, if ever, seen such weather conditions and weren't looking forward to the game. Psychologically, they were beaten before they took the field.'

The Germans, featuring the likes of Michael Zorc (later to play for Borussia Dortmund) and Roland Wohlfarth (Bayern Munich), took advantage of the quagmire by playing down the flanks and nullified Qatar's reliance on the offside trap by getting behind their static back four regularly. Two nil down at half-time, Qatar had nothing in their armoury to offer, and the Germans cruised to a 4–0 triumph.

Steve had seen a few of the Qatar games and was impressed by their defensive work. 'Qatar played the best offside trap I have ever seen. When I asked the coach (Evarista) why he did it, he replied, "We have a poor keeper, so we try to keep the ball a long way from him!"' It was the kind of brutal honesty Steve appreciated!

The Qatar team headed home from Sydney on their private jumbo jet with a burnished reputation and clutching tax-free cash bonuses of 100,000 Qatar Riyals and the promise of a Mercedes Benz and a bungalow awaiting their return in Doha, while Steve headed back to Hobart in cattle class on an Ansett flight, looking forward to what 1982 might bring him.

Certainly, 1981 had been an interesting year for Steve, but he wanted to be playing on a regular basis. So when he was offered a position at South Hobart, he leapt at the opportunity. South Hobart was the oldest football club in Tasmania, having been formed in 1910, but the team's more immediate history made for grim reading; they finished third bottom of the State League in 1981. In fact, since being crowned State League champions in 1959, South Hobart had won little of note until a couple of Southern Premierships in 1979 and 1980. Given his workload, though, Steve just focused on playing and left the coaching for others.

The Tasmanian authorities had decided to restructure the league for 1982, and the statewide league was replaced by northern and southern leagues with eight teams in each. South Hobart was in the southern league, along with Rapid, Hobart Juventus, White Eagle, Olympia, Croatia Glenorchy, Metro Claremont and Brighton, which would at least cut down on travel expenses for the clubs.

But before the new season kicked off, Steve sat down with Walter and summed up his first 12 months in the job. He had hoped to play for a team that year, but his schedule made that impossible. After finishing the instructor's course in New Zealand, he went on to teach or help out at 'two senior, four preliminary and ten basic coaching courses. These courses involved about 200 candidates, 76 of whom were physical education students.' However, he was also aware the garden wasn't full of roses as he bemoaned the parochialism that he saw as a threat to the game.

Looking back, he says, 'Tasmania is a small island, smaller than Iceland or Ireland, and it had a small island mentality, much like England does with the whole north-south thing. So much hot air was wasted on "north this, south that" I just felt the only way Tasmanian football could develop was by looking at a bigger picture.'

For Steve, it was all about football, and he had no time for egos or petty regionalism. He'd only been there a year, and he was already frustrated by the turf wars he was encountering. He told Walter, 'I feel we are at the crossroads. One path could lead us to a great future; the other path, if we succumb to parochialism, will lead to disintegration.'

Steve's first big task as director of coaching for the state in 1982 was a representative game against Australian Institute of Sport. Set up in 1980, as a direct result of Australia's failure to win any gold medals at the 1976 Olympics, the AIS was designed to 'identify and develop players for the national under-20 youth team and to develop coaches through the scholarship coaching scheme'.

Englishman Jimmy Shoulder, formerly coach of the national team, was its first head coach and said for the AIS: 'The first five years are going to be trial and error,' as he and his team developed a curriculum that would turn promising young talents from different parts of the country into top-class players. Like Steve, he had identified the glass ceilings that existed in state football. 'In our squad, we've got a kid from Cairns (Frank Farina), a kid from Hobart ... All of these could potentially get into the National League as Angelo Ambrosino has done. Now, if he had stayed in Hobart and hadn't come to the Institute, he would have played all his football down here (Hobart) and would never had the opportunity to have played at the top level, and maybe his place at Canberra would have been taken by an overseas player.'

Ambrosino, who had scored for Tasmania against the Rest of the World in the previous year, was now something of a local hero, having moved from the AIS to Canberra City in the National League, but in one of those 'This is Australian Football' moments, he was loaned back to AIS for this game and not his home state, as had been the case the previous year. There was another Tasmanian lad lining up for AIS, Luciano Fabrizio, who Steve had also called up the previous year as a precocious 17-year-old. Formerly of Hobart Juventus, Fabrizio looked in on his old teammates while back in town and, according to a match program, 'is looking forward to donning the Zebra stripes in front of his hometown supporters'. He came on as a substitute against Olympia, and his 'sheer brilliance' resulted in a penalty that helped Hobart Juventus to a 4–1 victory, keeping them unbeaten at the top of the table after four rounds. One wonders what Canberra felt about that.

AIS narrowly won the game 3–2, but Steve would have taken great pride in the performance of his lads against a strong young side which featured future internationals such as Tony Franken, Jean-Paul de Marigny and Frank Farina.

On the pitch, the 1982 campaign started poorly for Steve's new team, South Hobart; a 5–3 defeat away to Hobart Juventus was followed a week later by another reverse, this time at home to Walter Pless's Metro Claremont. A 2–0 win over Rapid in their third game suggested a corner had been turned, but was instead just a rare three points. With his club side struggling, the last thing Steve needed was any grief in his day job at the federation, but that is what he got when his mentor, Vic Tuting, stepped down.

In Vic, Steve had found his latest mentor, following in the tradition of teachers and coaches he had been inspired by. 'Vic was a football gentleman, old school and honest.' In Steve's eyes, there could be no finer compliment. The new leadership had new ideas which Steve didn't feel comfortable with, so 18 months into his three-year contract with the Tasmanian football association, he quit.

Walter Pless dutifully reported the shock resignation in *Soccer Action* with a short piece that was low on detail to the outsider, but full of meaning to the Tassie football fraternity. 'For various reasons connected with soccer, I was finding it impossible to do the job in a manner which I felt it deserved,' Walter quoted Steve as saying. 'I felt it was best, therefore, to resign. I couldn't condone, or be a "yes" man to some of the things that were going on.' He left his future in the air, saying that he had already received one unofficial approach from a Tasmanian team, but he said he 'would refuse any offers from within Tasmania', preferring to move to the mainland.

In fact, he got a teaching job at a university. In the middle of 1984 after a season playing for University, Steve was on the move again, and it was another decision that caught many by surprise. University was flying high, and Steve was relishing just focusing on playing, but he felt it was time for something different. 'At this stage in my career, I felt I needed a challenge, and Croatia (Glenorchy) offered me a very interesting challenge playing on the field,' he told his mate Walter Pless. 'I've also had trouble with my hands ever since I dislocated my finger saving a penalty against Billy Kirkpatrick of Rapid in a preseason friendly.'

He went on to explain he was enjoying the coaching sessions at Glenorchy under Frank Letec, which were more European in style than Steve was used to. He made his debut slotting in as a centre back in a 0–0 draw against Phoenix. Sadly, he wasn't able to influence a revival for his new team, and they finished second bottom of the league, while his former side University finished third behind Juventus. Ironically, Steve's past and present met in one of the last games of the season, and despite plenty of Glenorchy pressure, it was University who stole the points when an unmarked Peter Crowther headed home from a corner.

It was the third season on the spin that Steve's team finished in one of the bottom two places, and it wasn't a good feeling. Professionally, he had earned a good reputation within the Tasmanian football scene, and financially, thanks to his teaching work, he was doing well, but he knew his coaching resume needed burnishing. He had seen fellow Englishmen, Ken Morton and Peter Brine, arrive in Tasmania and make a good impression, and he wanted some of that. He was pushing 30 and still ambitious and having tasted international football with Bahrain, he felt the time was right to find a new club that matched his ambitions. 'All that, plus the money, was great!'

In 1984, White Eagles, who had suffered a relegation, earned promotion to the premier division of the southern State League, and they set about rebuilding for the new season. Unlike Devonport City, where the club kept him busy seven days a week for the 1985 campaign, Steve had enough free time to keep on lecturing at the university. 'I was full-time at both the university and the football club. It was hard work, but the money was worth it. I was able to buy a house, which got me on the property ladder, and I still had a team to build. White Eagles were ambitious.'

Any team building, though, was limited by cash, a situation familiar to coaches around the world. 'White Eagles decided that no players would actually be bought and that there would be no signing-on fees, so we had to try to get players who were free. So, we tried to get a mixture of young legs and older heads. I've certainly discovered a lot about players' attitudes,' he told Walter Pless.

The three Leszczynski brothers, Andrew, Mark and Richard, returned to the club, as did Bobby Rybak, while teenage goalkeeper, Mark Johnston, came from Olympia and immediately impressed the coach.

'The brothers all had their nicknames since they were kids. It was nothing to do with me not remembering which was which! Mark was Spider, Andrew was Dreamer and Richard was Daggy. Spider was one of my all-time favourite players. There was another brother as well, Chris. He was called Egg!'

Many years later, when Steve was coaching Thailand, they played a friendly against Poland. Remembering Spider, he met up with the captain of the Polish team and got his shirt, which he posted to Tasmania as soon as he could.

Despite the lack of funds, White Eagles proved to be a difficult team to beat. Against Caledonians, they trailed 2–0, only to fight back and nick a point, but there was an even more spectacular comeback in their next game. They hosted Rapid under the floodlights midweek. Within 30 minutes, the visitors were 3–0 up, and Steve was wondering where the switch was to plunge the pitch into darkness. He needn't have worried though. Inspired by the Leszczynski brothers, White Eagles fought its way back into the game and ended up winning 4–3, prompting Walter Pless to dub them 'the Houdini of Tasmanian football'. After eight rounds, White Eagles was fourth, two points behind leader Croatia and level on points with Juventus and Caledonians. Spider was on fire; he'd netted seven goals in eight games, while Dreamer had chipped in with five goals.

A week later, White Eagles was second after the team thrashed Olympia 5–2 with a hat trick from David Stoddard, Dreamer and Spider, and with Juventus having lost 1–0 away to Rapid, the Polish-backed team was dreaming of the title. Steve, however, was more cautious. Stoddard, Dreamer and Spider had contributed 21 of the team's 27 goals in the season so far; only leader Juventus had scored more, but the defence was looking shaky with only the bottom two teams having conceded more goals. He knew that if the team was to go on and achieve back-to-back titles, he would need to tighten the rearguard.

Next up was a double header at the Athletic Centre in Hobart with the top two in action against the bottom two. First up, the White Eagles thrashed hapless Metro Claremont 9–1, with Dreamer hitting a hat trick and Stoddard and Spider both on the score sheet. The win put White Eagles on top, for the moment at least, and put the pressure on Juventus who was to play bottom club University in the second game. Juventus may have been less ruthless than its rivals but still did enough to beat University 2–0 and give the watching White Eagles' coach plenty to think about.

Sure enough, White Eagles' form dipped with a couple of defeats, seeing Steve's team slip away, and when Juventus beat them 4-0 towards the end of August, it was their third loss in quick succession, and the gap widened to seven points, with only bottom side University having a worse defensive record. After losing 7-0 to Croatia, White Eagles' goal difference was now zero, and any diehard fan who had been to all 19 games would have seen a mind-numbing 104 goals. Entertaining? Yes, but do football fans want to be entertained? Is it a coach's job to entertain supporters? Former Welsh international, Alan Durban, didn't think so. After seeing his Stoke City team lose 2-0 against Arsenal in 1980, he was questioned by the media about his team's dour performance. 'If you want entertainment,' he replied, 'go and watch a bunch of clowns.'

The club shared Steve's optimism. 'I had a great president, Eva Plechta. She was a very intelligent woman who let me run the football side, and she could see the potential of the team.'

They also supported him as he set about the rebuild. One of the targets was, of course, to shore up that defence, and the White Eagles swooped to sign Peter Greenwood from Caledonians after he had impressed Steve while playing for Tasmanian Schoolboys in England. 'He told me he was looking forward to learning from me, and I told him, "You won't be doing that; you're going straight in the first team!"'

Steve had worked the team hard over pre-season, especially at the back and, with the arrival of young Greenwood also, it proved to be a master stroke. The nervousness that had been such a feature the previous season looked to be a thing of the past as White Eagles began the new campaign in emphatic style, defeating Metro Claremont 3-0, drawing 0-0 with Caledonia and putting four past Rapid without reply. Dreamer carried on his fine form with a hat trick against Rapid, while the ever-reliable Stoddard hit his first of the season.

With the World Cup in Mexico attracting most of the attention of the Australian sports media, the Tasmanian leagues carried on in a bit of a vacuum. Despite Juventus's trials and tribulations pre-season, the team still held a hex over White Eagles, being unbeaten over the previous two campaigns. When they met for the second time in the season, Juventus was three points clear of White Eagles, though the Polish side had the slimmest of superior goal differences. Steve needed a big performance from his team, and, not for the first time, it was the Leszczynski brothers who were there when needed. Andrew hit a hat trick, and Richard scored the other as White Eagles put the Juve hoodoo to bed once for all and, more crucially, narrowed the gap at the top to a single point. Just to add to Juventus's surreal season, keeper Damon Youl was sent off, and because the second-choice goalie, Tony Maccallini, was on holiday in Queensland, player-coach David Smith was forced to go between the sticks for the remainder of the game.

The result signalled the end of Juventus's title hopes as the team lost its next three games, while Croatia Glenorchy and White Eagles both embarked on winning runs that would take the title race down to the wire.

At the beginning of August, only a superior goal difference kept White Eagles ahead of Croatia Glenorchy, and the pressure was building. White Eagles defeated Howrah 4–1 in a bad-tempered game, during which Steve was sent off from the bench, and the game was delayed because of fan disturbance. A brace from Previdi, as well as goals from Andrew Leszczynski and Stoddart, gave the Eagles a 4–2 win to keep them top, while Croatia Glenorchy produced a less emphatic performance, beating Rapid 1–0, but the goal difference (+36) was double that of the team's rivals.

Everything was set up for a thriller in the penultimate round when White Eagles hosted Croatia Glenorchy, but the game proved disappointing for Steve's side as a 2–2 draw meant his former club was now the favourite going into the last match day of the campaign. White Eagles was up against Hobart Juventus, while Croatia Glenorchy faced Olympia.

White Eagles beat the bogey side quite comfortably, but the news from Olympia wasn't good. Croatia Glenorchy was drawing 2–2, which meant the team was to be crowned champion. Fortunately for the Polish side, Olympia hit two goals in the last ten minutes to win 4–2, and Steve could finally celebrate winning the first trophy of his professional career. Unfortunately, White Eagles went on to lose in the state grand final against the northern champions Ulverstone, while Olympia came out 5–4 in a thrilling Cadbury Cup final.

On the global football stage, winning the southern region league of a state where the round ball game struggled for column inches or airtime may not seem much, but as Steve and the players celebrated their triumph, he knew it was the culmination of two years of hard work with a great bunch of lads who responded well to his coaching. He also knew there was little else he could achieve in Tasmania. It was a cul-de-sac in a country that was itself not yet considered a serious football nation. In his six years, he had coached five teams and been the state's director of coaching, but he had grown frustrated at the small-town mentality that haunted the corridors of power.

He wanted a change so decided to further his studies in Canberra. In a final interview with Walter Pless, Steve said 'Devonport City, in hindsight, are still the best club in Tasmania. They're the most progressive and the most intelligently administered. I have no doubts if that club had been situated in Hobart, there would have definitely been a Tasmanian team in the National League competition.'

Steve was impressed by the quality of players coming through, as well as some of the imports, but was less impressed with how some of the clubs were run. 'Southern clubs should follow the example of those in the north and the north-west of the state by developing club facilities and training grounds, which would help to foster a good club atmosphere.'

Steve would not forget his time in Tasmania and over the years kept in touch with many of the individuals he had met, not least being Walter, and in their future chats Steve would often recall fondly some of the players he had known there.

4. A Coaching Smorgasbord

Canberra

It ought to be remembered that there is nothing more difficult to take in hand, more perilous to conduct, or more uncertain in its success, than to take the lead in the introduction of a new order of things. Because the innovator has for enemies all those who have done well under the old conditions, and lukewarm defenders in those who may do well under the new. — Niccolò Machiavelli, **The Prince.**

Initially, Steve had wanted to move to Canberra to continue his education and complete a Master's Degree in Sports Administration, but he continued to play until he could no longer justify his place in the team, and that is when he was able to call in his contacts to fall back into coaching.

While coaching the ACT state team, Steve got to work with a young lad who would go on to carve out a very successful career. 'I had Ned Zelic. He was about 17, 18, and you could see he was going to be a special player. We played Charlton Athletic, a team that was touring Australia, and they had Lennie Lawrence as manager, and I knew one of their centre backs. Tommy Caton played for Kirby Schoolboys, and he held the record, with 52 clubs approaching him. We drew 1–1, which was a major shock for us. A week later, we played Indonesia, and in the first half, they played a very good offside trap. At halftime, we worked on how to beat the offside trap, telling the lads to play deep and make late runs from midfield. During the second half, what did Indonesia do? Played deep! What a waste of 15 minutes but good coaching for them from an eastern European lad named Anatoli Polosin.

'Those two games were when I started playing with a sweeper, Ned Zelic, coming out from the back. Charlton didn't know how to deal with him. Their two strikers picked up our two defenders, and if they moved wide, their strikers moved wide, leaving great big open spaces. Ned was getting the ball and moving into those spaces. Someone had told me Zelic was too slow, but if he was, he kept slowly going past people. He had feet like Coco the Clown, size 15 feet, but he could do anything with the ball.' Tom Sermanni playing in his last ever game also ran the midfield that night.

Steve took over the Australian women's team in 1989. He signed a two-year deal, received an Australian passport, and his target was to help the team qualify for the first-ever FIFA Women's World Cup to be held in 1991. Women's football was a different world than men's in many respects, but Steve adapted quickly. 'I treated them the same as the ACT men's squad, which I also coached,' he said. He had to adapt quickly; Japan beckoned.

Australia women's first recognised internationals had only come in June 1988, when the team had travelled to China to play Brazil, Thailand and Norway. Despite now playing on the world stage, there was still a pub team feel about them, with players buying their own boots and equipment. The challenges Angela Iannotta faced were typical. She had grown up in a small town on the New South Wales/Victoria border famous for producing Australian rules footballers and vegetables. 'It was hard in Albury-Wodonga,' Angela said in an interview years later. 'There were only six or seven girls' teams, and the competition was bad, and we didn't have good coaching; we didn't have coaching at all. Where I got to, I was just lucky because I had a bit of natural talent. I was also fast, which helped. But my big problem was my father never wanted me to play. He was very against it.'

When she wanted to play for her high school team, she was initially knocked back because she was too young. She kept on at the PE teacher who eventually decided to give her a run out. 'I think I bugged him until he just said, "Okay, Okay." Then he saw me play and he was like, "Ah, nah, nah! We have to let her play!" I have a lot to thank that teacher for. He came home to my place a year later and talked to my dad and told him I was a good little player and to let me play. That kind of softened my dad a little bit. He was proud to hear someone say I was all right, and he came around a bit. So, I have a lot to thank that teacher for.'

With the backing of her father, Angela continued to make good progress, eventually being selected by the ACT squad which competed in the national championships. Steve noticed the 18-year-old and called her up for the trip to Japan.

Another teenager in the squad was Julie Murray who would go on to be the first Australian woman to play overseas professionally, as would Carol Vinson. Another member of the squad was the veteran Moya Dodd, who was the grand old age of 24 and on the way to becoming an influential figure, not just on the pitch, but off it as an administrator at the highest level with FIFA.

If the mixed assortment of teenagers from the countryside or more experienced old hands from the city were nervous about spending winter in Japan, which at that time was ranked third in Asia, it didn't show as they drew 2–2 and 1–1 with the Japanese national team. A couple of friendlies followed against Japanese club sides, which the Aussies won (2–0 versus Prima, and 1–0 versus Yomuri). The Female Socceroos (the name 'Matildas' would come a few years later) returned to Australia unheralded, but Steve had seen enough to feel pride in his players as he sat down to an interview with his old mate, Walter Pless, towards the end of 1990.

The reliable Walter was effusive in his praise of his pal, headlining the piece 'Continuous Progress Evident in Australian Women's Football', and the story focused on a number of areas close to Steve's heart. Describing a 'quiet revolution' in women's football, Walter pointed to a number of achievements since the new coach had taken over. The first, of course, was the successful tour of Japan. Then there was Julie Murray and Carol Vinson who had moved to Denmark, and there were also two players (Anissa Tann and Sunni Hughes) who were offered the opportunity to play in a men's team as a result of regular games being played against men's sides.

The crossover between the men's and the women's games extended to the training field as Steve roped in some of his pals to provide variety and experience to the sessions. Ron Smith, Eddie Thompson, Gary Cole, Eric Worthington and Tom Sermanni were among those who conducted sessions for the players.

Steve, though, would have taken just as much pride from seeing one of his players, Anissa Tann, become a professional player-coach and get a full-time job as a development officer with the New South Wales Amateur Soccer Federation. 'Anissa was top class at her job—so professional. She did so much unseen work for women's football, and I was delighted when she was the first to reach 100 caps and enter the Hall of Fame.'

The women's coach saw football as being more than just 90 minutes of kicking a ball around; he saw it as a vocation, albeit one that didn't seem like a job, so he was delighted when all of the national squad members had undertaken the level two coaching course and, having undergone a fitness program developed by his pals at AIS, two of the players (Tann and Oakley) were considered to be at an 'elite male standard'.

'I can't take credit for all these developments,' Steve told Walter, 'and in reality, the only thing that counts is their performance on the pitch,' but one could sense he was addressing his employer, rather than expressing what he really felt. He saw football and education as a way of bettering oneself, and he took great pride in helping others follow the same path he had taken back in the 1970s.

Apart from the mutual backslapping and the name-dropping, Steve was looking to the future of women's football. He wanted the Australian Women's Soccer Association to encourage state associations to be run more professionally and for National League sides to have a women's team.

The ideas flowed from Steve, and Walter, conscious of the space the paper allowed him, struggled to keep up. The coach still had a year to go on his contract, but he said the AWSA needed to be identifying potential replacements now and needed to be grooming current players such as Anissa Tann and Moya Dodd, so they could do on-the-job learning. 'We never stop learning,' he said, returning to a recurring theme. 'Whenever the national team goes into a camp, I go in with Thommo, and watch them work.'

By 1990, Eric Worthington finally stepped down as the national director of coaching with the ASF, and a number of people, including Ron Smith, suggested Steve should throw his hat in the ring for the position. He was up against some strong candidates, including Bruce Stowell and Alan Vest, both widely respected within coaching circles. Four of them were pals, and they would have been happy to work with each other as they all got along. The job went to another candidate, Mike Wells, and Steve describes feeling 'gutted' when the appointment was announced.

'It was politics. Mike Wells had helped get some votes for John Constantine in South Australia to help John be voted in as chairman of the Australian Soccer Federation, and this was his reward. I was gutted; I really was. It was the first time I had come across politics as it personally affected me. It had nothing to do with my ability, but I felt I had been done for non-football reasons. I should have realised I wasn't going to get the job. I was interviewed by a panel of four or five people, and one of them was reading *Australia Soccer Weekly* (a weekly newspaper which Steve frequently wrote columns for), and I sat there thinking,

He doesn't give a fuck, does he?'

A month later, in October 1990, Steve got a phone call from the CEO of the ASF, Alan Vessey. 'He told me he was sorry I hadn't got the job but that he still wanted me involved at the ASF in some capacity, so he wanted to create a position for me, National Soccer Development Officer. I didn't have a clue what the job was, but Alan said, "Don't worry. You'll be on more than Mike!" And it was a much bigger salary, funded by the ASC and the ASF, and I would be based in Sydney.'

He relocated to Sydney at the beginning of November and moved into an office next to John Constantine. Just down the corridor was Mike Wells, while Eddie Thomson, then coaching the Socceroos, was opposite. One day, he got talking with Constantine who asked him if he would be interested in working with the Sydney Olympic goalkeepers, Gary Maier and Clint Gosling, and from then, he was closely connected with the Greek-backed giants, initially unofficially, but later as their first team coach. 'Working with Sydney Olympic was like a foundation course for working in Asia,' he recalled later.

Working at the ASF was just as fascinating as Steve saw up close how the Italians and the Greeks vied for influence. 'But when it mattered, they did what was best for football.'

In the last issue of 1990, Steve wrote a column in *Australia Soccer Weekly*, in which he outlined some of his plans. He started the piece in his own inimitable style: 'If you are reading this column, then the first initiative brought about by the ASF development program will be of little use to you.'

With the manual he was developing, Steve wanted to reach out to the multitude of people who were enthusiastic coaches at the weekends because their sons or daughters were playing, but they had grown up with rugby league or AFL and were not natural football people. He wanted to give those coaches some ideas, so they would have fun coaching and, by extension, the kids would also enjoy the sessions.

The paradox of football is that the National League was the fourth most popular code of football out of four, but it was the most popular among kids to play. Steve wanted to translate that popularity into an organised system that would produce top class players who would go on to play for national and international teams. To do that, kids needed to be kept engaged. Recalling a nun he had seen coaching ten-year-olds in Tasmania, Steve wrote, 'All the educational and social research has shown that children in this era will stay in the sport that they get the most pleasure or fun out of.'

Steve was still conducting 'A' licence courses around the country, but the standard of coaches varied greatly, so he devised a task to sort the wheat from the chaff. He would set up a table tennis table in front of the coaches, spread some bottle tops around the green wooden surface, and give them some tasks while he watched with interest. 'Those who understood football understood about space and how important it is on a football field and how coaches seek to utilise it. Then there were those who didn't ...'

Meanwhile there was still the Women's World Cup. Women's football was changing internationally, and ahead of the qualification round, FIFA announced matches would last 80 minutes instead of 70 as they had previously, but Australia wasn't worried by this.

Qualification to the World Cup was by way of the Oceania Football Confederation Women's Championship, which Australia hosted in May 1991. Only three teams took part—the hosts, New Zealand and Papua New Guinea— with the AWSA selecting Bossley Park in Sydney to be the site for the match.

Despite all the fine words in the press, women's football was still massively underfunded, and the coach was only able to bring the squad together when the ASF chipped in with A$5,000. As it was, he only had a squad of 18 players to select from following injuries, but he was just relieved to be able to start work. 'They had to play club matches because we could not afford to call them together for training without affecting their finances. But the offer by the ASF has been marvellous and takes away 90 per cent of the worries. It means morale has immediately been lifted, especially if the players know they don't have to go into debt to represent their country.'

Steve was able to arrange a final friendly against a State League side before sitting down to watch PNG take on New Zealand in the opening game, and, as ever, he was positive about playing second. 'It will give us a good idea of the strength of the opposition because we meet New Zealand the following day. They will be our biggest threat to reaching the finals in China.'

Before the New Zealand game, though, there was an injury scare when Julie Murray went down with glandular fever.

Despite the lack of preparation and an injury to such an important player, publicly at least, imbibing at the fount of eternal optimism and could see no reason why Australia shouldn't finish top of the group. 'This side wants to get to China so badly it hurts,' he told the media.

Steve's optimism wasn't borne out as New Zealand flew out of the blocks, thrashing PNG 16-0 and then edging the hosts 1-0 when Wendy Sharpe headed home halfway through the second half. He wasn't impressed. 'We had no right to win; we had too many nice people out there,' the Australian coach said afterwards. 'We're now faced with the task of scoring a mountain of goals against Papua New Guinea and beating New Zealand in the return on Friday. I suppose the best we can say is that we have nothing to lose.'

It was 24 hours later, and the Australians did manage to score a mountain of goals as they beat PNG 12-0, but it wasn't enough. They were three points behind the Kiwis with an inferior goal difference, meaning their next meet would be crucial. Australia won 1-0 and played with a heart and vigour that had been missing in their first clash, and Murray, who had played through her sickness in the first two games, was back to her inspirational best.

The maths was easy. Australia had to beat PNG 16-0 in the final qualifier to overtake their Tasman rivals and book their flights to China. Unfortunately for the Australians, they hit eight goals in 80 minutes.

After ten years in Australia coaching at various levels and holding coaching courses around the country, Steve was aware of what needed to be done at a grassroots level to improve standards. He had tried to address this in Tasmania by encouraging coaches to undergo at least a basic course laying out what football is and how it is played.

'Mums and dads were out there doing their best to teach kids football, but they had little in the way of resources. I don't know a thing about netball, but if I'm going to coach netball, what I would need would be a series of netball cookbooks showing me little exercises and tricks of the trade I can take on to the training field and hopefully make training fun, instead of demanding kids replicate grainy images of Pele or Johan Cruyff and shouting at them when they weren't able to do so.'

Many of the coaches he was working with were excellent on theory. They had read the literature and seen the videos. But they couldn't always translate that theory onto the pitch.

'Theory is fine, but football is played on grass, and that is where coaches should be doing the bulk of their work. Coaching should be 95 per cent on grass and five per cent in the dressing room. Players can judge a coach by the work they do on the grass; they can soon sniff out the conmen. And that five per cent, the man management is vitally important, but no course tells you how to do that.'

Although there was a curriculum to follow on the courses, Steve started adding bits to it, drawing on his experiences. Presaging the John Terry/Wayne Bridge saga, he would ask what a coach should do if the goalkeeper was sleeping with the centre forward's wife? These days, of course, there would be a whole raft of counsellors brought in to deal with it, and the injured party would sell his story to a red top for a five or six figure fee, but back in the 1990s, every group Steve took came up with the same answer—it depended on who was the best player! 'If the striker was scoring goals every week, then basically, sod the keeper's feelings. Or if the striker was also firing blanks on the pitch, then get behind the keeper! Romance in football is for fans and writers; players want their win bonuses!

'I would tell coaches this story of the great Bobby Robson when he was coaching in the Netherlands with PSV. Romario would never turn up for training; he would drink, he would smoke. Hardly an ideal role model. Robson decided to get rid of Romario and told his captain, Belgian international Eric Gereets, about his plan. Eric said to his boss to do nothing yet; let him and the players deal with it. "Romario gets us our win bonuses, coach. We'll handle it."'

When he wasn't busy working with the ASF, AWSA and the Female Socceroos, Steve would sit down and devise a football version of Kanga Cricket, and after a long meeting with Ron Smith and Gary Cole, he eventually came up with RooBall. With Australia playing England in a friendly in June 1991, Steve took to the match day program to introduce his game to a wide audience.

'RooBall is designed to give every young player as many opportunities to kick a soccer ball as possible, while at the same time gaining the social skills from playing it in a team. Young children who want to play soccer want to enjoy it. They don't want to be running around without getting to the ball. A game of RooBall, while still competitive to score goals, gives everybody a chance to participate. At the level at which it is played, one is not looking for fitness or major tactics, but for smiles, laughter and enjoyment, and even if one can't do it very well, one can have a lot of fun. Roo-Ball is played on a "friendly" basis with no points, tables or trophies; therefore, there is no undue parental influence or pressure.' It was the 'friendly' nature of the game that was to be its death knell.

Steve was keen that every kid got involved in the game, so each time he had three substitutes, or interchange players, and coaches were encouraged to give each of them game time. Echoing Rinus Michel's Total Football, coaches were encouraged to rotate players, so 'they don't think of themselves as defenders or goalkeepers, but as soccer RooBall players'. Craig Johnston, who had been part of the great Liverpool side of the 1980s, was chosen to be RooBall ambassador, and he presented a demonstration of the game at the Sydney Football Stadium before the Australia versus England game kicked off.

In the short term, RooBall was a success, in part because it reflected how Australians saw themselves. The logo was a smiling kangaroo kicking a smiling football, and in Johnston they had an Aussie, albeit one born in South Africa, who had made his name in England boasting surfer good looks. Writing in his Development Program Report for the Australian Soccer Federation in 1990/91, Steve wrote, 'RooBall has been a greater success than I envisaged, in its most simple form, in that it has attracted Drug Offensive sponsorship, and Coca-Cola wished to also sponsor it. We have also the potential through the marketing arm to develop the game as a profit-making item. There has been a tremendous response to both the stickers and the posters, and of course the role of Craig Johnston is invaluable in public relation terms.

'The playing market for the RooBall age group is, at the moment, 87,516 registered players, with the potential due to a refined registration procedure and greater access to schools of over 150,000. We have gained a great deal of positive publicity and support from the game. It is an area where we can benefit in a tangible market sense and also in the intangible area of public relations and image.'

Going forward, Steve wanted the ASF to roll the game out across the country and introduce a structure to deal with states or associations who 'refuse to comply with ASF policy'. He could sense what was coming. The New South Wales Amateur Soccer Federation wasn't interested. 'It was very frustrating. I had a good product. I had sponsors. If we'd taken it national, it would have been very successful, but NSWASF wanted kids to play games on full-size pitches and have winners and losers, all that.'

Steve was frustrated by this intransigence from the states and took out his frustration on his boss, Constantine. Despite missing out on a plum job because of political machinations, Steve bore the chairman no ill will, and, indeed, they had developed a good working relationship in Sydney. Now it was time for the consummate political operator to give the football idealist some advice to help him negotiate the corridors of power. He sat him down in his office and told Steve to forget it.

'He told me to drop it. I was never going to win. I said, "But they're wrong," and he agreed but reiterated they weren't going to change their minds. He went all Sun Tzu on me and told me if I was going to get on in the offices of football administration, I needed to be more cunning. "You're too open. When you are with someone that you don't like, you let everyone see you don't like them." He was right. I didn't suffer fools gladly. "Don't. Don't give them the satisfaction of knowing they get under your skin." Then he said, "If there is someone you don't like, or they don't like you, keep them close. It's difficult to be stabbed in the back when they're looking you in the eye!" I sat there thinking that he was right, and it was good advice, but he hadn't finished. "Pick your battles. Sometimes you will win, and sometimes you will lose, and if you stick around long enough, you will know when you're not going to win, even if you have the best ideas. It's just the way it is."

'So, there I am working at the ASF. The director of coaching and the CEO didn't like me, the director of coaching especially, because I was on a higher salary, and I was getting coaching books published and was writing columns for *Australian Soccer Weekly* on a regular basis. I was higher profile than him, even though he technically had the top coaching job in the country. But Constantine liked me, partly because I was generating money, and partly because of the work I was doing with Sydney Olympic, and I got on well with Eddie Thompson.'

Constantine was voted out of office at the end of his five-year stint in 1994, and in came David Hill changing the political ecosystem one more time. Soon after he had taken over, he came into Steve's office and sat down. "'I hear you're doing great things," he said to me. "Good. That's good to know." Then he asked me what management text I was reading. Eh? I hadn't really thought about that since my talk with John Constantine a few years earlier, so I told him none. "Try reading *The Prince* by Machiavelli." I went out and bought the book. Woah! It is the football management textbook. Anyway, he asked me what I had planned, and he said everything was great, wonderful. I said I had been asked by Tom Sermanni to go with the Matildas to Sweden for the World Cup, and again, he was like, "Great! We'll pay you.'"

Steve returned to the women's setup when his pal, Tom Sermanni, was coaching and asked him to be technical director ahead of the World Cup the following year. After years of playing politics and sitting behind desks, he jumped at the chance to get back on the grass. Not much had changed. There still wasn't much money about, and the players and coaching staff struggled along with second-hand equipment and hand-me-downs from other quarters. There was one change, though. Australia national teams had been given "brands", so the national team were the Socceroos, the Olympic team were the Olyroos and the younger age groups were known as Joeys. With no Kangaroo derivative appropriate, it was decided to call the women's team the Matildas, from a famous old bush ballad, a move that was not initially met with universal popularity.

The Matildas were drawn in a tough group for the World Cup in Sweden, with United States, Denmark and China. The campaign started disastrously with Sonia Gegenhuber sent off in the opening game against Denmark. The Aussies went on to lose 5-0. Angela Iannotta wrote herself into Aussie football folklore when she equalised against China on 25 minutes, becoming the first ever Australian to score at a World Cup. Unfortunately, that was as good as it got. They went on to lose 4-2, and in their final game went down 4-1 against the United States.

Results may have gone against them, but the Matildas have gone on to appear in every World Cup since that Sweden adventure and appeared in four of the last five AFC Women's Asian Cups. Today's Matildas squad, featuring many players who weren't even born when Steve blew the whistle at his first training session, now play at some of the biggest clubs around the world and get well paid for doing so.

Goalkeeper Tracey Wheeler was with Steve in those formative days, and she is quick to credit the scouser for changing attitudes. 'Steve set incredibly high standards for players,' she said a few years later. 'But most of all, he was fair and consistent in these standards, and he dropped players who did not make them. It was the first time I had been treated like a goalkeeper, not like a girl who just played in goal. It was also incredibly hard work for all the players, but in reality, the girls who stuck with this fitness regime eventually made it through to the World Cup in 1995.'

And as for Steve, he wasn't finished with women's football yet.

Six weeks after returning from China, Hill returned to Steve's office to tell him he was no longer required. He was handed a cheque with the correct money owing, and he was gone.

'It was something that needed to be done. Somewhere in the machinery of Australian football some cogs were playing up, and I needed to be removed to get them working again.'

Not that he was out of work for long. Harry Michaels, president of Sydney

Olympic who was also a television producer, offered Steve a role providing commentary and punditry on National League and Series A games, while still working at Olympic.

'Harry was great. A larger-than-life character, full of passion, he loved football. He made series like *Aerobics Oz Style*, which was a massive success. His passion was to be a football director. He has done more for football behind the scenes than people know. If there was a player struggling, he would help them out, just like he helped me out after I was shafted by the ASF. I've got a lot of time for that fella.'

Steve worked with some different coaches at Sydney Olympic over the five or six years he spent with the club, since Constantine had first pointed him in that direction. 'Mick Hickman was a top lad, a very English coach. He would set his stall out early, wanted 4-4-2, and the players would go for that. Bertie Mariani was very different. I would say he was almost cerebral in his coaching philosophy.'

Mariani had been the architect of an excellent Marconi side which had dominated the National League at the end of the 1980s, and he took over at Sydney Olympic in 1993. 'He had players thinking, doing psychology. He would do interviews with players. He would do a personality inventory of all the players. He did one test, and Branko Milosević (who was born in the former Yugoslavia but moved to Australia and became a Socceroo) handed me the paper after five minutes. I asked what he was doing. He couldn't have finished so quickly, and he said, "I cannot read English. I just ticked A, B, C. I just want to play football!" But I enjoyed watching Bertie and his ideas.'

When Tom Sermanni left Olympic, the club appointed David Ratcliffe, a Yorkshireman who had moved to Australia in the late 1970s, just before Steve. Ratcliffe had played for St George, Sydney Olympic and Wollongong City, among others, as well as 21 games for the Socceroos before hanging up his boots. On John Kosmina's recommendation, Ratcliffe asked if Steve would like to be his assistant at Olympic as well as coach the goalkeepers. Having been out of club football since leaving Tasmania, he jumped at the opportunity.

One of the players Steve got to work with was Ivan Zelic, brother of Ned, who by now was playing in Germany for Borussia Dortmund. Ivan had followed his older brother's route through the AIS before signing for Sydney Olympic, and he was a player Steve rated highly.

'Ivan's debut was in the abandoned game against Daewoo Royals of Korea when he was elbowed in the head "off the ball, in the first minute",' he wrote in his column for Inside Soccer. 'And then followed three consecutive games in front of more than 10,000 people against South Melbourne (when he had come on as a second-half substitute), Sydney United and Marconi.' The 17-year-old had to mark the likes of Francis Awaritefe and Paul Trimboli in those opening games, a real baptism of fire, and after impressing against South Melbourne, he kept his place for the next game against United.

Coach Ratcliffe was more grounded, saying Zelic still had to focus on his schoolwork as well as his heading. In fact, Zelic was commuting regularly from Canberra, where he went to school, to Sydney to play football!

The 1996/97 season started well for Olympic with a resounding 4–1 away to newcomers Perth Glory, a five-hour flight away. As Steve tried to sleep, he wondered what his mates back in Tasmania would have felt about such a trek. For them, Hobart to Launceston was far enough! After a narrow 1–0 win over ten-man Canberra, Olympic was top of the table with maximum points.

For their next home game against Gippsland Falcons, Ratcliffe gave a debut to a teenager whose recent signing had caused some consternation within the committee. Brett Emerton had impressed at AIS, and Steve brought him to Olympic on a salary of A$35,000 a year. The committee was fuming! How could they commit so much money to a teenager? They later sold him to Feyenoord in the Netherlands for A$650,000, by which time Steve was coaching in Singapore. 'I never received a thank you email!' Years later, their paths would cross again when Emerton was with Blackburn Rovers, and they reminisced about the Olympic days. 'He was now earning in a week what he earnt in a year at Sydney Olympic.'

Also lining up for Olympic that day was Abbas Saad, making his return to professional football after a worldwide ban was overturned for his alleged involvement in match fixing in Malaysia. He lasted half an hour before going off injured. Despite the good start, Ratcliffe and Steve were hoping that by reuniting the Alistair Edwards/Saad partnership, which had been so successful in Singapore, and having Steve Refenes providing the ammunition, it would provide the impetus for a more sustained title challenge, but injuries were already having an impact.

Olympic's first serious test came away to Sydney United in front of 11,381 people. Saad started on the bench as Ratcliffe persisted with Edwards and Trajanovski upfront, but two second-half goals from Tony Popovic, either side of a consolation from George Sorras, ended their unbeaten run.

Sadly, the good run didn't last, and there were soon mumblings among committee members. It wasn't just the coach's office that had a revolving door. Presidents came and went with alacrity. One new guy arrived, and Steve instinctively knew he wasn't going to be able to work with him. One of his hangers-on went to his office one day and announced they were going to sack Ratcliffe, and they wanted Steve to take over. This offended Steve's principles, so he said he wasn't interested. He wasn't going to shaft his mate Ratcliffe. He had read Machiavelli and seen the likes of Constantine and Hill in action, but that wasn't his world. He wanted to stick by the moral compass he had developed growing up in Liverpool where you learnt to look after your own.

'"Okay, we sack you instead," was the reply, and I was gone! Dave went soon after.

'What an education Olympic was! After the game, the committee would gather the gate receipts and dump the cash on a big table, and they would literally carve it up. One pile went to pay bills, another for expenses, another for salaries. I learnt how to be a creative accountant watching them at work. In fact, I was having to pay the lads, and I was deducting tax as you were supposed to. Later, it transpired the tax I was taking from their salaries wasn't being passed on to the taxman! As someone said to me at the time, "It's no good owing the tax man a small amount of money. They'll shut you down. Better owe them heaps. That way, they'll want you to trade your way out of debt, and you can keep on operating. Sydney Olympic was the ideal finishing school for my time in Asia!'

Ever since he had done his FIFA lecturer course in 1981, Steve had been conducting courses around Australia and in 1997 was sent to Fiji by FIFA to take what is now known as an Oceania A license. Like any teaching, there was a syllabus to follow, and Steve would dutifully draw up lesson plans for the attendees before heading into the classroom. The trip to the tropical island of Fiji sounded wonderful to the Liverpool lad, and he set off with images of sun-kissed beaches, warm waters lapping round his ankles and lazing under coconut trees while the wannabe coaches went through their paces.

Steve arrived in Suva, and after getting settled in was soon teaching. It didn't take long before he was amazed by one particular individual.

'The best lad didn't wear boots! Here I was from a culture where footballers took boots for granted and expected a boot deal as a right, but this lad was having none of that. This lad would play barefooted; he would glide over the rough pitches, he could pass, had a good touch, but he could also coach, and he would sit in a tree to watch games. He told me he could see better from an elevated angle. He would sit in the tree, make notes, and then climb down and pass on his instructions to his players.'

While doing the course, he met an administrator, Ashok Balgovind, who he actually got on with, and they kept in touch in those pre-social media days by exchanging letters. He kept asking Steve to come back, and when his schedule allowed, he would fly out to the South Pacific Island to work with national youth teams as they attempted to win a cup. At one stage, there was an offer on the table to take on coaching the Fiji national team, which was tempting, but the politics scared Steve off. 'You had the Indian and the Fijian, and they weren't getting on well at the time, and I didn't want to get sucked up in all that. I was getting enough politics in Australia to last me a lifetime and then some.'

His coaching trips took him off the beaten track. 'I would tell friends I was off to Fiji, and they would say, "Oh great. You must go here, go there ... nearly all beaches." They would take me away from where the tourists went and inland ... that was like the Wild West! We'd go into villages along bumpy old tracks, and we'd get wild dogs jumping at the car, pawing at the windows, and they didn't want their tummies tickled. I'd get back, and my friends would ask how it was, where I'd been, and they couldn't believe it when I told them. Wish I'd had Instagram!'

From the madness of Sydney Olympic and the Fijian hinterland, Steve sought solace teaching in a maximum-security jail for young offenders in Sydney. 'I met my first murderer, but I found out most of the murderers there were nice lads. They weren't the planned murderer; they had just snapped, either under the influence of drink or drugs or glue. I learnt about gang culture from the Lebanese gangs in there. I spoke Arabic, of course, so I got on quite well with them. There were Vietnamese kids who ran certain areas, Aboriginal kids who were victims of alcohol or substance abuse. You had the Islanders from the Pacific Islands; you just didn't argue with them, but they were great—never disrespected a female teacher.

'It was massively eye-opening. I thought I knew Sydney, but they taught me about the drug trade—who runs which area. The lads were easy to teach because there were only six or seven in a class, and the last thing they wanted was to be thrown out of the classroom. Throw them out, and they would be sent back to their cells, and they spent enough time there alone with their thoughts. In the class, they could meet and talk, things we take for granted. Some were very intelligent, but some of the backgrounds they came from were scary.'

Whenever there was a new intake of offenders, part of Steve's job was to see if it was worthwhile putting them in a classroom. If they couldn't read or write, then they couldn't study, and they would be a danger to people around them because they would feel left out, frustrated, and kick off. Steve would show them a video of the film *Boystown*, a black-and-white film based on the story of Father Edward Joseph Flanagan who developed a lifelong interest in young people and their struggle to grow into responsible, productive members of society, and he would observe how they reacted to it. Initially, he was surprised to see how some of these tough lads would break down as they recognised scenes from their own lives.

For all his efforts to be a calming influence in the classroom, there was one incident where he nearly came a cropper. Steve would always count the pencils at the start and end of the lesson because if any were missing, they could be used as a weapon. One day, he was leaning forward helping a lad with the Australian equivalent of A-level maths, and the next minute, a thick arm was wrapped round his neck and a pencil stuck in his jugular vein. Instead of elbowing the lad in the stomach and throwing him over his shoulder as many a hero did in the movies, Steve froze.

'Come on, mate', the coach stuttered. 'You don't need to do that.' Amazingly, the lad laughed, released Steve, and returned the pencil to the box.

Steve reported the incident to the prison authorities and was somewhat surprised at their reaction. '"The reason he did that (release you) is because he liked you." He was a murderer and had never shown any emotions or been shown any emotions in jail, or in life. The only way he could think of showing me he liked me was to show me he had the power of life or death over me, and he chose life. I told the psychiatrist I would have preferred a box of chocolates! I saw him the next day, and he was fine, smiled, and said hello!'

Soon after the pencil incident, an old mate rang with an interesting proposition.

Part III:
The South East Asian Years

Notice that the stiffest tree is most easily cracked, while the bamboo or willow survives by bending with the wind — **Bruce Lee.**

5. Johor FA

Life was good for Steve in Australia. He had been there almost 20 years and had earned a reputation as a good coach, a coach for whom players enjoyed playing and a coach who spoke his mind, which helped him move into punditry as a way to top up his coaching salary. He had just been sacked by Sydney Olympic, but he knew that, aged 43, he still had years left ahead of him. Perhaps his dream job of managing Liverpool wasn't going to happen, but he was quite content to sit around and wait for the next job offer from an Australian club.

Malaysia and Singapore are relatively geographically close to Australia, but in the late 20th century, they were a closed book to the footballing fraternity down under. The Malaysia Cup may well have been one of the oldest football competitions in Asia, but when it came to football, Australia saw its heritage and its links to the UK and Europe.

That started to change in the late 1980s when Malaysian and Singapore football clubs started to realise the potential in Australian footballers and came calling offering unknown riches. Players like Alistair Edwards, Scott Ollerenshaw and Abbas Saad, who Steve knew well, were among the first, and soon there followed a steady trickle of Australian born-and-bred players being recognised in Southeast Asia, all the while being treated with disdain in their own backyards.

These Australians bought quintessential Aussie characteristics to teams, which were packed with flair but lacked discipline or a winning mentality.

They worked hard, they never knew when they were defeated, and they thrived on mateship, building a team spirit where little existed previously. And following in the flight paths of the players were the coaches, one of whom was Ron Smith.

Steve had worked with Ron, so when 'Smudger'—as he is known—called from Malaysia on a Monday in June 1998, Steve was all ears. 'Steve, what are you up to these days?'

'I'm teaching in a prison school,' Steve's voice crackled over the line. 'You're not going to believe what happened today! There was only a full-scale riot, people smashing each other and all that. I just sat down and waited for the guards to come in and calm things down. How was your day?'

Picturing the "woe is me look" on the other end of the line, Ron got straight to the point, already sensing what his mate's response would be. 'Fancy coaching? You'd have to be here in Malaysia by Thursday as there is a game at the weekend.'

'You gotta be joking. Anything has got to be better than this,' was Steve's response, and he booked the next available flight to Singapore.

'When he told me how much I'd be earning, I thought why not. It was only two months, and I thought I would return to Australia and a new club when I was finished. I had nothing to lose,' he recalls.

That phone call changed Steve's career.

Though he was well regarded in Australia, he was little known beyond the small insular football world. In Southeast Asia, he would be part of a footballing culture that dated back decades, and with it would come pressures he never could have imagined.

The promised driver at Changi Airport in Singapore failed to materialise, and Steve was forced to take a taxi across the narrow land bridge that links Malaysia and Singapore, and on to the Larkin Stadium on the outskirts of Johore Bahru.

JB, as it is often abbreviated, is the capital of the state of Johor, the southernmost state at the tip of the Malay Peninsula. At the time, it hosted two football teams, both under the ownership of the private Johor Corporation. Johor was the elder club; officially the team was known as Johor Football Association, while Johor FC was a newer club. Steve's pal, Ron, was at JFC while Steve was to take over Johor. Traditionally, neither club was particularly successful, though Johor had had its moments; they were both also-rans in the local league, and their respective fan bases reflected their lowly status and ambitions.

Steve's job was made slightly easier by having a number of familiar faces around him, not least being Smith, with whom he shared a flat upon arrival; while at the football club, he was grateful to see a couple of Australian lads in the first team.

'Thank fuck you're here; let's just get this (team) organised,' exclaimed Darren Stewart, a no-nonsense defender. Both Darren and his teammate, Milan Blagojevic, who was also known to Steve, explained to their new coach there was a nucleus of a good team; the local players were above fair quality, but the previous coach, nice guy though he was, just wasn't able to build a team from the disparate parts.

For that opening game, a cup tie against Perlis, Steve just sat in the dugout next to the coach he was to replace and fought against his jet lag. At half-time, his sole input was just to say, 'You can play better than this,' and the team would go on to win 3–2 and advance to the next round of the competition.

One thing that did stand out from that first game was the performance of a player in the opposing team. 'What a player! He was like a stick man, but what touch and vision,' Steve drooled. 'Can we sign him?' Unfortunately, that was out of the question, but the new coach filed the player away in his mental rolodex. The player in question was Kiatisuk Senamuang, nicknamed Zico, a Thai international and part of a generation of Thai players making a name for themselves across Southeast Asia.

Steve was, in some respects, lucky. He knew the job was short term, so expectations were realistic, and he anticipated leaving at the end of the eight weeks. It would hold him in good stead that he could call on the experience of Smith, Stewart and Milan over the coming weeks as he learnt to navigate the, to him, alien world of Malaysian football. The new coach was also lucky, in another respect, in a way he wasn't to fully appreciate just yet.

In Malaysia and other countries in the region, the coach doesn't have the power of a Mourinho or a Wenger or a Klopp.

In much of Southeast Asia, a coach's remit extends purely to getting the first team ready for match day and winning games. The actual running of the football club lies in the hands of an executive manager who may or may not be competent, may or may not be a football person, and may or may not be reliable.

Steve landed on his feet with Johor's manager, Haji Ahamad Mohamed, who spoke English fluently. As Steve struggled with adapting to the local culture, it was Ahamed who worked behind the scenes to soothe ruffled feathers. 'You're the CEO on the pitch, and I'm the CEO off the pitch,' he told Steve when they first started working together, and he was to prove as good as his word over the next few years.

Those early days taught Steve a lot about his new home, and Hajji Ahamad proved to be as good a teacher as Taffy Edwards had been at Collegiate, with one particular lesson still resonating to this day.

'You've got to be like bamboo,' he cautioned the coach one day early on. This was a bit deep for Steve, who hadn't seen much bamboo in Liverpool, Bahrain or Tasmania and was totally unaware of the quote at the start of this chapter. 'You've got to learn to go with the flow, bend with the breeze. If you try to fight the way things are here, you will lose. You're not going to change how Asia works; just concentrate on winning football games. That gives you power.'

Not long after that chat with Haji Ahamad, one of the Johor players approached Steve and said he couldn't make training the next day. 'My mum wants me to go shopping with her, so I can't make it,' explained the player matter-of-factly.

"This wasn't in any coaching manual I had read but I asked other senior players, and they said just accept it. Take him on, and you will lose the player and his mates in the team. It wasn't a power game in which a player wanted to get a mental edge over the new coach; his mother wanted to go shopping, and that was it. I was learning to bend. It was pointless wondering what Bill Shankly would have done had Roger Hunt asked for some time off to take his mother to Woolworths; I was in a different world with different rules, and it was down to me to adapt."

The family unit remains at the core of Malay society, and Steve would soon have players asking for time off to go to a wedding or a circumcision celebration, which would clash with training or a game. Steve knew these were battles he could not win, no matter how large a fine he imposed or how many football boots he threw, so he simply told the players to be upfront and honest with him, and there wouldn't be a problem. Lie and it would be the last lie they told at that football club.

Dazza and Milan also proved to be spot on in their analysis of the team's failings. With just a single win all season, relegation to the Malaysian third tier was a very real possibility and one the club couldn't countenance. The team was in a mess, bottom of the table after seven games, with just one win and one draw to show for their efforts. In an eight-team division, they were halfway through the season and odds on for relegation, but as the import players had said when Steve arrived, there was a good team waiting to be organised, and the new coach set about his task with gusto on the training field.

The first game wasn't long in coming, against the army-backed club known as ATM, and as the new man in charge, Steve wanted to lay down a few ground rules. He told his players, to all intents and purposes, a new season was beginning; everyone had a clean slate. He told them he had high standards, and he expected them to have high standards; cheating in any form, be it the training ground or on match day, was totally unacceptable. Be aggressive, get in your opponent's faces, support each other and enjoy winning. The latter may have sounded a tad optimistic, given the previous seven games, but as the coach said, they no longer counted. Everyone had a chance to impress.

Steve placed a lot of confidence in his Australian imports. He leant heavily on them for insights on their teammates, as well as knowledge of the league, and he essentially built the team around them, with Dazza at the heart of the defence and Milan the pivot in central midfield. They proved crucial in ensuring the new gaffer's messages were passed on to their teammates.

Whatever was said seemed to have worked, as Johor won 2-0 with goals from central defender, Azmil Azali, and a close-range finish from Azmi Mohamed. But ATM was also in a bad place in the table and was as gentle an introduction to Malaysian football as the new coach could expect. Tougher challenges lay ahead.

The wins kept coming as Negeri Sembilan were beaten 3-0, Perak was dispatched 3-1 in the FA Cup, and AIS were narrowly beaten 1-0 in a friendly. Ron watched the Perak game, and as they stood side by side on the touchline before kick-off, he noticed a large lump in Steve's back pocket. 'What's that?' he asked.

Steve took out a shiny black stone and showed Ron. 'It's my lucky stone.'

Forgetting the importance of the cup tie, Ron fell apart. 'What the hell are you doing with a lucky charm? You're far too intelligent to need any of that superstitious nonsense; give it here.' Ron grabbed the small rock and threw it away.

While Steve was doing wonders with the players on the pitch and adapting to life without a stone in his back pocket, things were not going so well off. He struggled to adapt to his new surroundings. At an early training session, Steve was putting his players through the paces when he suddenly saw a man on a horse riding across the field. This wasn't something covered on any training course Steve had attended, and just as he was about to respond in his best scouse 'Get off my fucking pitch, you ...' he was rugby tackled by captain Azmil Azali who had seen enough of his new coach to anticipate how he would react.

Azmil bundled Steve to the ground, and, with his hand over Steve's mouth, said, 'You were about to tell him to fuck off, weren't you?' Steve managed a nod before Azmil said, 'Don't. He's the crown prince of Johor, and he owns this field. Say anything like that, and it's bye, bye, Coach.' Needless to say, when a princess was riding around the pitch a few weeks later, Steve offered nothing more than a cheery wave and a 'How do you do?'

While he was getting to grips with royal etiquette, Steve also made some tweaks to how he operated. It was said of Arsene Wenger towards the end of his Arsenal career that he was an analogue coach in a digital age, the inference being he was stuck in his ways and not adapting to the way the game was developing. Steve embraced change. He had always thought deeply about the game, had been an early convert to player psychology and statistics, and he saw no reason to change that just because he had more than 20 years' experience and earned a well-paid job in Malaysia.

Malaysia, as a country, is made up of a number of different races, with the Malay being the most numerous, alongside large numbers of Chinese and Indians, as well as indigenous peoples. Malay culture places great emphasis on *jaga maruah*, or 'saving face', which essentially means the no-holds-barred banter and abuse of an English or Australian dressing room is not replicated in Malaysia, where being too direct or too forthright would be considered rude. Modesty rules, and players would change into their kit on match day by wrapping themselves in a towel before removing their trousers and putting on their shorts. Status also plays a role with passive obedience to superiors seen as a core tenet of being Malay, which helps explain why a footballers' union was struggling to make an impact in the country.

This obsession with face and status made for a very different dressing room environment than what Steve was used to in Australia. The players would just sit quietly on their benches, perhaps nervously puffing on a cigarette, and listen to their instructions. No one really wanted to ask questions; they didn't want to be seen as being too big for their boots or, even worse, suggesting the coach hadn't been explicit enough in the instructions. Most players came from the villages of Malaysia where deference and respect are ingrained into them at an early age; they can earn good money being a footballer, but they just prefer to keep their heads beneath the parapets. Among themselves, they get on well, though respect would automatically be extended to a player who was seen as more pious than the rest or had had a more successful career. Club management members, though, were always treated with deference, whether it was deserved or not. These were the people who could decide whether a young player stayed at the club or was moved out, and they decided whether those players would be paid or not.

Football in the state of Johor in the 1990s bears no resemblance to the current setup. Now, thanks in part to the backing of the current Crown Prince, Johor Darul Ta'zim are, by far, the most professional football club, not only in Malaysia but probably in all of Southeast Asia. Today, they have their own training facilities, and any trip to the royal polo grounds is far more genteel than it was in Steve's time. Back then, Steve would turn up for training in his beaten-up old Proton with bibs, balls and cones in the boot, and in the absence of any changing facilities the players would get kitted and booted either in the open or in their cars. For him, it was another challenge, and he took it in his stride the same way he dealt with being battered black and blue in mining villages or did training on sandy pitches in the desert.

The whole club festered through a lack of investment and a lack of care. There were parts of Larkin Stadium that hadn't seen a dustpan and brush in what seemed like years, and other areas were positively off-limits to anyone who didn't have an interest in herpetology. 'The scoreboard wasn't working, so I sent a couple of the odd-job men up there to fix it because, of course, as a coach, that is my job. I forgot about it for a while, and we got on with our training session. Soon, we became aware of loud screams, and we looked up to see the men scrambling down from the scoreboard screaming, "*Ular, ular, ular!*" About ten snakes had made their homes in there, presumably because it was warm and quiet.'

As he had in Bahrain, he set about learning the local language, Bahasa Malay, and would sit at home watching local TV, while his players helped him with local slang, key football words and the odd swear word.

He also introduced days off, something totally revolutionary in Malaysian football where players were expected to train, train some more, and then continue training, even after a game or a gruelling away trip. These small steps helped endear Steve to the local players in the squad and made him appear as a coach who had their backs. Of course, in all this he was helped by his CEO off the field who offered his full support in the face of club officials, with little to no understanding of football. Even now most officials' responses to a defeat are for more training and more running. While this was a great frustration to the ambitious young coach who thought so deeply about the game, he would always fall back on some key advice he had received from Ron Smith soon after arriving in Malaysia. 'If you get one thing done in a day, you have done well.'

Things continued to go well on the pitch, with back-to-back 2–0 wins over struggling Police and promotion-chasing Terengganu, making it four wins on the spin since taking over and, just as importantly for the coach, four clean sheets. He had been brought in to beat the drop, and it looked as if safety was being secured. Malaysian football fans, more than most, love a winning team, and Johor supporters responded to the club's revival by returning to the stadium, and with a big state derby looming against Johor FC and progress being made in the FA Cup, the whole area was buzzing.

Historically, Malaysian football has been dominated by Selangor and Singapore, though since the latter went its own way in the mid-1990s, the picture has become more mixed. Selangor is a big boy when it comes to crowds— when the team is doing well, it's capable of attracting 60,000 or more people to the home games. Other states like Pahang, Kedah or Perak can attract around 20,000 or more people if they are on a good run. But when teams are losing, supporters just stop going, which is what Johor fans had done in the first half of the season.

For the derby, recent results gave Johor the edge, and their supporters headed to Larkin Stadium in an optimistic mood. For Steve, it was just another game, albeit one against his erstwhile flatmate! He neither knew nor cared about any rivalry that may have existed between the two teams, and while he was slowly becoming aware of fissures with Johor Corporation, which backed both clubs, he was kept well insulated from that by Haji Ahamed. Johor FA won the big Derby!

Other games were also an education in a different manner. A trip to Kelantan was a major experience!

'The dressing room was disgusting; there were cockroaches everywhere,' recalled Steve. 'As we got off the bus, Haji told me, "Whatever happens, just take it on the chin."'

Until then, working in football had been genteel for the coach. East Riffa is never going to be on a par with Liverpool, Tasmanian football is little more than a kick-around with mates, and in the early days in Malaysia, expectations had been so low that Steve fully expected he would be gone at the end of the season, no matter what. Suddenly, he was being thrown into a cauldron, an atmosphere he hadn't experienced since standing on his milk crate at Anfield watching in awe as Celtic fans drank themselves into a stupor.

As he took his place in the dugout, the noise levels increased, and if for one moment Steve felt he was being singled out for attention, then he was, as plastic water bottles not filled with water but another liquid and stones rattled off the Perspex dugout. It seemed such a feeble defence against such vitriol, but once the game started, the coaching team was able to shut out the din and focus on the game, while Johor dominated on the pitch. The visitors ran out 3-0 winners, and with the home support turning their ire on their own team and the match officials, Johor was able to savour the moment before heading back to their bus once the streets had cleared of home supporters unhappy with the defeat. Steve returned to KB and sat in the opposition dugout on a number of occasions over the next few years but would never forget that first trip.

Johor finished the season in second place, five points behind Terengganu, but with a positive vibe surrounding the club. Had the league season continued for another three or four games, the team was confident it could have finished top and earned promotion, a far cry from early June when Steve had arrived. As it was under the new coach, the team had seven straight wins and not conceded a goal. As well as escaping relegation, Johor had reached the Malaysian FA Cup final where a trip to Kota Kinabulu in Sabah waited, along with a match up against the local heroes. An unlikely glory beckoned.

While Johor's defence had been unable to replicate their league meanness, they had still been strong enough to get past Perak and Kuala Lumpur to set up that date in the middle of August in distant Sabah. The hosts most definitely had the cup pedigree, reaching the final three times previously and triumphing in 1995 against Pahang in Kuala Lumpur. This time, of course, they had home ground advantage and boasted an England international in their ranks, former Arsenal midfielder, David Rocastle, having signed for them soon after being released by Chelsea.

However, it was Johor who lifted the trophy that sultry night in Kota Kinabulu with the reliable Milan Blagojevic scoring the only goal of the game on 32 minutes. Steve was effusive in his praise for his two Aussie stalwarts, describing after the game how Milan 'never let him (Rocastle) get a touch. He was just brilliant against this hardened former England international. And as for Stewart?

Not only is Darren my captain, but he was also our goal scoring sweeper. That's just how competitive and proud a professional this Australian player really is. In fact, he has been at Johor now for six straight years, which has now made him the longest serving foreign player ... he's treated like a king!'

The team's strong end to the season bought Steve more political power than any shiny black stone did, and he used that to negotiate a new two-year deal, though he was later advised for the 1999 season that he would have to do without both Milan and Darren Stewart as the league had decided no more import players were to be used. As if that wasn't bad enough, he learnt that the club's budget for the new campaign would also be substantially cut. As rewards went, the double whammy wasn't the best, but at least he had the security of a two-year deal and the knowledge Haji Ahamad had his back in the internal bickering that went on higher up the food chain.

When it came to assembling a squad for the season ahead, Steve relied heavily on the manager who not only had the contacts but also had the added bonus of understanding the game. The team was built around a core of local Johor-born players, but the absence of foreign players meant the duo had to look further afield for key players who could have an impact. It was on the recommendation of Haji Ahamad that the club snapped up Hashim Mustapha.

Hashim, 33 years old at the time, was Kelantan born and bred, and apart from a short spell with Kedah, he had spent his whole career in the north-east with his hometown team. His career was winding down, but the former Malaysian international still had a thing or two to offer on the pitch and was happy to make the journey south where Steve would make good use of his experience. The coach still had the nucleus of the 1998 team, and he was looking to players like Azmil Azali (think Harry Maguire, a big, powerful defender) and Azmi Mohamed to fill the void left by the departures of Dazza and Milan, both on the pitch and in the dressing room, while at the same time prioritising players who could play in a number of positions. This is where Haji Ahamad proved invaluable.

Ahamad quickly grew to respect Steve and the way he operated, and he knew his coach would appreciate the addition of Hashim. Strong people in the dressing room were as essential to moulding a good football team as silky ball skills were on the pitch, and he had seen how much Steve relied upon the likes of Dazza and Milan for getting his messages across. Azmil was developing into a good leader, but another old head wouldn't go amiss!

'Half-time in the dressing room is where Steve performs his best, giving personal attention to all in that limited time, saying good words to the performers, and putting an arm round those struggling,' Ahamad recalls. Hashim and Azmil made sure the half-time messages were carried out in the second half.

There was one other change the team would have to get used to. The Football Association of Malaysia had decided they didn't want any more drawn games, so if, after 90 minutes, the scores were level, there would be a penalty shoot-out to decide which team would get the three points. Steve shrugged his shoulders and got on with his job. He would soon get used to all the chopping and changing, and anyway, he soon discovered a more sinister problem that ate away at the integrity of the game itself, one that forced him to ask some searching questions not just of those around him, but also of himself.

Preseason commenced a few weeks after the FA Cup triumph, and with the Aussies gone, he called on the local players to offer their own ideas and, much like days off and ball work, this was quite a revolutionary idea in a country where players were often seen as little more than chattel by club officials and were expected to keep quiet and do as they were told. To Steve, it made absolute sense; he was still a newcomer to the league, and the players knew the conditions, the opponents and who to watch out for, so why not pick their brains? Others were less enthused, and little did he know that behind the scenes there were people who were not taking kindly to all these new-fangled innovations. Then, however, they bided their time, letting Haji Ahamad know but waiting for their moment. They may not have been football people, but they knew teams lose, and they knew where the axe was kept.

With time to kill between preparing for the new campaign and the actual start, Steve sat down and codified his approach to football and how he wanted his teams to play. The journey to understand how football could be played came to fruition in Johor in a series of bullet points that set out a philosophy Steve had developed through 20 years on the training field, coupled with conversations with peers and mentors along the way.

Analysis came easy to Steve. 'My foot in the analyst's camp is that as far back as 1998, I was sitting in front of a VHS (remember them?) with a pencil and paper (remember them?), spending hours trying to analyse games to help me make my training sessions more realistic and applicable to the game,' he wrote in an article for *Total Football Analysis* website in 2019. 'So, I analysed firstly where were goals coming from and how were they being scored.

'I found that at whatever level, the same principles were applying: goals were coming from approximately 80 per cent inside the penalty area and were mostly scored from one or two touches by the opposition player. It got me thinking that if goals were mostly being scored in the box, then how do you get the ball into the box as often as possible? And the more players in the box, the greater the chance of scoring!' With opposite applying to defending.

The last thing Johor needed was a trip back to the north-east to play Kelantan TNB, but fixture lists aren't kind to beleaguered football coaches, players or supporters. Little did Steve know that for this game, he wasn't only up against 11 opponents and a hostile atmosphere.

'I'd spent most of my time talking, playing or watching football since I could remember, and you'd have thought I had covered everything, whether it was in Stanley Park with my father, playing Subbuteo with Paul Bennett, or discussing psychology with Merv Beck going to and from Yorkshire League.

'But nothing, no training course, could have prepared me for match fixing.'

There had been rumours of course. Anyone who spends any time close to football in South East Asia will soon pick up hints and mumbled conversations or will see some eye-catching results. However, you hope, and you just shut your eyes and ears, praying there is no truth in the murmurs. It's football, the beautiful game of Pele and Cruyff. Surely the beautiful game could not be sullied by dirty cash, or by players or match officials on the take.

Unfortunately, Malaysia has form when it comes to match fixing. In 1994, '21 players and coaches (were) sacked, 58 players suspended and 126 players questioned over corruption involving match-fixing' wrote B Suresh Ram in the *New Straits Times*.

Dr Declan Hill, who has researched extensively the prevalence of match fixing around the world, said in the *Sydney Morning Herald*, 'In Malaysia, the corruption was so bad that following a national police investigation in 1994, one cabinet minister estimated 70 per cent of matches in their leagues were corrupted.'

The date is carved deep in Steve's memory, April 9, 1999, when Johor played away to Kelantan TNB. Johor was trailing 2–1; ironically, Hashim had scored his first goal of the season when, with five minutes to go, the Johor goalkeeper palmed the ball into the back of the net. That kind of thing happens all the time; players make mistakes especially at set pieces. It's easy to misjudge the ball, to lose it in the floodlights, to be temporarily unsighted. Then, with moments left, a long-range effort made it 4–1 to the home side; the coach started asking questions. 'I hadn't been expecting much from the game to be honest. It's a long way to go and a hostile atmosphere; away teams don't often do well there but the manner of those two late goals irked me.'

The players, too, hadn't expected much from the game and had backed themselves to lose by three clear goals. 'They didn't think they were doing anything wrong! The way they saw it, they were going to lose anyway, so they had no chance of getting a win bonus. This way, they got some money to mask their disappointment. Why go on a 28-hour round trip with nothing to show for it? Anyway, from the players' point of view, this was a victimless example of throwing a match. They had initiated the fix; no one had got hurt; no one had been threatened. I was soon to learn match fixing is not just black and white. There are so many shades of grey it is difficult to take a moral stand and remain involved in the game in the country.'

Steve's willingness to listen to anybody would soon give him a lesson in match fixing he would never forget, and while he would never condone it, he had an understanding of the root causes and how it could affect players if they ever decided to mount a moral high horse.

'Players are easy targets. Most footballers are on low salaries, and sometimes they are paid late or not at all, and often they are far from home, meaning they lack strong support in difficult times. Everything costs money. Basic healthcare costs, getting married costs, having children costs, kids going to school costs. Match fixers are experts at sussing players who are weak, vulnerable, and that's who they target.

'Sometimes players do resist the efforts, but not for long. Having a couple of men on the back of a motorcycle and suggesting they know which school his child goes to sounds like something from *The Godfather*, but it is a reality naive young men are left alone to face. It becomes easier to do as the bookies ask; at least that way there is a regular income to supplement the erratic earnings of a professional footballer.

'Match fixing is a complex issue and don't think it doesn't go on all over the world. There are many reasons for fixing and many ways to fix a game. The actual result is often of little interest; it's the factors within that matters, such as the number of goals. I got better at spotting it, but when you are winning you never believe it's due to fixing!'

It was a sober lesson to learn, coming alongside a greater awareness of the battles behind the scenes at Johor and Ron Smith's maxim that if you have successfully completed one task in a day, you have done well.

You could be forgiven for thinking Steve was looking wistfully elsewhere to coach, but he wasn't. He had fallen in love with Malaysia, with the people (well, some of them!), the country and yes, even the football. He had given up on Liverpool calling and offering him a job; he was in a good place and despite all the trials and tribulations, he was loving life in the tropics.

The defeat at Kelantan, and the manner of it, proved cathartic as the team regrouped and went unbeaten for the rest of the season, finishing champions, a point clear of Selangor, and thus qualifying for the Malaysia Cup where they finished bottom of their group. There was another early Cup exit, but overall the 1999 season came to a successful but premature end. Steve, Haji Ahamad and the players could look forward to life back in the top flight after an absence of a couple of years.

There was, of course, a sting in the tail befitting a team nicknamed the Scorpions. For the 2000 season, Johor would have to operate on an even tighter budget, making an already difficult task all but impossible. Sure enough, Johor would spend the season struggling to get to grips to life in the top flight, much to the delight of some club officials who had spent preseason sharpening their swords. The politics Steve had so assiduously been avoiding were poised to explode.

Football is a harsh mistress at the best of times, and success is soon forgotten as fans and officials focus on the now. It didn't matter Johor had won the FA Cup and the second division in successive seasons yet now faced life in the top flight with a shortage of funds.

Thanks to Haji Ahamad's sterling work massaging egos behind the scenes, Steve managed to hold on to his job. Following a defeat to Perak, he switched to a 5-3-2 and saw his players recover enough to earn a win over Sabah. However, the recovery was short-lived, and Johor went on another poor run, losing four and drawing two of their next six games.

Back in Johor after the next loss, Steve was called to a meeting with Haji Ahamad in Dunkin' Donuts. It was over, the manager told his coach, they want you out.

Haji Ahamad had fought tooth and nail for Steve over the last two and a half years as the coach's unorthodox style had grated against the formality and stiffness of officialdom, defending him each time he or his players had stepped out of line. All the time the team was winning, he had the most powerful arguments. Steve's combative, no-nonsense style gained him plenty of admirers in the game, among players and other coaches, but in the boardroom, people were less enamoured with his efforts. In their world, appearance and etiquette were everything; players and coaches served at their behest and theirs alone.

Some officials resented Johor's success early on under Steve. Their "flagship" club was JFC, and they were getting the bulk of the resources in their bid to be the first privately owned football club to play in the top flight. Maybe some of them felt put out that their ambitions were being blunted in part by the upstarts being the more dominant team on the pitch. And doubtless there would have been some among the committee who objected to the way Steve tried to empower his players, whether it was actively seeking their opinions or allowing them days off once in a while.

Whether or not this thinking was behind the subsequent budget cuts Johor suffered from is not clear.

As ever, Steve didn't get involved, but he knew that one day, the officials would seize their opportunity and act. So here he was, sharing a final, amicable coffee with the man who had just sacked him. Haji Ahamad, who 'felt the sacking was an injustice', told Steve that he had had enough of the posturing and politicking going on behind the scenes, and he too had resigned, and they parted friends. The first part of Steve's Malaysian trilogy was over.

6. Vietnam Women

If you want to ever achieve happiness, don't dwell on the past. Instead, start living. What is the point of obsessing over something that has already happened, and that you cannot change? Live! — Kien Nguyen, *The Unwanted: A Memoir of Childhood.*

With the Malaysia chapter of his life seemingly over, Steve returned to his beloved Liverpool and his parents' familiar home in West Derby, so he could consider his options. It was 20 years since he had moved to Australia, and he made a point of returning home every couple of years. He wasn't short of offers, and a return to Australia was always a possibility, but his work with Johor had raised his profile in Southeast Asia, and despite some of the many off-field battles and the frustrating lack of infrastructure, he had grown to love the area, Malaysia especially.

The Lao Football Association wondered if he wanted to coach their national team, a position probably as relaxed as any managing position in the world. Lao was no great shake, even in Southeast Asia, and expectations were low. Steve could have seen a contract out eating *laab gai* (a spicy chicken salad) and watching the sunset over the Mekong River from a restaurant in the sleepy capital Vientiane, but Malaysia had given him a taste of proper football culture.

Then there was an offer from Lancaster University for teaching and coaching. That was tempting, for it was close to home, and it would be a return to what he had prepared for when he had gone to Carnegie all those years back. But for a coach approaching his peak years, Steve desired challenges, something different, and something new.

He soon found all that and more in Vietnam with the men's Southeast Asian Games squad. That was the position he was initially sounded out for, but it wasn't the position he eventually took up. When the Vietnam Football Federation made contact with Steve, they saw him taking over the national team ahead of the biennial competition later in 2001 hosted by Malaysia. They wanted to get rid of the incumbent who had fallen out with a number of key officials and players. Terms were agreed and discussed, and Vietnam had their new coach.

Then they got thinking. Nobody rated their national team; not even the most patriotic official felt they had a chance of a medal in Malaysia. Sacking the coach and bringing in a new man just for a tournament they had little chance of winning seemed a waste of time. It was better to keep the existing coach in situ; failure in Malaysia would be good enough reason to fire him and to focus on the women's team as they were widely seen to be among the favourites.

So it was in 2001 that after a three-month break from the game and an English winter, Steve accepted the offer of national team coach of the Vietnam women's football team. The offer came from the Football Federation with the remit of preparing the team for the upcoming Southeast Asian Games to be held in Kuala Lumpur that September.

If the job may have surprised some, it certainly ticked Steve's boxes. New language? Tick. New names to learn? Tick. Off-field politics? Tick. Seemingly impossible deadline? Tick. Very little prior knowledge? Tick. Oh yes, this job was Steve down to a tee.

The SEA Games, initially known as the Southeast Asian Peninsula Games, is a multi-sports event which had been introduced back in 1959 as a biennial sporting extravaganza that helped promote cooperation and understanding among the nations in the region. However, that was a time of unrest as newly independent nations struggled to form their own identities after centuries of colonisation.

By 2001, the area was home to a number of Asian tigers who had turned their AK-47s into mobile phones and MBAs, and they had seen impressive economic growth come to the region. Even Vietnam, which had for so long held on to a more isolationist path, was slowly opening up to the outside world. The SEA Games, a kind of micro-Olympic Games/Asian Games, had become part of the ASEAN sporting calendar, with national honour being broadcast live around the region.

Before introducing himself to the team, there were a couple of important people Steve needed to meet. One was the technical director, who was also a communist party representative. He made it his business to know everything about everything and rinse through the hue of ruling party doctrine before deciding what was best for the party. The other person was the translator who would be a vital nexus between the coach and the players, so she was someone Steve needed to have complete faith in.

It took time to find a translator; a few tried out for the position but were considered not competent for the role. One would earnestly take notes at meetings, then go home and translate before proudly handing over her notes the following day. She didn't last long. Next was a woman who said yes to everything, no matter what the question. One day out of frustration, Steve turned and said, 'You're a giraffe,' to which she replied, 'Yes.' She was soon to be an out-of-work giraffe. One of the players did a good job for a while, but that was never going to be sustainable. Finally, Steve found the right person.

'I walked into the office one day, and this woman calls out, "G'day, mate," in the finest 'Strine you heard north of Darwin.'

Bui Thuy Linh had gone to Australia to train to be an accountant, and she had totally immersed herself in the language and the culture. Not only was her English excellent, but she also wouldn't take shit from communist party appointees who tried to interfere with Steve's running of the team. She was perfect for the job!

To anyone coaching abroad your translator is your most important asset for both linguistics and for understanding the culture. Linh was brilliant. Though, there were a few hiccoughs.

'I once told her to tell the players to hit the far post with their crosses. Next minute balls were pinging to the corner flag! She said "you said hit the furthest stick!" Also, one game in the heat of the action I said "fucking welly it". This time she was unusually using her electric translator. What are you doing? I asked. She replied, "I know what fucking is! I quite like it. But what is this welly?" It shows you can't use slang in overseas coaching!'

Early training sessions were getting-to-know-you exercises as Steve struggled to get to grips with the unfamiliar names—there were plenty of Nguyens, for example—while finding out what there was in the way of equipment (30 bibs, 30 balls and 40 cones, as he recorded in his notes after the first day of training). Meanwhile, the players were put through their paces with plenty of fitness and weights to build up their body strength.

Within a few weeks, Steve had an idea of what his ideal team would look like, so he arranged their first full-scale friendly against a men's over-35 side. In a close-fought game, the women came out narrowly on top, winning 3–2. The coach came away gushing at what he had seen, taking time to praise his players for their fitness and discipline, and how they had kept on going, even up until the 90th minute. All that fitness work was paying off.

It was Linh who first pointed out to Steve the negative press he was receiving in the local media. Now in his 40s, his desire to learn the language had dimmed, and he saw little benefit in making the effort for what he assumed was a short-term position. Linh showed him some of the stories that came from the technical director who was voicing his concerns about the tactics the team was using, which surprised Steve, as the team was unbeaten and he had never attended a single session. He obviously had a spy in the camp! Which in fact he did.

A full-scale game was later organised in the middle of June against a team made up of staffers at the British Embassy in Hanoi where diplomats of various shapes and sizes fancied their chances against a team of women.

For Steve, this was an opportunity to see how his team performed against a strong, physical opponent before they headed their own separate ways ahead of the national championships. For the diplomats, it was different; there was male ego rubbing shoulders with national pride. One of the embassy players was certainly up for the challenge, flying into challenges with all the grace of a hungover Sunday league player. Next time he caught Steve's eye, the coach said, 'You don't want to be doing that,' but the diplomat was nonplussed. 'She's got to learn,' was the reply of this Roy Keane wannabe. 'Don't do it,' Steve repeated.

The next challenge saw his captain, Hien Luong, take out the upper-class Brit in proper Roy Keane style. 'I told you not to be a silly lad,' Steve explained to the embassy official as he was carried off.

Steve's women had shown they weren't going to be intimidated by anyone on the pitch. They chewed up party cadre for breakfast; they weren't going to let bigger and more physical players dominate them on the pitch. Steve was delighted. They possessed that all-important mental toughness to go with their skills. He felt they had a chance in Malaysia.

Following a month's break, the team returned to Hanoi to start the serious preparation ahead of the SEA Games. Steve had them do a few light training sessions before heading to Australia for more intense training, along with friendlies against tougher opponents. As many of the women had never travelled outside of Southeast Asia before, they were called to a team meeting where they were given a crash course on how to behave.

They were warned several times not to take their own food with them. Australia has very strict quarantine laws, and food would be confiscated. Australia also has many restaurants and a large Vietnamese community, so they needn't starve. They were also advised not to hang their laundry out of the hotel windows as they were accustomed to doing at home.

'The hotels have washing machines; they can do the laundry for us. Do not hang your laundry out of the windows.' Linh faithfully passed on the dos and don'ts, and the players politely nodded their heads without listening to a word that was being said.

Sure enough, at Australian Customs in Sydney, officials were confiscating enough food to feed a starving football team for a month. The highlight came when the communist apparatchik attached to the team walked straight through Customs instead of queuing with the rest of the travelling party, a privilege he was afforded at home. But Aussie Customs was having none of it, and called him out, much to the amusement of the squad.

The merriment didn't end there. The following morning, the team was patiently queuing for the breakfast buffet, and in came the apparatchik taking full advantage of his own sense of superiority by pushing in front of the players and coaching staff to grab his breakfast first. The restaurant staff members weren't amused by the man's arrogance with one of the servers calling out, 'Oi! Who the fuck do you think you are?' He would not forget the burning indignation he felt at these public slights to his person.

Apart from enjoying a rare chuckle at the cadre's expense, the team was in Australia to prepare for a big competition, and within a couple of days of landing, Steve had them playing New South Wales in a friendly. Being August, it was quite chilly, and the pitch was quite slippy. Vietnam was out-muscled by their hosts and lost 2–0.

Back at the hotel, the players felt sorry for themselves and did their own laundry, hanging the clothes out of their bedroom windows.

On the pitch, things improved as Singapore was beaten twice, 6–0 and 4–0, with a loss to Australia sandwiched in between. Despite the laundry issues, Steve had been impressed with how the squad had conducted themselves on the trip. They had trained hard and seriously for the whole stay and put in good performances against tough opponents. Having worked with the Aussie women's team a decade earlier, he was well placed to judge how the Vietnamese ranked against their hosts.

'Technically, the Vietnamese were far better with the ball than the Australians, but they were no match physically. If anything, the Vietnamese worked that little bit harder. Many had come from impoverished backgrounds, and they felt very lucky, and immense pride, to be offered the chance to represent their country overseas.'

Steve felt the players were ready; many had the Vietnamese down as favourites to win the SEA Games, and a major part of the coach's job over the next few weeks would be to manage expectations and hope the upset communist cadre would not cause any problems.

Before leaving Australia, the team was let go for one last night out, and they decided they wanted to go to McDonald's, which had yet to spread its golden arches to Vietnam. The coach-driver who had driven them everywhere during their stay had been seduced by their charms and their mischievousness, and he offered to treat them all.

'I fought in the Vietnam War,' he explained to Steve. 'I never knew any Vietnamese; they were all seen as the enemy, and we had no contact with them. This is my way of apologising for our actions.' Whatever the reason, the players loved their first Big Mac and fries, and their coach appreciated the efforts of a kindly coach-driver and his burger diplomacy.

A month later, the Vietnam squad was ensconced in the hotel in Kuala Lumpur, preparing for the tournament. Steve felt confident. 'I was only worried about Myanmar. If we could get past them, we would win the trophy,' but he wasn't telling the players that.

Their first game was against Indonesia at KLFA Stadium, and an early goal from Doan Thi Kim Chi on two minutes somewhat settled the nerves. Nguyen Thi Mai Lan made it 2-0 on 20 minutes, and when Luu Ngoc Mai made it 3-0 five minutes before half-time, the Vietnamese were coasting. Three second-half goals in 11 minutes confirmed Vietnamese superiority, with Luu completing a hat trick and Bui Thi Hien Luong rounding off the scoring.

A second convincing win two days later, 5-0 over Singapore, with Luu netting another two goals, meant Vietnam had reached the knockout stage where they would come up against their toughest opponents, Myanmar. The players knew this was the big one. Also, the Vietnamese media was taking notice. Luckily, the reporters tended to be females, and they were quite sane compared with some of the male media members.

However, 24 hours before the semi-final, there happened one of those incidents no training course could be expected to prepare a football coach for.

It was September 11, 2001, and on the other side of the world, two aeroplanes were crashing into the World Trade Center in New York as TV viewers looked on in shock and horror. As the fireballs engulfed the buildings and thousands lost their lives, the Vietnamese squad, who barely five weeks earlier had been enjoying McDonald's Happy Meals in Sydney, were whooping and a-hollering in their rooms and the hotel corridors. Every member of the squad had their own memories or tales of the Vietnam War, of families ripped apart, or homes and possessions destroyed; in their eyes, 9/11 was a moment of *schadenfreude*.

Vietnam had a complicated relationship with the United States. Diplomatic relations had only been restored six years earlier, and 1997 had seen the US send their first ambassador to Vietnam. Rapprochement had accelerated since, especially through trade and tourism, but as is often the case, it takes longer to conquer hearts and minds at ground level, especially when those hearts and minds had been brought up on napalm, Agent Orange and incessant communist party propaganda. The burning injustice and anger over what had been visited upon their country, through no fault of their own, exploded just as the Twin Towers came crashing down.

This would later be expressed by former Deputy Prime Minister and poet laureate To Huu just months before he died in a poem that appeared in a Saigon newspaper the following year.

The one who brags about "human rights"
Is still dropping bombs
And then suddenly calamity fell
Upon an arrogant superpower

However, Steve was a football coach, and he had no interest in any geopolitical justification of the atrocity. He wanted the squad focused on the game with Myanmar and nothing else.

'It was a confusing time, as of course the players had no English, so the news they were getting was via Vietnam. We had a meeting where the fitness coach who had actually fought in the war explained this was not the correct behaviour. After that, the players were top class, except for the incessant hanging of laundry outside the windows of five-star hotels!'

As expected, Myanmar proved a far trickier opponent than either Indonesia or Singapore, and despite another goal from Luu, the opponents proved a tough nut to crack. Vietnam won after a tense penalty shoot-out, and the reward was a final against Thailand, and Steve's second cup final in three years.

It was Cup final day against Thailand, and the team was gathered together in the dressing room. Rather than dealing with nerves and giving out some final instructions to his players, Steve was on the warpath. All the talk of respecting others that Ron had highlighted when Steve first moved to Malaysia had gone out the window.

'Fuck off! Just fuck off!'

Incandescent with rage, the coach was in the face of the team manager. Translator Linh joined in as well with a couple of choice 'fuck yous' to the hapless cadre, while a couple of players were in tears on the bench.

'Coach, he said I play,' cried the reserve goalkeeper. 'I don't play. She should play,' as she pointed to Steve's first-choice goalie.

'Coach, he said I don't play. She should play. I should play,' sobbed goalie number one.

In his infinite wisdom, the manager decided to change Steve's starting line-up and play the second-choice goalkeeper in the final. Not because she was a more commanding presence in the box, not because she was a better shot stopper, not because she was better in the air, but because she came from the north of the country, and the team manager/communist official said there were too many players from the south in the starting 11. Perhaps worn down by the crescendos of "fucks" being levelled at him, the official backed down, and logic prevailed with the number one keeper playing. The number two keeper was brought on with five minutes to go to make sure every player could say they got on the pitch.

Steve was proud of the way his players were standing up to the interfering official, as well as their contextually correct profanity use. No team talk was needed after seeing the team rally round the goalkeeper. They were riled, and they were ready.

There were two goals from Bui, a penalty from Nguyen Thi Thuy Nga and another from the reliable Luu, and the Vietnamese defeated the Thais 4–0. They lifted their first-ever SEA Games title, launching an era of unprecedented success in the region as they had four of the subsequent six events, finishing runner-up on the other two occasions.

Nicknamed the Golden Girls, Vietnam has been the most powerful team in women's football in the region for the best part of two decades, with impressive performances in the AFC Asian Cup as well as wins in the ASEAN Football Federation Championship in 2006 and 2012 and finishing fourth in the Asian Games in 2014.

The players left a great impression on Steve, not only as professional footballers, but as people who battled many obstacles and succeeded, and many of this team are still involved in the game, either coaching or in administration. 'The delight and pride these players felt I have never seen replicated anywhere else. When they sang the national anthem, they meant it! It would bellow out. You could see the passion in their eyes. Winning that first-ever trophy was a special moment, and they were a special group of players.'

It was fitting that Steve would close the Vietnam chapter of his career with a trophy and an argument with officialdom!

7. Home United

*It has to be good to live in Singapore because otherwise, nobody will stand for it—***Lee Hsien Loong**.

Following his success in leading Vietnam to Gold in the SEA Games, Steve didn't stick around. He had been offered the opportunity to take the team to the Asian Games in October 2002, but he knew that was a completely different level. There, the Vietnamese would have had to go toe to toe with the likes of China, Japan and the Koreans, and Steve was realistic enough to know his players weren't at that level. Coaches are remembered by their last game, and he had just won a trophy; he saw his legacy being damaged if he chose to go to the Asian Games in South Korea, and he was proved correct as the Golden Girls finished bottom of their group, suffering heavy defeats along the way.

Anyway, he had been appointed youth coach at Sheffield Wednesday alongside his old mate from Australia, Jimmy Shoulder, who was heading up the academy.

Looking back at his career, it is easy to see this short stint as an aberration, Sheffield Wednesday standing like a beacon among a list of clubs unfamiliar to most British football fans, but while Steve relished the opportunity as he did with every job he took on, there was a part of him hankering for foreign shores.

He was in his 40s and had made a name for himself in Southeast Asia, but back in the insular world of English football, he was a nobody, and there was little chance of him working his way up the ladder in England. Despite the success English coaches have had overseas, they are still seen as unknown quantities and a risk within their home shores, while a foreign coach, known or unknown, is often seen as a safer bet. For example, it took Roy Hodgson 30 years before he made an impression in his homeland, and he had won titles across Europe and reached the World Cup finals. If a coach with that kind of pedigree struggled to break the glass ceiling, then what price would an unknown scouser have to pay who had won a gold medal with a women's team in Asia?

It was little wonder that when a Singapore side called Home United came calling, Steve was all ears.

Coaches enjoy working with young players; it is where they feel they can have the most influence on the direction a player's career takes, but there is nothing that can replace the buzz of being the man at the top who has to build a team to challenge for trophies. Having a couple of medals tucked away in a tatty old shoe box had given Steve the thirst for more. Plus, there was the chance of Asian Champions League and AFC Cup.

Steve arranged a meeting with the Sheffield Wednesday manager, former Leeds United and Wales midfielder, Terry Yorath, and explained he had received an offer that was tempting. Basically, Terry told him to go for it. The Welshman said there was little chance of Steve being appointed first team coach with the Owls, and he would not stand in his way if he received a better opportunity. Besides, he had worked overseas coaching the Lebanon National Team, so he had some empathy for where his youth team coach was coming from. It was an amicable parting of ways, and soon after, Steve boarded a flight to Singapore.

They were heady days for Singapore football. The S-League was the destination of choice for the finest generation of Thai players ever produced, while local players came through who would go on to form the nucleus of a national team. It wasn't just the Thais who were adding exotic quality with exciting Brazilian and Iranian players, and even Grant Holt, who would later go on to score over 200 goals in England.

Steve liked what he saw in the squad over those final few games of the 2002 season. The players were genuinely nice lads, there was a good team spirit, and training was serious but fun. However, some of the squad just weren't good enough for where Steve wanted to take the team, so at the end of the season, he sat down with the club management and started planning for 2003.

'You talk about luck in football, and I had luck in buckets at Home United. Not only were the players good, the management off-the-field were excellent, very easy to work with. The manager was a guy named David Conceacao, a policeman seconded to the football club, and he was excellent, a really good negotiator. Like Haji Ahamad at Johor, David just told me to look after the team;

he would take care of everything else, and he was as good as his word.

'Then there was the president. Again, he was a government appointee as Home United were a club that had its origins in the police, ambulance and fire services, much as SAFFC had military roots. My first president was Tan Boon, a great bloke who loved football. But he was replaced by Lee How Sheng, who was probably the cleverest guy I ever met. He had a degree from Oxford and a Master's from Harvard. He once asked me if I knew of Oxford University, and I said yes, I'd played there!

'"I was taught by Stephen Hawkings," was his reply! Sheng had unusual ideas about football, which was fine as, like David, he was happy to let me do my job and always gave me 100 per cent support.'

Behind the president and the manager was a committee much like there was at Johor, but Steve had nothing to do with them, and that suited him just fine also.

Completing the Home United setup were two gems. Kit man Rosli Dollah and goalkeeper-coach Francis Thomas would prove to be invaluable to Steve as he moulded his team. All the players, senior down to the youngsters, loved Rosli. Francis was the Singaporean equivalent of Radar O'Reilly from the US series *M*A*S*H*. He knew everyone who mattered and could find anything that was needed.

The first challenge Steve faced when building a squad for 2003 was the salary cap. He had never come across this before, and all he had to play with was SG$70,000 a month for the whole squad, just over £25,000 at the time.

He sat down and juggled the numbers with David, and they agreed the best they could do was to have 16 first team players and four young lads who could run all day! Steve wanted Khairul Amri in the latter category, a promising teenager at the time, but was overruled by the Football Association of Singapore who said players his age needed to be at the Young Lions, a developmental squad of promising young players competing in the S-League against fully seasoned pros. Like a salary cap, this was something Steve had never encountered before, and he was miffed, to say the least. This wasn't to be his last run-in with the suits at Jalan Besar.

The cap made it difficult to accommodate the demands of Brazilian import Peres D'Oliveria who was hankering after a pay rise. Peres had arrived in Singapore in 2001 and made an immediate impact, scoring 42 goals in his first two seasons and impressing the new coach with his technical ability. Steve wanted Peres to stay, but there were fears that meeting his demands would upset the salary cap calculations. The club also wanted to do everything by the book, which tied their hands further.

'As I wasn't covered by the salary cap, I suggested I hire Peres' wife as my maid, admittedly a well-paid maid, and could funnel the extra wages to him that way, but the club weren't keen, citing tax difficulties!' Eventually, David was able to reach an agreement, and Peres would go on to play an important role in the coming season.

With the squad assembled, Steve started preparing for the 2003 season and soon came across something else he hadn't seen before. Before a new season, the Singapore FA (FAS) insists players must pass an endurance test. If they failed, they wouldn't be cleared to play. Steve didn't like this and was vociferous in his criticism, at one point earning himself a 500 Singapore Dollar fine from the FAS after going public with his thoughts. He had good reasons to be critical.

His willingness to speak his mind and support the team quickly won him the support of the players.

Steve made a few slight changes to the training regime he had inherited. He had the lads training at 9 o'clock in the morning as he had done in Johor, the reasoning being most rains or lightning came in the afternoon, which could decimate training for the day. He also gave the players over 30 years old a day off a week, which was received with mixed feelings. Peres spent all day in bed; Brazilian-born striker Egmar Goncalves, who had taken Singaporean nationality, played with his children. The only player to be upset by the extra free time was Thai midfielder, Surachai Jaturapattarapong. On his first day off, he turned up for training as normal, only to be told to go home by the coaching staff and his teammates. He ended up playing golf, and rather than be traditional and use a buggy or a caddy, he slung the clubs over his shoulder and ran around the course! He played off a single handicap, so the extra exertions had little impact!

The first game of the season was against the previous season's champions, SAFFC, hyped locally as the Uniform Derby, and Steve was feeling confident. He had gone with 3-4-1-2 with Peres playing just behind Egmar and Fahmie Abdullah, which had raised a few eyebrows as it meant Indra started on the bench.

Fahmie had been signed preseason from Clementi Khalsa and was seen as a talented player, though he carried a reputation as a bit of a wild boy—well, he dyed his hair. However, this was Singapore, where jaywalking and chewing gum were considered crimes. As far as Steve was concerned, he was 'super talented', and his performances preseason meant he fully merited his starting place on the team sheet. Egmar gave Home the lead on 35 minutes, though SAFFC levelled early in the second half through V Selvaraj. With both sides going for the three points, Steve threw Indra into the fray and, lo and behold, he scored the winning goal on 71 minutes.

Indra responded in just the way the coach hoped he would. He went on to score nine goals in the opening seven games, as the Protectors embarked on an 11-match unbeaten run. Indra was ably supported by Egmar and Peres in the goal scoring stakes, with the latter benefiting from his extra time in bed, netting ten times.

Home's first loss of the season came in their 12th game as they played SAFFC in the second Uniform Derby of the season, but while Steve, the coaching staff and the players were disappointed by the result, they responded in a manner befitting of champions by winning their next six games, scoring 26 goals along the way.

Sadly, being Singapore, the team's efforts went relatively unheralded locally. The S-League had opened in a blaze of glory a few years earlier, and large crowds were seen at many games. That initial buzz soon dissipated, and fans started staying away, preferring the hype that accompanied the burgeoning English Premier League, rather than the game in their own backyard. Home United was undoubtedly the great entertainer in 2003, and in players like Indra, Sutee Suksomkit and Peres, they possessed players of immense technical ability who could thrill and delight fans. However, local media was more interested in promoting the Thierry Henrys and David Beckhams from thousands of miles away, and affluent Singaporeans flocked to support English clubs.

Maybe the lack of external pressures, the sheer absence of non-stop analysis worked in Steve's favour. In most countries with a strong football culture, the media are masters at digging out and making up stories to justify their existence. If things are going swimmingly at a club, then a newspaper is not above printing stories hinting at unrest in the camp, planted by players or agents with their own agendas. This was not the case in Singapore where dirty linen is kept in-house. There, a coach is unlikely to pick up a local paper and read that a rival is considering bidding for his top scorer, or a club source has gone public about a training field bust-up. Coverage was limited to match previews, match reports and the odd player interview.

'This was the best family atmosphere at a club I had ever experienced. Everything clicked. I was surrounded by good lads who did their job and did it well. I would never hear about any problems or bust-ups, though I'm sure they happened. In fact, I would have been surprised if they hadn't happened. But there was a good dressing room, and there were a couple of hard-bitten pros who knew the score and would nip any sign of trouble in the bud.

'Aide Iskander and Subramani were as professional as I have ever come across. They were both experienced players—talented players—who bossed the dressing room. They knew what it meant to be a professional footballer and led by example. Excellent role models. They made my job much easier just knowing there were people I could trust to keep discipline. Mani and Aide could take care of themselves and were as hard as nails on the pitch and in the dressing room.'

The two veteran defenders were modest about their roles at the club. Aide says, 'Actually, both me and Mani were fortunate to have good professionals such as Egmar, Peres, Surachai, Sutee, Lionel, Sivakumar, (his brother) Aidil, Indra, because these players are naturally talented, and Steve was the perfect coach to motivate them to win trophies, and me and Mani were there to make sure everyone was on the same page to create legacies for the club.'

Discipline was rarely an issue. 'If a player came in late for training, all it would take would be a quiet word from either me or Aide, and that would be enough,' says Mani. 'We had good players. They knew what was expected of them,' said Mani.

On the pitch, the wins and the goals kept coming as Indra, Peres and Egmar engaged in their own personal battle to be top scorer, and Home United had the title sewn up in their 29th game of the season when they defeated Tampines Rovers 3–1 towards the end of September. The game at Home's Bishan Stadium was a nervy affair, with Peres opening the scoring just after the hour mark. The Stags soon equalised, Australian George Goutzioulis setting up a tense finale under the lights. In the final minutes, first Fahmie and then Indra settled the game and the title, fitting that the two players involved in Steve's first big decision of the campaign should come together to confirm the title.

Home United's reward for having won the title so early was to have their squad decimated for their next game as Singapore bid to qualify for the AFC Asian Cup. Immediately after the title had been clinched, six players, including Indra, Aidie and Subramani, headed to Kuwait with the national team hoping to overturn a 3–1 loss in the first meeting. Steve was irate about the call-ups and was soon calling publicly for his team's game against Sembawang Rangers to be postponed, but the S-League was having none of it, insisting the game went ahead as scheduled. They fined Steve for his outburst.

Steve had no choice but to accept the decision and set about rejigging his team. He knew he would have to call upon a slew of youngsters, and while he had no problem in calling on the reserves from time to time, at the start of his time with the club, he had explained to the players how he would make two substitutions per game for tactical reasons, with a third giving one of the younger lads valuable minutes subject to match conditions. It would also help the younger lads feel part of the squad and of course allow them to pick up a few bonuses along the way. But this was different. This was the league body effectively forcing him to select a much-weakened team. As usual the players rose to the occasion and won 9–2!

With the title won, Steve's attention turned to the Singapore Cup.

The Cup final was played at Jalan Besar Stadium towards the end of October, in front of almost 5,000 fans, and it was to prove to be an eventful and a fitting climax to the season, featuring the best two teams in the country, with Steve and Geylang United's Australian coach Scott O'Donnel both nervously prowling their respective technical areas.

Sutee gave Home the lead on 15 minutes, and as the game wore on, it looked like the Protectors were on course for a historic domestic double, but Australian Brendon Santalab equalised for Geylang on 34 minutes to send the teams in level at half-time.

The second 45 saw Geylang increasingly dominate the game, causing nervy moments in the Home defence. Up top Indra was struggling to make an impact, and a frustrated Steve started mentally making preparations to replace his striker. It was then that Indra decided to take the game by the scruff of the neck and score what would prove to be the winner. It was a nice habit to have, and one Steve was fully aware of. 'Strikers score goals; it's their job, but the top strikers, they score crucial goals, goals that count.'

It had proved to be a good first full season in Singapore. Two trophies to add to his growing reputation, Peres was the player of the year and top scorer of the year, while three of the top four scorers in the league were Home United players Peres, Egmar and Indra. Scott O'Donnel was named coach of the year, a decision which seemed to upset Peres more than it upset Steve. 'He was swearing, saying

I should have won coach of the year, but I wasn't too bothered. We'd had a good season, the team had played well, and anyway, how much money did I lose by not winning the award?'

Two members of the victorious Home side could look forward to their very own special preseason. Indra and Suttee had been given the opportunity of two-week training stints with Chelsea, at that time flush with cash from Russian oligarch Roman Abramovich. Arranged by an international airline which had sponsorship deals with both clubs, it was a once-in-a-lifetime opportunity for the two players to enjoy a bit of football stardust, albeit with the reserves. And for Indra, as a serving policeman in his day job, it meant more time off work.

The idea that one of his star players happened to be a copper in his day job and was being invited halfway round the world for a trial by an English Premier League may once have seemed strange to Steve, but he now took it in his stride.

He was less relaxed about one incident, though. He had started receiving phone calls from an unidentified number, offering unsolicited advice about the team. 'He was telling me who to pick, who to drop, pick a weakened team for such-and-such a game. I was having none of it, of course, and together with David Conceacao, who was a policeman, filed a report with the police and the FAS. When the cops reported back, it was bad news. They told me they were unable to trace the call because it was being made from a fax machine! I was disappointed because I didn't enjoy having threats to my life made.'

Soon after, Steve was in a meeting with David and some of the club sponsors when they rang again. 'The sponsor signalled for me to hand the phone to him and spoke quietly and firmly to the mysterious caller in the local dialect Hokkien. There were no more phone calls after that! I found out later the sponsor had mentioned a few names who were higher up that particular food chain, and the caller quite rightly decided to do his cold calling elsewhere! The FAS, by the way, never did get back to me. They'd fine me because I said the beep test was daft, but when it came to investigating alleged match fixing, they didn't want to know!'

Run-ins with the FAS were all part of the learning experience in that first season in Singapore, as Steve took great delight in highlighting the inconsistencies and inaccuracies that were a daily feature of football in the city state. He was a regular visitor at headquarters for one hearing or another.

One particular time, both the referee and the linesmen accused Steve of verbal abuse after a game. 'They're right. I did abuse them after the game. But

I did not make the comments they alleged I made in their reports. For a start, I've been an English speaker all my life. I am a qualified English teacher. What they alleged I said was grammatically impossible for a well-educated native speaker, not to mention physically impossible. Then David applied the coup de grâce. He stood up in front of the panel and told them in all the 25 years he had been a policeman, he had never once come across witness statements which matched so completely. It just doesn't happen. People see different things, remember different things. He really laid it on. He was basically calling the ref and linesmen liars but in an Asian way. It was great to watch! I got let off, but I could sense the disappointment in the panel as I walked away without having any kind of sanction imposed. I knew though it was only a punishment delayed. They would get me soon enough!'

Steve packed his medals into a shoe box and sent them off to his mum, soon to be forgotten. The year 2003 was over. It was time to plan for 2004 and the challenges that lay ahead. 'Even to match our 2003 record will be a difficult task with the reduction of teams and the introduction of a Japanese side. At the same time, our resources will be devoted to the inaugural AFC Cup.'

Planning for the new campaign began before Suttee and Indra were enjoying the bright lights of London as Steve sat down with manager David and thought about 2004. The S-League was being restructured, a regular occurrence in Southeast Asian leagues, with just ten teams entering instead of the 12 which had battled it out for 2003 with Albirex Niigata, a satellite Japanese team. Teams would still play each other three times over the course of the season, but instead of 33 league games, there were now 27. For Steve and Home United there was, of course, the AFC Cup to take into account.

They had to because the S-League wasn't going to be of any help; despite the extra demands on the team and the players, the salary cap remained the same, and like 12 months earlier, it seemed to Steve much of his preseason planning involved finding a few extra dollars to meet Peres' wage demands.

Singapore is small, and every game is a derby. Home United's furthest away game for 2004 was to the league new boys on Albirex Niigata that played at Jurong East Stadium. The AFC Cup was different of course. Home was drawn with Happy Valley (Hong Kong), Valencia (Maldives) and Perak from Malaysia, and the fixture list compilers at the S-League were not much given to taking Home's travel plans into account when they were doing their work.

'One of the good things about Home was how they treated players and coaches. As a club, we were massively restricted in what we could pay players, but when it came to the AFC Cup, they treated the squad superbly. Players would be on a good travel allowance, something which was over and above salary, and the club would ensure players could maximise their income. For example, flights would be arranged so that players would arrive before midnight to allow them an extra day's allowance. It was the small things like that which made Home such a special club and saw players happy to keep signing on, even Peres!'

As a veteran coach with nearly a quarter of a century's experience, Steve had amassed an impressive collection of contacts around the region and was soon able to get the rundown on Happy Valley. He was of course familiar with Perak from his time in Malaysia, but Valencia was very much an unknown quantity. He hadn't come across many people who had worked in Maldives football.

The AFC Cup began in February with Home hosting Happy Valley, winning comfortably 5–0 with the holy trinity of Egmar (with a hat trick), Peres and Indra getting on the score sheet. Then came what was, for many of the squad, their first experience of a proper away trip. Singapore is criss-crossed by a number of expressways known by their acronyms. However, Valencia away was the real deal, over land and sea. The club had done its homework, and rather than have the travelling party stay on the main island, they were booked on a private resort island called Paradise Island. It is the archetypal beach resort, with white sands, crystal-clear waters where holiday makers could snorkel, parasailing, canoeing, windsurfing, or just sitting on the beach and taking in the views.

Of course, a football team is not your usual holiday maker. They were there on business, and their days were interrupted by short boat rides to the main island, so they could train and prepare for their big game against Valencia. The club's preparations were meticulous, and as they lounged round the pool, the players doffed a metaphorical cap. As professional footballers who took care of their bodies, they steered clear of funny-shaped glasses filled with fruits and umbrellas. Unfortunately, when making the bookings, no one had thought to check if any of the travelling squad had issues with boats, so it was to everyone's surprise when both Suttee and Surachai, their tender Thai tummies upset by the gentle rocking of the water taxi, threw their heads over the side of the vessel and vomited their guts into the previously crystal-clear waters.

The game itself was scheduled to kick off at 3.00p.m.; in other words, in the hot afternoon sun. This was mentioned at the managers' meeting, and when

Steve pointed out the ground had floodlights, so a later time was possible, he was abruptly told they were broken.

Lacking any background knowledge of his opponents and frustrated by the treatment they were receiving, Home's players did their talking on the pitch, winning 3–0, with Egmar getting two and Peres scoring the other. Heading back to their resort for the final time, Steve made sure he was sitting as far from the Thai lads as possible, while mentally praising the team's efforts. For all the distractions on the trip, they had performed heroically and came away with an excellent result. But he wasn't fooled. Winning the double last season had been a monumental achievement and one unlikely to be repeated. Steve knew his squad was paper thin, and they were only a couple of injuries away from possible disaster.

Steve was looking towards the Perak game and was soon approached by Perak officials, and the start of a complex mating dance began. Under contract with Home until the end of the 2005 season, there was no way Steve would countenance fishing for another job, and besides, Perak already had a coach in place and wasn't doing too badly. His rule has always been never to stab another coach in the back. However, football people talk to a great many people, and they file that information away for another day. It may prove to be useful somewhere down the road, or it may not. In this instance, it would be the genesis of a future move though neither party could have known it at the time.

On the field, Home impressed, fully deserving the 2–2 draw in front of a hostile crowd. It was a decent enough result for an AFC Cup away leg but seen in the context of the dropped points in the last two league games, Steve was right to be concerned about his meagre resources for this tough campaign. Soon after returning from Malaysia, Home dropped more points, losing 2–1 at home to SAFFC before drawing 2–2 against title rivals Tampines Rovers, for whom Aliff Shafaein had equalised in the 90th minute. The second leg against Perak saw a similar result, meaning Home conceded two goals in each of its last six games.

Unfortunately, time is a luxury successful football clubs around the world don't have. It wasn't until midnight after the draw with Perak that the Singapore team could board their coach and face that long drive home. It wasn't the best recovery finely tuned athletes need after a tough 90 minutes, being cooped up on a bus for 12 hours, especially for the older players who were finding their bodies needed a bit longer to recover than they used to.

'No elite team would allow their players to travel straight home like we had to, but what could we do? There wasn't much in the way of flights from Ipoh to Singapore in those days, and while the club had treated us royally in the Maldives, some of the lads had to get back for their day jobs, and even our younger players had to report to their base for national service duty. I was only grateful I was given the freedom to coach how I wished; believe me, plenty of clubs would have insisted the players hit the training ground once they had arrived home. At least I could give the players a day off.'

The players with day jobs had added pressures. While the foreign players could draw a decent wage, many of the local lads had parallel careers to ensure they earned enough to survive the high prices in Singapore, and as coach, Steve needed to be sensitive to external demands being placed on his players.

In a perverse way, the AFC Cup was providing some respite from the domestic drudge. Four games in, Home United was well placed to qualify for the knockout stages having won two and drawn two games, and next up was a potentially tricky trip to Hong Kong to face Happy Valley. If the travelling squad was expecting suites overlooking Hong Kong's spectacular harbour, they were to be disappointed. 'It was a small hotel with small rooms, organised by the home team. You'd open the door to your room and immediately bang your toe on the bed. To get to the bathroom, you had to walk sideways between the bed and the wall. To be fair to Happy Valley, the team that had made the arrangements, the team wasn't trying to make things uncomfortable for us. This was Hong Kong, and it was what was available for the budget.'

Home won 2–0, thanks to the tried-and-trusted pairing of Indra and Peres, and the Singaporean side could look forward to the knockout stages.

'There was nothing easy or glamourous playing in Asian club competition in those days. While the beaches were nice in the Maldives, our hosts went out of the way to make things awkward for us. No professional football club in Europe would allow their players to travel for 12 hours on a coach in a prestigious tournament, but in a way, these trials brought the players closer together as if the shared hardships were just one more challenge to overcome. They were such a positive bunch of lads; they laughed off the pokey bedrooms and service station halts at 3.00 a.m. and let their football do the talking. Victories in the Maldives and Hong Kong, and a draw against our toughest rivals in Malaysia are testament to the character of the squad, and I think, like so much in Singapore football, they were not given a fraction of the credit they deserved.'

The triumph in Hong Kong was sandwiched in the middle of a seven-game winning run that included a 5-0 thrashing of Valencia in their final group stage game of the AFC Cup, but rather than seeing this run as a springboard to climbing the table, there was always a sense a hiccough was just around the corner.

Just to add to the fixture congestion, the Singapore Cup started in April, not without elements of farce. The ten S-League teams were joined by DPMM, a team from Brunei, Tampines Rovers reserves, Sembawang SC and Cosmo League, a combined team drawn from a mostly expat-based Sunday league. Meanwhile, Sinchi appear to have changed his sponsor midway through the competition, going from Sinchi TV in the first round to intriguing Sinchi Golden Throat by the time they met Home United in the semi-finals. In appreciation of Home United and Geylang United AFC Cup adventures, they were both given a bye in the opening round.

It was becoming clear to Steve and his coaching staff that Home's inconsistency, coupled with their lack of depth, was costing them in their bid to hold on to the title. They still had it within them to win games comfortably, but what they couldn't do was grind out results.

Home was struggling to match Tampines' consistency, and it became increasingly certain that if Home was to have any success that season, it would have to come in one of the cups.

From the end of July to the end of August, Home played six games, scoring 29 goals and conceding 14. It was peak Home United as they carved open defences at will. Home's holy trinity upfront of Egmar (14 goals), Indra (6 goals) and Peres (9 goals) was purring, but what hurt Steve was the single defeat that season with Young Lions completing its whitewash of its more experienced opponents with a 4-1 romp. Still, Sinchi Golden Throat had been brushed aside 10-5 on aggregate (5-1, 5-4) to set up a Singapore Cup final against Tampines Rovers at the beginning of October.

However, before then was the return of the AFC Cup.

Home's reward for finishing top of its group was a tie against Lebanese side Olympic Beirut, with the first leg to be played in Lebanon in the middle of September.

Lebanon was still tense in the early years of the 21st century, and the first shock was when Steve found out they were playing in Tripoli and not Beirut.

Singaporeans are brought up thinking their country is safe, so for young lads grown used to the security their own country offered, their journey into Lebanon was certainly going to be an eye-opener.

The drive from Beirut to Tripoli is just over 50 miles along the coast taking in the wide vista of the Mediterranean deep blue waters. However, most of the travelling party had no interest in the surroundings. They were more focused on their armed police escort. They'd seen Rambo movies and had no intention of being caught up in a real-life version.

Tripoli in 2005 was like a war zone. It certainly wasn't anything like the tourist destination it mostly is today. The hotel was large and empty, and although the staff members were gracious and kind, the warnings not to leave the grounds were firm and intimidating, designed to be taken seriously. The squad was only too happy to heed the warnings.

The stadium itself was empty, with army personnel providing security. As the players trawled the bowels of the stadium, looking askance at the dirty dressing rooms, they prepared for the game dreaming of nasi lemak and teh tarik. It was like they were sitting in the set of a movie in an alternate universe.

The referee snapped them from their reverie, and it was time to play football.

Yet again Steve could only watch from the dugout in admiration at the sense of togetherness and professionalism his team possessed. Aide and Subramani had been questioned during the season, but they had really come to the fore during the AFC Cup campaign. They led by example on and off the pitch, and their calm, unruffled demeanour was soon shared by the younger players in the team. Suttee remained Suttee, unflustered by his surroundings, while Peres was in his element; his left foot was his wand, and it really didn't matter how rough the canvas was; he would stroke and caress the ball—make it do exactly what he wanted.

Home chased the game for most of the 90 minutes with Olympic taking the lead on 18 minutes but, not for the first time, Indra scored when it mattered, levelling within ten minutes. Beirut went in 2-1 up at half-time. and when Faisal Antar made it 3-1 on the hour mark, it looked as if Home was done for.

On the bench, Steve knew better, and so did the players on the pitch. First, Indra pulled one back with just 11 minutes remaining, and when Egmar made it 3-3 on 83 minutes, Home United was on course for a famous result. It was again a result they could only share among themselves. In the days before social media, and without a media presence from Singapore, the folks back home would have seen the result, a cursory match result, and little else. Perhaps some would have complained the team hadn't won, but they wouldn't have been fans anyway. In what may well go down as the best result by a Singaporean side in Asian club football ever, the players were alone in their celebrations in their dirty dressing room.

Unlike Malaysia, there was to be no midnight drive following a game. The security officials accompanying the party deemed the roads too unsafe, so the squad returned to their dirty hotel and tried to sleep, adrenalin still pumping after the result. A week later, a brace by the talented Fahmie Abdullah confirmed Home United's place in the AFC Cup semi-finals. As Steve waited for the draw, he recalled some words from a Lebanese official: 'Be careful of Syria.'

It was indeed to be a Singapore Syria double with Geylang United also reaching the semi-finals. Awaiting them stood 180 minutes against either Al Wahda or Al Jaish.

With second place guaranteed, Steve rested some of his more experienced players for the last two S-League games. Before the AFC Cup semi-finals there was still the small matter of the Singapore Cup final, but in many ways, it was a game too far. The Tampines, unhindered by jet setting round Asia, took control in extra time going on to win 4–1.

Steve had just over two weeks to try and lift his players for Al Jaish—two weeks of recovery, recuperation and, of course, day jobs. The Singapore season was over; other teams were planning for 2005, but Steve and his coaching staff did their best to lift their players for the final hurdles. The players had seen Lebanon, they had heard Syria was even worse, and they could be forgiven for feeling less than thrilled at the prospect of visiting Damascus. Aide and Subramani did their bit to rally the troops; they knew they were on the verge of becoming the first Singaporean team to reach an Asian club final, and they also knew this could be their last chance of glory. Lebanon had been bad, but could Syria be much worse?

Sadly, it could. Steve had no complaints about the match officials or the opposition team and even felt the coach-driver who drove them around was 'excellent, but often drunk'. But that was it. In a letter to David Conceacao that would form the basis of an official report to the AFC, Steve didn't hold back. Sadly, the club never even got a reply from the AFC.

It wasn't easy for the younger lads in the squad, but there was Mani and Aide present to keep their feet on the ground. While their combined experiences may not have prepared them for anything as hostile, they knew at the end of the day there was a football match to be played, and they did their job well by working with the younger lads and trying to keep them focused on the 90 minutes, nothing else. And then there was the food!

Being Ramadan, food was an issue for the whole trip, with the players struggling to overcome their jet lag before an important game, but at least Sutee could be relied upon to provide some light relief.

'I had taken the lads to see Sultan Salahdin's tomb and a local mosque, but Sutee had ducked out of those visits. His stomach was rumbling, and he'd gone off in search of some food. We're waiting by the bus to go back to the hotel when he finally comes running down the street with his usual big grin. He had tracked down the only fish and chip shop in Damascus open during the fasting hours! I thought he was going to be killed!'

As for the game itself, Al Jaish ran out comfortable winners 4-0, and Steve had no complaints about the result. Al Jaish is backed by the Syrian Army and is able to use its power and influence to attract all the best players in the league. The side that lined up against Home United was, in essence, the Syrian national team, and they remain the most successful club in the country. They went on to lift the AFC Cup in 2004, their first and only triumph in Asian club football.

After the game, after changing in the squalid dressing rooms, and after pushing their way through Syrian supporters to get on the bus, the squad settled back to enjoy the ride back to the hotel, knowing they only had a few more hours in Damascus. Fans outside threw rocks and spat at the windows of the bus as they drove.

Steve and the Home United squad were grateful to return to the welcoming embrace of Changi Airport and the anonymity of Singapore. To their credit, there was no talk of playing dirty when the Syrians visited for the second leg, and they were able to enjoy Singapore at their leisure, winning the second leg 2-1 to set up an all-Damascus final.

Home United could finally end a long season, but the team was to end it without a trophy. Some called for Steve to pay the ultimate price, and he had been in the game long enough to know there would be someone keen to sharpen the axe. He came out fighting, pointing out the limitations he faced with budget and the squad.

'Success is a comparative definition,' he wrote in his post season report. 'After doing the double in 2003, it was always going to be difficult in 2004 to repeat the scenario, especially with the new philosophy of Young Lions, having foreigners and over-age players, and the introduction of the well-organised Japanese team Albirex Niigata.

'The team did, however, continue to sustain the highest standards, coming second in the league and losing in what was considered the best-ever Singapore FA Cup final. Add on to this the team reached the semi-final of the inaugural AFC Cup, only losing to the eventual Syrian winners. This was a great achievement, for whilst a number of Singapore teams (Sinchi, Albirex and Young Lions exempted) are restricted to a salary cap in the S-League, this impinges greatly on AFC development. Perhaps best summed up when I looked at the bench of Perak in our group game and saw five full Malaysian internationals, and we had on our bench three Youth League players, and nobody a current international.'

No doubt there were some on the committee who would have taken exception at Steve's definition of success, which in football is usually measured in trophies won. Steve was thinking holistically. His aim was to make Home United the biggest club in Southeast Asia, this at a time when there was no Johor Darul Ta'zim or Buriram United being funded by deep pockets, and the team's progress to the AFC Cup semi-finals was evidence the club was heading in the right direction. He pointed to one particular gong to support his argument.

'Our overall successes led to the club receiving the unique honour of being the first Singapore team to be nominated for the Asian Football Confederation (AFC) Team of the Year, competing with giants from Saudi Arabia and Korea. We were nominated for ongoing achievement and for playing with an attacking and entertaining style. We play on the best pitch, we have the most attractive Stadium and HUFC as one leading AFC administrator said to me, "Always do everything the right way."'

It is telling Steve chose to highlight that particular quote. 'Values' is a word tossed around all too easily in football and having experienced some tough old away trips in the AFC Cup, he could have been forgiven for thinking that perhaps the only way to be successful in the region would be to master those dark arts he had seen so potently on display in Syria and elsewhere. However, he stuck to his footballing principles, not just about playing the game the right way on the pitch but being professional off it as well. Take care of players, be good hosts, and do things the right way.

Steve wanted to be a force for good in the way he had seen Bill Shankly at his beloved Liverpool. He saw his role extending beyond the training field and 90 minutes on match day, and into how the club was run on a daily basis. For many in the region, these remain alien concepts. Too many club owners and managers see coaches as a necessary evil, someone to blame when things go wrong, and they feel they can benefit from appearing to act tough. There is little in the way of day-to-day management, and too many clubs seem content to just get by week to week without any kind of vision or master plan in place.

By now, Steve was 48 years old and a highly sought-after coach in the region. He was at a club he loved, working with players he loved, and although he was entering the final season of his contract with Home United, one of the clauses stated he would be offered a new deal if the Protectors won a trophy during the 2005 season. With Peres, Egmar and Indra showing no signs of losing their potency, and Subramani and Aide Iskandar the wise old heads at the back, as well as the trusted shoulders of David Conceacao, Steve was feeling confident.

His primary aim was the AFC Cup. 'I felt there was unfinished business there. I wanted it, and some of the older players wanted it. We had won leagues and cups. We wanted to take on Asia's best. I wanted Home United to be the first Singaporean team to win an Asian club competition. Singapore, under my old mate Raddy Avramovic (another member of the goalkeepers' union, Raddy had played for the Yugoslav national team as well as playing for Notts County and Coventry City before beginning his coaching career in the Middle East), had won the ASEAN Football Federation Championships the previous year. Singapore football was on a roll, and I believe Home United winning the AFC Cup would have further burnished the island's reputation as a growing football powerhouse.'

There was another reason. Both Steve and David were disappointed at the lack of support they had received from the FAS on their AFC Cup travels in 2004.

'The attitude was certainly one of, "Well, it's your problem. You sort it out," rather than seeing our exploits as something Singapore football, as a whole, could take great pride in. The national teams kept calling up our players, and fixtures were arranged with little attention being made to our travelling. Small stuff perhaps, but typical of the lack of vision in the corridors of power at the time. And as for the AFC, well, they just ignored our comments over the way we had been treated in Syria, so we thought bollocks to them both; let's win this bloody thing!'

Steve again took the team to Bangkok for preseason. Part reward for their efforts the previous season, part preseason, the trip also served to give the inspirational Surachai Jaturapattarapong a well-deserved testimonial. However, a game against Chonburi took the players out of their comfort zones. They knew Bangkok and all it had to offer—the humidity, the traffic, the other stuff—so they weren't too keen on travelling beyond the city limits. Chonburi seemed quite a trek. Steve sensed the doubts and called a team meeting. 'You get to stay in Pattaya.' That stopped the grumbling dead in its tracks!

The team returned to Bangkok for the testimonial, which was as much a treat for Steve as it was for Surachai. Ever since that first game in Southeast Asia when he sat on the bench at Johor and drooled over Kiatisuk, Steve had fallen in love with Thai players. Then there at the Supachalasai Stadium, the biggest names in Thai football had gathered to pay homage to one of their own.

'That was a bit special.' Kiatisuk Senamuang, Dusit Chalermsaen, Tawan Sripan, Therdsak Chaiman, Thawatchai Dumrong-Ongtrakul, Kittisak Rawangga, Nirut Surasian, Worawuth Srimakha, and Anurak all featured, and we were just happy to get out of our own half! What magnificent players! The Thais won 3-0, and we did well to get nil!'

For 90 minutes, Steve was a kid in a candy store. Little did he know, a few years later he would have the keys to the store.

The AFC Cup had seen Home drawn with Pahang (Malaysia), Happy Valley (Hong Kong) and New Radiant from the Maldives, with Pahang providing the first opposition at Bishan Stadium. When the Malaysians got a penalty within the first three minutes, Steve's head was in his hands. Cameroonian international Bernand Tchoutang stroked the ball home, and Home was playing catch-up. Fortunately, Peres equalised, and Fahmie hit the winner in the second half, but it made for uncomfortable viewing.

Three days later, Home lost the first uniform derby of the season, going down 0-1 against SAFFC. There was hardly time to analyse the defeat as within hours of the referee's final whistle, the Home United travelling party was heading to Hong Kong to face Happy Valley for the second successive season. Yet again it was Peres who scored, this time the only goal of the game, underlining the importance Steve attached to the Brazilian in securing his services for another season.

Back in Singapore for their fifth game in 20 days, Home took a 2-0 lead against Balestier Khalsa, only to lose the game 3-2. Back in the dressing room,

Steve looked at his gallant troops. Two wins in the opening AFC Cup were just what the doctor ordered, but one point from the first three games in the bread-and-butter S-League was not. Steve was fully aware of the limitations of the squad, and he knew the demands on the squad would only increase as the season unfolded when international call-ups and injuries would take their toll. He needed everyone to pull together, and he needed David and club president Lee How Sheng behind him. However, cracks were being to show.

In a letter to a local newspaper in April, an 'avid S-League fan since its inception in 1996' found himself really irked by the fact professional football coaches were being 'employed as pundits on ESPN on days when their time should be better spent scouting round the island'. The writer then went on to express concern over the coaches' sleeping habits, wondering if they managed to wake up in time to take morning training after a late shift covering Champions League games in a TV studio. The writer then wondered whether this moonlighting was allowed by the S-League and asked whether it was any coincidence Scott O'Donnel's Geylang's title challenge had withered or Home United failed to retain their title because of their coaches' late nights. Manager David Conceicao responded with a letter of his own defending the coach to the hilt and saying Home United was proud to have Steve in front of TV cameras on a regular basis, and as they had won the double with their coach doing punditry, they were not too concerned.

It was this togetherness, this willingness to support each other, that made the atmosphere inside the Home United camp such a happy one and highlighted the important role David played in building and keeping that harmony.

However, David wasn't to stick around much longer. Enforced committee changes saw new faces come in, and the smooth-running football club soon became a place where players and staff spent as much time looking over their shoulders as they did looking to release Indra into space.

The new president wanted his own people in place, and David was out, sent back to police duty. A new guy came in, and it was no more, 'You be CEO on the pitch, and I'll be CEO off it.' Those days were gone.

Steve had been lucky in his time with both Johor and Home United to be working with managers who understood enough about football to allow the coach the time and space to work. That all changed at Home as the new manager tore up the unwritten covenant which had operated between Steve and David and sought to impose his own will upon the playing squad. It wasn't long before he was known as Alex Ferguson, and it was certainly no compliment as he was upsetting the positive vibes which Steve had built over the years. He was talking to players, suggesting who would stay, who would leave, making team selection suggestions. In short, he was the nightmare Steve had heard much about from his time in Southeast Asia but had seldom come across.

The dressing room harmony was ripped apart as it was soon made clear the new manager had his eye on a new coach for the following season. As it happened, this particular coach had already told Steve about the approach, making it clear he wasn't actively seeking to usurp his position. Steve respected his honesty, but he was past caring. He couldn't work in an atmosphere like this and had let it be known on the coaches' grapevine he was looking around for a new club. He told the manager he didn't appreciate his constant interference, that it was upsetting the atmosphere within the club, but it was pointless.

On July 7, 2005, a number of bombs ripped through London, killing dozens of people. Thousands of miles away in Singapore, Steve was preparing his team to play Woodlands Wellington later that evening when the news broke. He met up with Woodlands defender Daniel Bennett, a cultured English defender who had made Singapore home, and they discussed the incident in the tunnel.

Bennett had heard that one of the bombs had gone off in Liverpool and was concerned about his family, but the coach replied that it was, in fact, Liverpool Street station in London. The Woodlands coach, Karim Bensharifa, walked by at this time, and perhaps misunderstanding the conversation or not knowing the events earlier that day, swung around and accused Steve of 'trying to psyche my players, you English bastard'. Steve just laughed it off, but Karim went to the media accusing the Englishman of racism. Despite Steve's best efforts to work with journalists, there were always some who couldn't wait to dig him out for something or other, true or not, and the story was soon all around Singapore.

Woodlands filed its complaint, first accusing Steve, who had of course lived and worked in Bahrain, of making racist comments about Arabs. Home filed a counter complaint on behalf of its coach. The story made for sensational headlines in the normally docile Singapore press. In one long-winded column, the reporter, who had been humiliated at a Home United training session previously, managed to squeeze in references to Hillary Clinton, Muhammed Ali, the IOC and the London Olympics before saying, 'If found guilty of making a racist comment, Mr Darby should be sacked.'

At the subsequent hearing, Steve admitted to calling Bensharifa 'an Arab twat. He called me an English bastard. I am English, but my parents are married, so obviously I'm not a bastard. He is an Arab, and I think he is a twat.'

Both Daniel Bennett and the Woodlands kitman supported Steve's version of events. Both coaches were subsequently fined. Steve received a fine of S$500 for using bad language and was told it was not in the spirit of sportsmanship to talk to an opposing player before a game or refuse to shake hands with an opposing coach after a game. Bensharifa got S$100, with one newspaper filing a story under the headline 'Darby Fined Again'.

The journalist who wrote that particular story was later jailed for his role in attempted match fixing. He was found guilty of offering prostitutes to match officials in return for throwing a game!

Steve is invariably positive about people he has encountered along the way, but mention of Bensharifa sees his demeanour change. The idea of a coach going behind a fellow coach's back, of bad-mouthing fellow coaches, went totally against the principles Steve had developed over the years. In Tasmania, he had responded to some negativity by doing an interview saying coaches shouldn't be knocking each other and should be working together. He saw coaching almost as an Arthurian brotherhood above the cut and thrust of day-to-day football where coaches would nobly prepare players to do battle for 90 minutes. What happened on the pitch or in the dressing room stayed there.

On the pitch, Home United was consistently inconsistent. Against the Young Lions, they let slip a two-goal lead and were glad to escape with a draw. A few days later, they thrashed SAFFC 5–1. The AFC Cup seemed to offer some respite from the pressures of the domestic league as Home finished top of its group to be drawn against Al Nejmeh from Lebanon in the quarter finals. Unfortunately, Home didn't turn up in the first leg, going down 3–0 at home, effectively ending their dreams of Asian club glory.

The second leg may have been a formality, but the players were determined to go down fighting, and Steve was delighted to see Indra give Home the lead, shocking the partisan home support. Al Nejmeh was a good team, though, and inspired by a young striker named Mohammed Ghaddar, they fought back to win 3–2. In one of those twists of fate football loves so much, Ghaddar would later play for Darby in Malaysia.

Out of the AFC Cup, and with Tampines Rovers looking imperious in the S-League, the Singapore Cup was all Home had left to play for.

The first leg at Bishan Stadium was a hard-fought affair between two very good teams. Aware of this final chance of a trophy, the Home players let their football do the talking. They took the lead twice, and twice the Tampines fought back. With a draw looking likely Noh Alam Shah, the Tampines' talented striker, scored in injury time to set up an intriguing second leg three days later.

If any game highlighted what might have been, it was the second leg at Tampines when two first half goals were defended by Home, superbly marshalled by the wily veterans Subramani and Aide who set up a third successive final.

The final against Woodlands would be the final act in a three-year drama that had seen Home United dominate the domestic game and come so close to making a name for themselves in front of a wider audience.

Unfortunately, one of Home's leading actors would miss the final curtain call. Peres had been sent off in the semi-final against Tampines, meaning he would miss the final. Still, Steve could call upon Indra, Suttee and Egmar upfront. It wasn't all gloom and doom.

Woodlands took the lead on seven minutes through Romanian Lucian Dronca and proceeded to batter Home. The first half didn't make for comfortable viewing, and being forced to replace Azhar Baksin with Imran Sahib on 33 minutes didn't help. Steve was glad to get the team in at half-time with no further change to the score, and he used the break to make some changes, replacing Kamal Nasir with Fadzuhasny Juraimi.

Imran was one of the unsung heroes at the club, and Steve knew that he could always be relied upon to do a good job. 'He was a wonderful pro, a great lad with a positive attitude, and a good athlete. Never caused any trouble. My instructions to him were brief. Get the ball, run with the ball and try to find Indra.'

Somehow, Home found itself 2-1 up. First Indra and then substitute Juraimi scored in quick succession, but any hopes Home was winning were soon squashed when the inspirational Subramani was injured and had to go off with 20 minutes remaining. Deep down, Steve knew it was only a matter of time until Woodlands clawed its way back into the game. Sure enough, just minutes after Subramani had been replaced, defender Azmi Mahamud levelled the tie.

But Imran had remembered his instructions. He hadn't needed an iPad or reams of a PowerPoint. His gaffer told him to run and to look for Indra, and that's what he did, right to the end. Sure enough, in the third minute of injury time, Imran received the ball. He looked up, saw Indra, and sent the police officer on his way. Indra did what Indra usually did. He finished calmly, and Home United was the Singapore Cup winner for the second time in three years.

Up in the stand, the manager accepted the praise from those who sat around him, while on the pitch, Steve and his players celebrated wildly.

There was still time for a final cameo, an encore that you won't find in any coaching manual. The Home United players, led by Subramani, collected their trophies and medals, and there were two medals remaining, one for the coach and one for the manager. Steve went up and collected both. One he hung round his neck; the other he presented to David Conceacao who was seated near the new manager. It was a deliberate slight towards the new man, but Steve didn't care. Once the party was over, he would be ready for the next chapter in his career. And for Home United, it was to be their last trophy for six years.

Mani was sad to see Steve go. 'We had something special at Home United, and I do think that had Steve stayed, we would have gone on to win the AFC Cup. We were getting closer and closer, and those teams which were beating us in the later stages from the Middle East, they weren't better than us technically. They boasted superior physique and strength, but a couple of signings, and I think we would have been serious challengers.'

The respect between the two men was total. A few years later when Mani announced his retirement from the game, Steve put down in words how he felt about his stalwart defender.

I once described Mani to a Lebanese newspaper as a virus! Once he got hold of you, he was impossible to shake off. I don't know if they understood, but the opposition players soon did. He was a magnificent professional who was an outstanding captain for me for three wonderful seasons, dedicated and hard working with a massive love for the game. But also, of a more vital note, he was an honest and good person off the pitch as well. I sincerely hope he stays in the game as the Singapore game needs people such as Mani.

Mani also wrote:

'We had a good team, good players and played good football as well as winning trophies. We believe we did Singapore proud in the AFC Cup. I don't think that team got the credit or recognition it deserved. Singapore football history is all about the Malaysia Cup and 1994, and I feel that does a disservice to those of us who followed, including our Home United team.'

At Anfield Road Primary School, 1964 (5th from left, back row)

At Hayfield Street with my friend,
Kevin Price

Liverpool Schools FA

The Carnegie Berlin side in Leeds, 1975

The Tasmanian state side, 1981

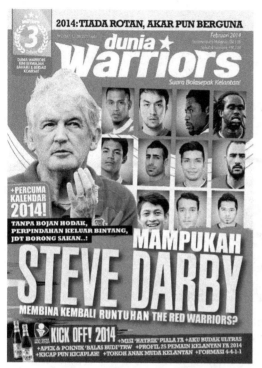

Cover page of a local football magazine when coaching with Kelantan in Malaysia

A promotional poster of the Matildas produced by then sponsor, Coca-Cola, in 1992

At Johor. Australian Milan Blagojevic is shaking hands (L) with Salim Khamis with Darren Stewart just behind, 1998

AFC Cup press conference with Kelantan, 2014

Presenting a certificate to Hamad Mohammad, Bahrain's most capped player, in Bahrain in 2016

With Jamie Carragher in Thailand, 2009

With Bryan Robson in Thailand, 2010

Working as part of a commentary team for Malaysian TV with
(LR) Adam Carruthers, Jason Dasey (an Australian journalist in Asia),
Emile Heskey, Abbas Saad and me

Working with Sunil Chhetri, India's most capped player, at Mohun Bagan in 2011

Grounds people in the Indian Super League

Sachin Tendulkar with Peter Reid

Chatting with the coach of South Korea, Uli Stielike, before a World Cup qualifying match between South Korea and Laos, 2017

The Lao national team, 2017

8. Perak

Steve had opened talks with the Malaysian side Perak once it became known that a new coach had been lined up to replace him at Home United, regardless of the results for the season. A couple of other Malaysian sides had expressed an interest, as had a Vietnamese side, but Steve felt more comfortable with Perak.

'Basically, I met the club president, it helped he was the son of the then Sultan and he said, "Tidy the club up." I also liked the fact he didn't want to get too closely involved with the running of the football club. He only wanted to know if there was a problem. I got the impression things had been a bit of a shambles, especially when one of the foreign players came to me and asked me how he had to pay me to play! I said, "Just score some goals, son, and that'll do me!" So you can guess what had been going on previously.'

There was little time to get a feel for his new squad as the Malaysian football authorities had decided to change the calendar for the new season. The 2005 campaign had only finished in October with the usual show-piece Malaysia Cup final, which Selangor had won. The 2006 season was brought forward a few weeks and was now to be known as the 2005/06 season, meaning Steve literally had a month's preseason to get his squad prepared.

A lot of the more experienced players from the previous season had moved on, leaving Steve with a core of good players he could rely upon and some talented, but untested, youngsters including one lad, Dominic Minsi, who had just turned up at training one day and asked to join in. 'No one had a clue who he was, but I liked his attitude, and as we needed players, I took a punt.'

He was also missing a few lads who were with the Malaysian national team at the SEA Games in the Philippines.

The season-opening Charity Cup in those days, better known locally as the

Piala Sultan Ahmed Haji Shah or Piala Sumbangsih, pitted the winners of the Malaysia Cup against the winners of the FA Cup, but as Selangor had won both, it was decided they would play FA Cup finalists Perak at Bukit Jalil Stadium.

Unlike similar curtain raisers in England, the Piala Sumbangsih was part of the regular fixtures. At stake was not only a trophy and the bragging rights that went with lifting silverware, but also three points. The large crowd at Bukit Jalil Stadium certainly caught out one of the Perak players. Croatian defender Vedron Kukoc had just arrived in Malaysia, and Steve was confident his experience at the back would come in handy over the season. However, there was a moment of concern when the coach saw him on the pitch before kick-off gazing in awe at the crowded stands holding 80,000 people towering above him. The defender turned to his coach and said, 'This is not what I thought. This is bigger than Croatia.' He was soon to find out that not all games in Malaysia attract such big crowds, but it wasn't a bad first impression.

With first choice keeper Hamsani Ahmed injured, Steve sprang a surprise by giving his 18-year-old third choice goalkeeper Nasril Nourdin his debut. The lad did so well in that cauldron of noise that he kept his place in the first team, even when the veteran Hamsani was fit again. Within 12 months, the Blackburn Rovers, who had won the English Premier League ten years earlier, was rumoured to be interested in him.

Selangor would be no pushover. The most successful in the history of Malaysian football, the team had not only won a domestic cup double, but they had also won the second tier Premier League the previous season. With Khalid Jamlus, ironically a former Perak striker, and Indonesian Bambang Pamungkas upfront, they boasted two of the most exciting strikers in the region.

Steve had spent the best part of a month looking at his players, and he liked what he saw. Captain Ahmad Shahrul was the Malaysian Subramani or Aide Iskander.

'A leader, a great pro, and widely respected in the dressing room,' is how the coach recalls him. He was also impressed by the other two foreigners he had inherited, Guinean Keita Mandjou and Abdoulaye Traore, who hailed from Burkina Faso. Traore was as urbane as they came. Fluent in five languages and a qualified medical doctor, he was another who provided a positive influence in the squad, especially among the younger players.

With an eclectic mix of Malaysian Malays, Malaysian Indians, Malaysian Chinese, a Sabahan, a Croat and the two lads from West Africa, all coached by the multilingual lad from Liverpool, Perak wasn't going to be worried about its more illustrious opponents or be awed by the occasion.

Steve went 3–4–1–2 with his captain operating just behind the diminutive Danial Fadzly Abdullah and Keita Mandjou, Traore given licence to get forward when he saw fit. After coping with the initial Selangor onslaught, they brought a larger number of supporters than Perak given their proximity to the stadium. Perak was happy to go in at half-time. 0–0.

Early in the second half, Perak took the lead. Mandjou showed great desire to get in front of his marker and lobbed the keeper from ten yards. Perak was piling on the pressure. At the back, Dominic Minsi, Vedron and Khairi Zainuddin handled the much-vaunted Selangor strike force while more debutants, Yoganathan and Ganesan, bombed down the flanks providing width. Within minutes, Perak was 2–0 up, and a free kick into the box was won by Traore whose knock down was expertly flicked past the keeper by Mandjou for his second of the game.

Selangor did pull a goal back a moment later, which caught the TV station broadcasting the game out; they were still showing replays of Mandjou's goal before cutting back to the live action, just in time to see a Selangor player place the ball on the centre spot.

On 78 minutes, the Selangor keeper failed to deal with a cross, and the ball fell nicely for Traore to get his name on the score sheet, looping the ball over his shoulder to make it 3–1. Selangor's coach, the legendary Dollah Salleh, responded by replacing the hapless keeper, but the problem lay further forward. It was a futile gesture. Perak was getting behind the Red Giants defence almost at will, and they were showing greater desire to win the second ball. It was no surprise when a lovely through ball released Mandjou, and the Guinean striker finished with all the calmness of a player full of confidence.

Selangor had no answers, and a rash 35-yard effort flying harmlessly over from Amri Yahyah summed up their frustration moments from the end. With Nasril in no rush to take the subsequent goal-kick, the referee rather dramatically showed the young keeper a yellow card for what he interpreted as time-wasting, a harsh decision that bordered on bullying given the handful of seconds remaining. Perak got to retain the trophy it had won the previous season, and as midfielder Wong Sai Kong raised the Piala Sumbangsih, the crown fell off right in front of the impassive officials on medal duty!

Steve had another medal to put alongside his Singapore Cup gong, and as his players celebrated in front of the Perak support, he stood slightly apart at the back of the bouncing group, enjoying the moment.

The players on national team duty returned from Manila, but if they thought they were going to walk straight back into the first team, they were mistaken.

'They (the players that had won the Piala Sumbangsih) played hard for the big win, and they deserve another match together. I personally believe that if you perform well in a match, you should get to keep your place for the next match.'

It wasn't the players' fault they would miss out. The biennial SEA Games is seen as a prestigious tournament, as Steve knew well, but why was it being allowed to clash with the start of a domestic season? Reputations are fine but a new coach can only work with what he has in front of him, and if the new players perform well, that means a stronger squad and more competition for places.

Among those keeping his place in the team was the third-choice keeper Nasril. The 18-year-old appreciated the trust the new coach was showing him and was determined to show his debut hadn't been a one-time success.

A week later, Perak was sitting pretty on top of the eight-team Super League after defeating Perlis 4–0 in front of a delirious crowd at their Perak Stadium in Ipoh, but Steve wasn't getting carried away. Winning the Piala Sumbangsih had given him a boost, but he knew the football team was a long way from challenging for honours. Besides, the president had tasked him with, in effect, rebuilding the football club from top to bottom. He set about developing the football club infrastructure, a task which became much easier when manager, Datuk Jamil (though Jamil was supportive), was suspended by the Football Association of Malaysia, prompting the president to ask Steve to take over his duties as well. It was a headache, but he thrived on the challenges, taking full advantage of the hands-off approach taken by the club president.

New Year's Eve bought a top-of-the-table clash as Perak hosted league leaders MPPJ. To add some spice, the big spending Selangor-based side had signed defensive duo K. Nanthakumar and Chan Wing Hoong from Perak. The Perak coach especially rated K Nathakumar and had tried to sign him for Home United. 'He is a good and tireless player, and his work rate is high. He certainly can do a lot of damage to opposing teams if not taken care of.'

Nearly 30,000 supporters descended on the Perak Stadium hoping to see a thrilling game ending with a Perak win, before going off to enjoy the fireworks seeing in a New Year. Instead, the fireworks were on the pitch as MPPJ shocked the home support into silence, netting inside 16 seconds when a statuesque

Perak defence allowed Zimbabwean international Newton Ben Katanha to nod the ball home. Mandjou restored parity on 30 minutes when he powered home a cross from Daniel Fadzly. Kit Liew Kong made it 2-1 to MPPJ in the second half with a header from a free kick.

Everything kicked off 20 minutes in. The Perak captain had to be held back by Steve; Ahmad Shahrul Azhar confronted the referee after he was given a red card for an incident involving Rachid Zmama. Supporters reacted, and smoke bombs added to the fog as events unravelled quickly. A linesman was seen to fall to the ground, apparently after being hit by a water bottle which had been thrown from the ground. With Perak officials rushing to get in the ref's face, the goalkeeper-coach was having a go at the fourth official. Security personnel rushed on to the pitch to escort the match officials back down the tunnel, and the game was halted while tempers calmed down. Play did continue after seven minutes, and MPPJ held on against the ten men of Perak, keeping the team's place on top of the table.

The Football Association of Malaysia threw the book at Perak. Ahmad Shahrul was banned for 12 months and fined approximately $1,000 for elbowing an opponent and confronting the referee. Perak was also fined approximately $5,000 for the incident which saw a linesman hit by a water bottle. The Perak manager Datuk Jamal Nasir Rasdi also faced charges of entering the field of play illegally and speaking out against the referee, but he didn't turn up. He was later suspended from all football activities for 12 months.

The team returned to winning ways, defeating Negri Sembilan 2-1 which heralded a good run of form as Perak climbed to the top of the table by the middle of March.

Steve's focus was on the next game, of course, away to Penang, but when the Seladang lost 3-1, a third defeat in four games, there were questions to answer. As ever, he stood by his players.

The next game was against Negri Sembilan and the Seladang players were hoping a new striker would ease the burden on Mandjou and Traore. Zambian international Emmanuel Zulu had been impressing in training, and Steve had no doubts about giving him his debut.

There was some bad news though. Zulu's international clearance was sent to the wrong number, and the Croatian defender Kukoc had to go into hospital. He was injured in a collision away to Perlis at the beginning of February and had been complaining of a headache ever since. He went into hospital early March where he underwent a CAT scan which didn't reveal much. He was kept in hospital for observation but was released after missing a crucial game against Pahang. However, with Steve looking forward to having the defender's calming presence back for the return meet with MPPJ, Kukoc was diagnosed with a brain tumour and was likely to be out of action for a couple of months.

The 2-0 win over Pahang had seen Perak go top of the table on goal difference ahead of MPPJ, but the coach didn't get carried away.

A week after an FA Cup tie with Perlis, another tie was played in Singapore between Young Lions and Sarawak. Steve's pal Dave Roberts refereed the game, and he went home thinking nothing of it.

'The game was relatively straightforward which finished 7-2 to the Young Lions. It was only the next morning Steve called me and asked, "At what point did you realise?" I still didn't, and he had to explain the game had been fixed and that there was a lot of money on nine goals being scored. To this day, I still cannot see how it was done as I made decisions in the game that would have impacted the result, that is, not awarding a penalty, playing an advantage that directly led to a goal being scored.'

'I had been called the night before from a Singaporean mate asking if I wanted to put a bet on the score,' remembered Steve. 'Obviously I said no, but the fix had been leaked, and everyone in the game was talking about it, everyone except the Sarawak coach, Jalil, who was honest and devastated when he found out.'

Perak did beat Perlis in the second leg of its FA Cup tie. It was not enough, and only a win in their penultimate league game of the season away to Penang gave them a respectable third place finish. That final victory was inspired by the return for their captain and the continuing excellence of a teenager. Malaysian football works in mysterious ways, and one of those ways could be seen in the disciplinary system and the inevitable appeal process that follows a discovery that a player had been wrongly charged in the first place. Steve couldn't wait to welcome back his talismanic skipper Ahmad Shahrul Azhar and, while saluting experience, didn't forget to heap praise on the teenaged goalkeeper who had surprised everyone in the first game of the season, keeping his place ever since.

His joy at the win, though, was tempered by the knowledge the team had come off an eight-game winless streak and that a tough group in the Malaysia Cup lay ahead, including some international travel. Perak had been drawn with DPMM from Brunei and Melaka from the second tier, as well as MPPJ, and despite the lowly status of two of the teams, he knew there would be no easy ties, especially in their first game in Brunei.

DPMM was backed by the deep pockets of members of the Brunei royal family and because of their spending power often plied their trade in Malaysia or Singapore's professional leagues. Perak's first Malaysia Cup tie was in Bandar Seri Bagawan, and Steve knew how important a good start was if the team was to add to its trophy haul.

He would not be able to field a full-strength line-up as a number of his younger players were away with the Malaysian Olympic team in South Africa, and Dominic Minsi was suspended after being sent off in a league game. To add to his woes, defensive midfielder K Yoganathan was missing after being involved in a motorcycle crash! At least Kukoc and Ahmad Shahrul Azhar were available, and of course there was Mandjou upfront.

Perak came away from Brunei with a useful 0-0 draw and went on to win four of the next five ties to leave them top of the group, as well as a quarter final against Penang. Again, national team call-ups left the coach frustrated as he would have to be without three key players: goalkeeper Nasril Nourdin and defenders V Thirumurugan and S Subraminiam.

It wasn't a bad first season considering the budget Perak had was one of the smallest in the league, and there was plenty of promise being shown by the younger player who had been promoted to the first team. And then there were the facilities.

'I had problems with local governments. The state of the facilities in Ipoh (were) appalling, and all I wanted was to improve them for the sake of the game. For example, the toilets in the Stadium (were) disgusting. Fans deserve better than this. Also, we had no training facilities. But I discovered that telephone calls don't get returned, people pass on the blame, and most of all never reply to letters, which I found the most discourteous. Also, a football pitch needs a groundsman, not good-hearted, hardworking general workers,' recalled Steve in an interview with a local paper at the end of his spell in Ipoh.

He was ably assisted in his efforts by the unstinting Bobby, a young administrator who was tireless in his support of the coach. 'Bobby was great. He didn't ask questions, which I appreciated! Knew that he had the interests of the club at heart, and I could trust him to get things done for the benefit of the club and not his own benefit. Believe me, people like Bobby and (Home United kitman) Rosli Dollah in Singapore are more important to the atmosphere round a football club than some suited manager with their own agenda playing the big "I-am".'

Of course, there was very little Steve could achieve, even with a two-year contract and a hands-off boss, but he kept recalling his pal Ron Smith's maxim: 'If you get one thing done in a day, you have done well.'

Despite a poor season results-wise, Perak had actually turned a small profit, and Steve wasted no time in adding to his squad. He needed to strengthen his attacking options; Danial Fadzly Abdullah had been a willing foil for Mandjou, but he was too slight to impose himself on opponents. Steve swooped for Khalid Jamlus. The former Perak striker was seen as a colourful character in the somewhat strait-laced world of Malaysian football. Back in 2001, he, along with a couple of teammates, had been dropped from the Malaysian World Cup Qualifying Squad after having been caught out partying at Hard Rock Cafe. It was hardly the infamous Arsenal Tuesday Club, but by Malaysian standards, pretty raunchy. A subsequent successful trial with Eintracht Frankfurt failed to wash that stain away, and there were people who warned Steve that Khalid would not be a good signing.

'I had people tell me he was lazy, he doesn't give 100 per cent in training or games, and he was a bad influence. But these were not football people. My captain, Ahmad Shahrul, told me he was a good lad; treat him with respect, and he wouldn't cause any problems. It was a no-brainer. I listened to Shahrul and brought him back to Ipoh and never had any problems with him.' Khalid went on to form a lethal partnership with Mandjou, scoring 15 of the 36 they bagged between themselves in the 2006/07 season.

Steve was also able to bring back another Perak old boy. K Nathakumar was a local lad who had made his debut in 1998 before being released at the end of 2004, along with a number of other experienced players including Jamlus, as Perak had faced financial problems. With some more money in the kitty, the coach was delighted to have the 29-year-old defender return to bring some much-needed experience and guile at the back. With the younger lads having had a vital season under their belts, the mood was one of cautious optimism for the new season.

While Steve was able to add to the squad for the new season, there were a number of players he missed out on. 'After I arrived in Ipoh, I was approached by some agents who offered me a kickback on any deals I did with their players. I've never gone down that road and wasn't going to start now. Word soon got around, and some agents refused to work with me, for being honest!'

No agent was needed for one player. S Subramaniam was playing for the wonderfully named UPB, a palm oil company, training 80 miles south-west of Ipoh out in the *hulu*, a Malay term for the boonies. Steve saw him while his team was playing a friendly against Perak, and he was so impressed that he wanted to sign him there and then.

In an example of how channels of communication worked, he was told that Subramaniam was, in fact, a Perak Youth player, and he was spending the season on loan with UPB. No one had seen fit to tell the new coach there were players out on loan, and of course he had never asked. Like many coaches around the world, he just assumed this key information would have been forthcoming when he had taken over, especially as he was missing a number of key players at the start of the season on international duty.

Subramaniam was instantly recalled from his loan spell and thrown in the first team for the Malaysia Cup. He was soon called up for the Malaysian Olympic squad. Subramaniam was quick and aggressive, and his natural leadership skills meant sure he was soon captaining the national team, completing a fairy tale rise for the 21-year-old who had been all but forgotten by own club at the end of 2005. Subra was quick to credit his coach at Perak as he said, 'Darby changed everything for me. He drafted me into the Malaysia Cup squad. Suddenly, I found myself in the Olympic team and then the national team.'

As was often the case, the format for the new Malaysian Super League season was changed with an increase in the number of teams from eight to 14. The fixture list saw Perak take on four newly promoted teams in the team's opening games, defeating Sarawak 2-1 at home, Mandjou and Traore starting the new season as they had ended the last, 0-0 away to Terengganu and a disappointing 0-0 at home to Johor FC. Next up was a local derby with northern neighbours, Kedah.

The Red Eagles were ambitious. Coached by Azraai Khor Abdullah who had spent much of the previous 30 years associated with his boyhood club, unfashionable Kedah had invested in excellent foreign players including striker Marlon Alex James, Bernard Huggins and midfielder Nelson San Martin. They had secured the Premier League title at the end of the 2005/06 season and were poised to write the names in the history books as one of Malaysia's best-ever sides.

In January 2006, Perak made the short journey from Ipoh north to the Darul

Aman stadium in Alor Setar for the first of what would be six monumental bouts that would decide the domestic season. Neither team had found its groove yet, with having just earned four points from those first three games and struggling to stay close to Perlis, another northern side, who had started the season with an unbeaten three-match run. With Nasril away on national team duty, the experienced Hamsani was back in goal, but he was sent off just before half-time, meaning 19-year-old Kamarul Effendy was thrown on for his debut. The Kedah goalkeeper was also sent off in a tempestuous game, but sadly for Perak, they lost 4–3, and the trip home was made worse with the knowledge table-topping Perlis had made it four wins from five.

Kamarul kept his place in the starting eleven for the next game at home to Johor FC, but a 0–0 draw meant Perak had just a single win and three 0–0 draws after five games of the new season. Boasting one of the most exciting forward lines on the country, Steve publicly wasn't too worried about Mandjou, Traore and Jamlus's lack of penetration in front of goal. He preferred to blame the other team's goalies.

It was to be a few weeks before Steve felt Perak had turned a corner and Jamlus was finally gelling with Keita. A trip to Selangor was one of Malaysia's more daunting away days. The proud heritage of the club seeps through every page of football history, and when they are being roared on by a large, passionate crowd, more than one player has been known to buckle. Six games in, Steve was not sure which Perak would turn up. They'd shown glimpses of their talent but had yet been able to sustain it over 90 minutes, especially against the newly promoted sides. While the coach was not feeling particularly worried about form, he knew a couple of victories could transform the season. As they set off to the Shah Alam, the team was boosted by the return of both Nasril and Kukoc.

Suddenly, all the hard work in training seemed to seep through, and Perak impressed as the players defeated Selangor 4–2 on their own pitch and followed that up with a 2–0 home victory over last season's nemesis, Perlis. They had finally found their mojo. An early exit in the FA Cup from Kedah proved to be a minor irritant as Kedah embarked on a nine-game unbeaten run that cemented the team's place as title challengers along with the Red Eagles' Perlis.

Despite having some more experienced players he could call upon, Steve was still not averse to calling upon youngsters if he felt they were ready, much as he had done in the Piala Sumbangsih in 2005 with Nasril between the sticks. Towards the end of March, it was Perak's turn to host Negeri Sembilan, and the

coach sprang a surprise by giving 18-year-old winger Fakri Saani his debut.
'It was a super performance from the young lad (Fakri). He showed no jitters
in his big match debut. Fakri won over the fans with a convincing performance.
Frankly, I thought he had done enough in the first half, and I contemplated
replacing him in the second half. But he scored again to complete his hat trick
and then set up Keita for the fourth goal. I can't ask for anything more from a
rookie. He has the physique and football talent. The match against Negri was
good exposure for him. But I am not going to rush him. I will continue to bring
in young players for exposure when the need arises under the rotation system
because of the tight schedule.'

Years later, Fakri met up with Steve again in Lao under very different
circumstances.

Around this time, the ugly aroma of match fixing tried to stink out the now
buzzing dressing room.

One of the young local players was approached by a match fixer. Suspicious,
the player had arranged for a pal of his to be close by for the meet, and hidden
from view, he took a few photographs. The player, feeling a bit nervous and
exposed, went straight to his coach and reported the incident, and Steve passed
on the approach to the new club president, Dato Muhiyuddin. The Perak secret
police were called in, and they interviewed several people at the club, mostly
concerning recent results and why certain players weren't playing well. After
collecting a few autographs and taking some photographs, they went off, and
nothing further was heard. Meanwhile, Dato had gone to the FAM and told
them what had happened, but again they didn't seem too bothered.

Steve was disappointed with the lack of response from the authorities, but he
felt that when they did take action, they targeted the wrong people. 'We always
target the tail of the snake, which is the players. The real reason for match fixing
lies at the head of the snake. They are the ones that should be targeted. Often,
young uneducated players are blamed, and sometimes they don't even get paid
for three months.'

Rumours of match fixing persisted for much of the season. However, while
there were many who were suspicious, no one was sure who was behind it.

There remains one game Steve can't get out of his head. 'We were away to
Melaka, and they were awful. They finished bottom of the table with just two
wins and conceded 72 goals in their 24 games. We knew they weren't a good
side, but I couldn't help noticing they were holding an especially high line and

kept catching Mandjou offside. Their defenders were so high up they were almost in our half. And every time they pushed up, they would catch Mandjou. We eventually dropped him deeper, so he timed his runs later, but why were Melaka playing such a high line? It made no sense.'

Perak won the game 9-0 with Mandjou scoring five and Jamlus hitting a hat trick which made for a joyous trip back home after the game. The Perak coach was delighted, but the deeper, more thoughtful football man tried to understand the logic of his opponent's tactics.

Matters came to a head in the penultimate round of the season. Perak and Kedah were battling it out for the title, and with the Red Eagles at home to Negeri Sembilan, Steve's team hosted Terengganu.

'They certainly made things hard for us, but it was a good game of football. I was sat in the dugout focusing on the game, but we kept hearing updates from Alor Setar: 1-0, 2-0, 3-0 and so on. They ended up winning 7-0 while we could only manage a draw.' Kedah went two points clear and, just as importantly, made big inroads to the Perak goal difference. Coincidentally, both teams had to fly to the island of Borneo for the last round of fixtures with, rather unusually, both games kicking off at separate times. Kedah beat DPMM in the earlier game 1-0 to secure the title, leaving a deflated Perak, who were without Nasril, Traore and Subramaniam to turn on the style against Sarawak. The Kedah versus Negeri result did, however, play on his mind. 'It was frustrating as I knew Azrai their coach was honest as were their players, but you never knew what was happening behind the games.'

There was still the Malaysia Cup, and the two northern sides were drawn together in the same group. Honours were shared as each won its respective home tie by two goals to one, and both qualified to the knockout stages. In the quarter final, Perak was drawn against Perlis, the same team which had ended Perak's cup runs so dramatically the previous season. After losing the first leg in Kangar 2-0, it looked like history was going to repeat itself, but Perak reversed the result with a 4-0 win.

However, first there was the small matter of Sabah in the semi-final with the first leg away. Ordinarily, Sabah played its home games in Kota Kinabulu, the state's capital, but in a move Sir Alex Ferguson would have appreciated, they decided to host the semi-final in Tawau, some 280 miles south east of Kota Kinabulu. Although perfectly within their rights to do so, the move was calculated to inconvenience Perak as much as possible as it entailed extra travel time and costs. Perak had left Ipoh at 9.00 a.m. on the Friday, not returning until 4.00 a.m. on the Monday.

Perak had the last laugh as Jamlus scored on 21 minutes; although Sabah soon equalised, Perak held on for a draw. After the game, Steve sent a cheeky SMS to Kedah coach Azraai Khor saying, '*See U in Bukit Jalil!*' His rival was feeling equally confident, later revealing Kedah had already booked hotels in Kuala Lumpur for the weekend of the Malaysia Cup final despite being held 0–0 in Terengganu. Both coaches' optimism proved well-founded as they won their respective second legs and could look forward to the Final. Steve was looking for his third trophy in Malaysia, while Azraai was after his third for the season.

Tired legs and "hidden hands" finally caught up with Perak. Ahmad Shah was sent off on the 20th minute of the final in an incident when replayed on TV which seemed to have the ref reaching for red before the tackle was done. Azraai looked across at Steve and smiled more out of sympathy than a desire to gloat. Kedah bossed the game and won 3–0, leaving Steve to rue a couple of his selections. He'd taken a punt on Mandjou and Jamlus who were both carrying injuries, and it hadn't paid off.

Finishing runner-up to an imperious Kedah, in both the Super League and the Malaysia Cup, hurt after a season that had shown so much promise, but there was worse to come. With a new 12-month contract, Steve set about building a squad for 2007/08 and another attempt at the AFC Cup, and as he had at Home United, he started by trying to tie down two of his most influential foreign players, but both Keita and Traore rejected the offer to stay citing personal reasons.

Perak would eventually bring Chilean striker Carlos Caceres in to replace the much-loved Mandjou, but he struggled to win over the supporters who had really taken to the Guinean's all-action style.

'He always gave 100 per cent in training and games, and these efforts made him a hero. It also made it difficult for the next foreigner, Carlos, to follow him. He actually scored more goals per game than Keita, but his languid style was so different to Keita's robust figure. An unusual incident happened when Carlos scored his first goal for the club. He ran to the crowd and crossed himself! Keita was a Muslim, and when he ran to the crowd, he made an Islamic gesture, and believe me, it influenced some of the crowd.'

Shorn of two key players before a ball was kicked, Steve was forced to look elsewhere. With AFC Cup adding to the fixture list, he was fully aware that, as with Home United in previous seasons, he would be severely hampered by budgetary concerns and a less-than-sympathetic national association. However, as he sat down after the Malaysia Cup final loss to plot the way ahead in the new season, little did he realise how much of a role finances would play. He managed to bring in a couple of experienced local players, Hardi Jaafar and ex-international Mohd Nor Ismail, and he promoted Fakri, who had impressed when scoring a hat trick on his debut.

Once a budget had been arranged, Perak was back in the market, bringing in two more Chilean lads, defender Mario Berrios and playmaker Jorge Munoz, who had been recommended by Nelson San Martin who had been so impressive with Kedah. Berrios, who spoke good English, was looking forward to the new season in a new country. He turned out to be an excellent acquisition both on and off the pitch.

Perak was going to need all the experience it could get. The AFC Cup draw saw the team going up against SAFFC (Singapore), Kitchee (Hong Kong) and New Radiant from the Maldives. However, that didn't start until March, and by early January, there was an element of the Perak support which wanted Steve out.

Perak hadn't started the season badly and after six games had 12 points on the board having suffered two losses. In January 2008, they hosted Kedah in a rerun of the 2007 Malaysia Cup final. Perak started brightly with early goals from both Jamlus and Noor Hazrul within 15 minutes, but each time Kedah levelled within minutes. The turning point came when Jamlus was sent off soon after half-time. Steve felt his striker had been hard done by.

With a one-man advantage, Kedah scored another three goals, leaving Steve a disgruntled man when the ref blew the final whistle. Members of the Perak Football Fans Club later accused Steve of calling them stupid and called for the Englishman to be sacked. 'He also made an obscene gesture at the fans. His behaviour is unacceptable, and we want him to be sacked,' said a spokesman at a press conference. 'Unlike our previous coaches, he is arrogant and never listens to the opinion of the fans.' The supporters group also said they would boycott the next home game against Perlis.

'I had been spat on by a so-called fan while I was holding my three-year-old daughter in my arms. I called him *kampung bodoh*, village idiot, which I think upset him, but things would have been even worse if my daughter hadn't been with me. Two weeks ago, the president of the fan club said that I was the best coach they (Perak) ever had. I never made any obscene gestures (to the fans). The Perak fans have been fantastic and very supportive of me, and I respect them,' said Steve at the time, before refusing to make any more comments on the matter.

The club management came out and supported the coach and blamed the supporters for overreacting. 'As far as we are concerned, Steve has done a good job for Perak and has been managing the team very well,' said Perak FA vice president Datuk Mahiyuddin Arshad. 'What happened at the Perak Stadium after the Perak–Kedah clash (on Saturday) was just unfortunate. I have studied the matter and have concluded that it was our fan club that had erred. It was wrong of them to confront the coach when the team lost, and highlighting the matter in the press will not solve anything. They should have instead forwarded all complaints to me or to the Perak FA so that the problem can be solved amicably.'

Not all Perak fans felt the coach needed to be in a constant dialogue with them. Ah Wa was a familiar figure home and away, and everyone at the club loved him. He only finished primary school and had grown up living on a police base in Ipoh. He followed Perak around the country; one time, Steve saw him after a game in Kuantan looking lost, so he opened up the team bus so he could spend the night in safety. Another time, the coach paid for a hotel room for him to stay in and let him travel back on the team bus to Ipoh.

The team struggled to find consistency on the field. A 6–0 win away to PDRM would be followed soon after by a 4–1 reverse at home to Selangor.

Steve admitted things weren't going according to plan but refused to admit there was a crisis at the club, and the team wasn't doing much wrong.

The AFC Cup got off to a good start in March with a 3–1 win in the Maldives against New Radiant, and hopes were high the team would continue that form in the second group stage game against SAFFC from Singapore, a team with which Steve was very familiar.

Recalling how the Singapore Football Association had not helped its sides in Asian club competition when he was at Home United, Steve called on the FAM to do more. Again, he was looking at the bigger picture. For Steve, success shouldn't be just confined to the domestic setup, and if a team was to dwell in Asian club football, that would be a big lift to everyone, not just the team with the medals.

For once Steve's prior knowledge counted for nothing as SAFFC brushed aside Perak in Ipoh 6–1. Evergreen striker Aleksander Duric hit four as the Singaporeans relished the space provided by Perak's three-man defence. The coach, as ever, refused to blame the players and offered no excuses beyond a congested fixture list. 'They were the better side and deserved to win. It would not have mattered what shape or system we employed because our opponents defended and attacked better.'

Six days later, Steve was less reticent to criticise after Perak was roundly beaten 5–1 by Kedah. 'In the first half of the season, Perak enjoyed the best defensive record. For the first time now, I am feeling ashamed of my team's performance, especially in defence. I went ballistic in the dressing room during half-time. because we just donated the goals to Kedah with schoolboy errors. What I cannot understand is that these errors were committed by experienced players, and they failed to cope under pressure. My defenders need to be mentally tougher.'

But it was not like Steve to stay angry for long, and after his rant, he went on to praise Kedah and the conveyor belt of talent the club had. As a coach employed by Perak to get results, he was fuming, but as a football man he was big enough to praise the work another club was doing whether it went down well with supporters or not.

Those supporters spoke with their feet for the next AFC Cup tie with just 1,000 people turning out for the home game with Kitchee, compared with 5,000 against SAFFC in the first game. The busy schedule had taken its toll on the Seladang, with strikers Jamlus and Caceres both absent, but Berrios earned the three points in injury time, and Steve admitted his team had got lucky.

Both Jamlus and Caceres were fit again for the game away to Kitchee, and it was Caceres Steve had to thank as his brace secured an important point. With SAFFC surprisingly being held 1–1 by New Radiant, Perak was second on seven points behind leaders SAFFC who had ten, and Steve was optimistic his team would reach the quarter finals. But on the eve of the tie with New Radiant, hepatitis decimated his plans. Nor Ismail was in hospital on a drip, while Ahmad Shahrul and Dan Fadzly were 'dead men walking'. Goalkeeper Hamsani had turned up for training, only to be sent directly to hospital for tests as he reported feeling unwell. With those four key players missing and Jamlus under the knife for a knee operation, Steve was forced to look to the youngsters to fill the bench and hope none of his starting 11 received any serious knocks.

He wasn't going to underestimate the Maldives side after the results achieved in Singapore in the last game. Perak put its woes behind, and two goals from Jorge Munoz either side of one by Razali Kandasamy gave the Seladang one foot in the quarter finals, and a 2–0 win in Singapore meant Perak finished second to SAFFC only on goal difference and kept Steve's dreams of an AFC Cup medal alive.

Behind the scenes, though, things weren't going so well. The Super League campaign ended with a whimper. Just a single win in the last five games saw Perak finish fifth, 15 points behind champion Kedah. Malaysian fans aren't known for sticking by their teams through thick and thin. A couple of defeats meant they stayed away, and that's what happened in Ipoh. If there was a positive, the sparsely populated terraces meant the volume of fan dissent was limited. 'We could hear every word, and I was surprised at some of their English vocabulary!' And finances, always tight in Malaysian football, raised their ugly head and threatened Perak's future in the AFC Cup and the Malaysia Cup.

Towards the end of June, Steve was telling the local media the club hadn't paid any salaries since the end of March, and loan sharks were circling some of his players sensing easy marks. Ordinarily he preferred to keep things in-house, but he sensed what he was hearing was only the tip of a very unpleasant iceberg.

'This is an unhealthy situation. Desperate players are vulnerable, and it could lead to other undesirable things like illegal bookmaking and match fixing. But my players have been magnificent. They have turned down the offers and approached me for help.'

The club wasn't in a position to help. They had a Malaysia Cup tie in Johor on the horizon and were struggling to get the team there.

The final league game of the season saw Perak flying to Brunei, but when it came to reserving the flights, the airline rejected the booking! Steve contacted the airline direct and was told the Perak account was empty, and there was nothing they could do. The coach ended up paying for the tickets himself, and it wasn't the only time he dug deep into his pockets for the team. With some of the younger players being approached by loan sharks, he paid them out of his own pocket rather than run the risk of them coming to the attention of match fixers.

The team was able to meet its commitments in Johor, and the next game away to Perlis was down to the generosity of supporters. The Perak FA acting president, Datuk Mahiyuddin Arshad, blamed the state government.

Despite all the nonsense going on behind the scenes, Steve had nothing but praise for his players. 'I have no problem for the Malaysia Cup as real match atmosphere kicks in automatically, and the players give their best. But it is a different story on the training ground. They have many things on their minds. The real hard work is done in training, and it is difficult when the players' hearts are not on the task. It does not help when we are forced to train on an awful pitch at a public park that does not have facilities like toilets or parking spaces. In fact, a few players have received parking fines.'

But with the club struggling to even afford to get to away games a short drive away, there were serious concerns about the AFC Cup Quarter Final tie in Lebanon in September. Perak had appealed to the FAM and state government but had heard no reply, and Steve warned if Perak was forced to withdraw from the AFC Cup, it wouldn't just have consequences for the club.

'I was sick of hearing how the new party in power were the party of the people. When I finally got through to the chief minister and demanded he pay his players, the politician wondered why the players weren't playing for the love of the state and the honour.'

Steve agreed it was a good point and innocently asked the minister whether he was serving for the love of the state and the honour. No money came from the meeting, but oh boy, it had felt good, and Steve says it made him feel better!

It would cost about US$26,000 to bring 18 players and six officials to Lebanon. Although they sliced the budget by US$6,000 by trimming the squad to a minimum of 15 players and four officials, Steve feared that if they could not make it, Perak would be suspended and fined, and Malaysian teams also faced expulsion from the AFC Cup competition next year.

Quarter finalists get a grant of $20,000 to cover their expenses for the away leg, but they don't receive that money until after the round has been completed. The club tried to sell some land to help overcome the financial crisis, but property sales take time. Players were taking loans from their parents to help make ends meet.

If there was no cash coming soon, they would have to withdraw from the AFC Cup. Perak was one of four teams in the last eight from Southeast Asia. Kedah had been drawn against Al Muharraq (Bahrain), SAFFC versus Al Nahda (Oman) and Steve's former club Home United against Dempo from India. Perak had drawn SAFA from Lebanon with the first tie at home. Fortunately for the club, the FAM stepped in with a $20,000 loan, so they could go ahead and make bookings for the second leg in Beirut. All of a sudden, the state government was interested in its local football team.

As if the team's preparations for the quarter final weren't being hampered enough by financial issues, Steve had plenty of problems putting a strike force together for the first leg. The FAM had announced there would be no foreigners in the league for the next season, so striker Caceres, knowing he was not wanted, headed home to Chile. He was an out-and-out striker and was positively lethal in front of goal, but he had never really bonded with the team in the way Mandjou had. Fakri Saarani was away with the national team in Vietnam, and Razali Kandasamy had missed training for six days.

For two seasons, Perak had boasted one of the most potent frontlines in the country. However, on the eve of their most important game, they were down to Jamlus. Within 12 minutes of kick-off, Jamlus was carried off injured, forcing Steve to look to the lightweight Danial Fadzly, a competent-enough player in the domestic league, but not what was required against the bigger, more physical Lebanese, and with little penetration upfront, Perak was lucky to get away with a 2–0 loss.

The day of the second leg in Beirut, Steve had a few moments to gather his thoughts before the team headed to ground. The loan from the FAM had been greatly received, and he had looked forward to the trip, even though he knew there was little chance of overturning a two-goal deficit in this part of the world. Things had taken a turn for the worse, though, when some officials from the state government tagged along for the ride. The same people who hadn't bothered replying to requests for funds to pay salaries travelled first class to Beirut and enjoyed themselves on a shopping trip to Damascus. As can be imagined, this didn't go down well with the players, and at a training session, they used the officials for target practice, while Steve whispered as quietly as he could to stop.

'The invisible committee that had been shopping for two days was sat in the dugout at the stadium, soaking up what they felt was the big time, so we decided to return all the balls at great pace to that area. They soon realised they were not wanted! It really annoyed me the players were giving 100 per cent for their team and country, yet these officials had jumped on an expensive trip to go shopping. Only one of them had the decency to even talk to me.'

He headed to the Corniche and enjoyed the gentle sea breeze rolling in off the Mediterranean. He knew his time with Perak was over, and looking back, it was surreal. Steve had worked under three club presidents (a Regent, a future deputy PM and a Dato.) Normally it was the other way round! To be fair they had all supported Steve and the players in any way they could.

Were his AFC Cup ambitions to be thwarted by a team from the Middle East again? He knew that many back in Malaysia didn't care about Asian club competition, they saw it as a distraction from the domestic league and cups, but Steve knew the AFC Cup posed more of a challenge. Terengganu away was never an easy trip, but travelling around Asia and playing different teams in difficult environments was a challenge he embraced. Losing to SAFA in the first leg hurt his professional pride, and he wondered whether he would be getting another chance to bury his AFC Cup demons again. Just as he was nearing the place where Lebanese Prime Minister Rafic Hairi had been murdered in an explosion earlier that year, his phone rang.

'All right there, Darbs?'

Steve groaned. 'All this shit going on, and now I get one of my mates ringing to take the piss.'

9. Thailand

'Made in Thailand', made in our own land,
the land of the meaningful songs and dances.
Foreigners secretly are admirers of Thai products, but Thais don't see their worth.
Scared of being looked down upon, that liking Thai products isn't fashionable.

—*Made in Thailand*, by Carabao.

'Darbs, it's Reidy.' The accent was broad scouse. 'I thought someone's having a laugh here. One of my mates is pulling my leg. Although we'd gone through the Liverpool schools' football system and played against each other a few times I'd only met him once, and that was a long time ago.'

Eventually, Steve was convinced the voice on the other end of the phone wasn't one of his mates with too much free time on his hands, but Peter Reid, ex-player of Bolton Wanderers, Everton and England midfielder.

'Well, I'm in Lebanon. I've got a game tonight …'

'You're joking, costing me a fortune this phone call!' Steve's antennae were up. A former manager of Manchester City, Sunderland, Leeds United and Coventry City wasn't calling because he was interested in how Pahang lined up.

'Do you fancy coming to Thailand to be my coach?'

Coach in Thailand? Steve wasn't a kid in a candy store. He was being locked in the candy store with the keys and being told when to expect new deliveries. Ever since he had seen Kiatisuk Senamuang playing for Perlis against Johor, he had been enamoured by Thai footballers and their professionalism.

'I understand you speak fluent Thai …' Reid was still speaking while Steve was mentally flicking through his rolodex of Thai footballers. Surachai, Sutee, Kiatisuk, Teerathep ...

'Yes, yes, I speak fluent anything me,' he mumbled. Mentally, he was salivating at the opportunity of working with the best players in Southeast Asia.

Steve was thinking it was going to be fun comparing notes with a former England international.

'He's played against the best players in the world at a World Cup. I was paying players' salaries from my own pocket and booking flights because the club I worked for had no cash. He's had everything on a plate in his career; if I wanted a plate, I had to bring it myself. I don't know who's gonna get the worst culture shock, me or him!'

Peter gave Steve a phone number. It was Worawi Makudi, president of the Football Association of Thailand, and within a few hours, a deal was agreed. The timing was perfect. Steve knew his time at Perak was over, and although he had been informally looking around, there had been no responses.

Steve returned to Malaysia to clear his desk in Ipoh and headed north to Bangkok to meet Peter and start his new job. Rather unusually, Peter's job title was manager, using a role given to a favoured apparatchik in Southeast Asia. Steve was coach, an arrangement that served them both well and ensured there was no interference from the FA or any other outside influences, as can often be the case.

'It's great you're here. You speak fluent Thai and ...'

'I don't speak fluent Thai. I know about three words! I know Malay, Vietnamese and Arabic.' The contract had been signed now, so it didn't matter! 'What I do know, though, is the best players, and that is the most important thing.'

Once the former Everton midfielder had been appointed, he started tapping into his vast footballing network to find someone who might have an idea about Thai football because his knowledge was somewhat less than zero. Dave Roberts, having recovered from his time in a Damascus prison cell, had returned to England and had found some media work in his native north-east.

'I would interview Peter each week, who was at Sunderland at the time each week. When I heard he was looking at the Thailand job, I spoke with Steve to see if he would have any interest in working with Peter and explained my connection with Reidy. Steve was keen, so I called Peter and made the suggestion, pointing out Steve's experience in Asian football but more specifically his first-hand knowledge of Asian football culture, something I knew Peter would need to succeed. He would need someone close to him who was watching his back,' recalls Dave.

'I brought Steve because I knew I was going to need his local knowledge and also his cultural understanding because everything about Thailand was totally new to me,' Reid wrote in his autobiography *Cheer Up, Peter Reid*. A lot of the advice Steve gave was to do with bollocks. He told me I couldn't bollock anyone because that isn't the done thing, and neither could I walk around the dressing room with my bollocks hanging out because that isn't acceptable either.'

There were communication problems in the early days, with Peter speaking hardcore scouse and Steve, scouse light. At first, Steve translated Peter's instruction into an English that was easier on the ears, but it was obvious a translator was needed. A locally based English guy found out, and he came along to training one day to offer his services, but he didn't last long. He would be trying to explain things to the players, and you could see they weren't understanding a word. Steve asked Teerathep, who spoke public school English, if the lads understood anything the translator was saying, but he politely said not much. A Thai translator was found next, and he struggled when Reid wanted a player to change direction. Peter would say, 'Youse go left. Youse go right,' and the translator would stand there looking blank. 'Sorry, sorry. Who is "Hughes"?'

Both Englishmen hit the ground running. There was a friendly tournament in Vietnam at the end of October before the ASEAN Football Federation Championship, better known as the Suzuki Cup, at the end of the year.

In Southeast Asia, the Suzuki Cup was the biggie as far as supporters and players were concerned. The World Cup and the AFC Asian Cup may have more status around the world or Asia, but within the bubble that is Southeast Asia, they were impossible goals. The likes of the Japanese, Koreans and Iranians were just so far ahead of the region when it came to qualifiers that national pride was sated when defeats were narrow. However, the Suzuki Cup was different. The perception was anyone could win it even though, factually speaking, only the Thais and Singapore had since its inception in 1996.

A training camp had been arranged by the Thailand FA, but Steve was not impressed because the best players were not there.

'I knew Peter was going to struggle with the Thai names. I did, and I'd been working with them for years. So, we drew up a system. We gave each player a squad number, and I drew up a list with three columns. First was the number, then the player's nickname, and finally, their complete Thai name. Goalkeeper

Sinthaweechai Hathairattanakul's nickname was Tee, to our relief!'

Another player missing was one of Steve's players at Home United. 'You'll like this lad. Great player. He'll lighten the place up,' he told Reid. He rang Sutee Suksomkit. 'Why aren't you here?'

Sutee was soon joining the rest of the lads at the camp. Reid saw the impact of Sutee's arrival on the rest of the squad. 'Is there any more like that?' There were and Steve called them up. 'We've got to start getting to games. There are plenty more out there better than what we have here.'

With the squad now in place, Peter and Steve set about working with the lads on the training ground while Peter also learned about his new home.

Coming from a professional setup in England, Peter was used to having people around doing the most mundane, but essential, tasks, and that included getting materials ready for training. He asked for the balls, bibs and cones to be laid out ready for training the next day. Everyone smiled and said yes, and when he came in to take the session, people were standing around waiting to be told what to do. In his autobiography, Peter describes that as his biggest frustration and one that even Steve, with all his experience in the region, was not able to solve, though to be fair to the coach, all too often he was the one setting out the balls, bibs and cones!

The duo's first challenge came on their way to the T&T Cup in Hanoi. It seems nobody at the FAT had thought to provide Reid with a work permit, so he was still on his 30-day tourist visa. When it came to flying to Hanoi, the former England international was pulled over by immigration and fined for overstaying his visa.

While the new manager was enthused about the striking options available to him, he was less happy with the stamina of the players.

'They can only run for 50 minutes. They lack fitness and stamina,' he told the local media. 'The game of football is played over 90 minutes and not 50 minutes. The first thing I want to do during the training is improve their fitness. We know that every team wants to win the tournament, but our players have just finished the Thai Premier League, and their fitness is not 100 per cent. We do not expect much from the tournament. Teams like North Korea and Uzbekistan are much better than Thailand.'

The T&T Cup was an annual event in Vietnam and in 2008 saw North Korea and the Thais invited by the hosts. Uzbekistan had withdrawn. Thailand won their first game under the new management team 1–0 against ten-man North

Korea with a 90th minute goal from substitute defender Patiparn Phetphun.

After the game, Reid said, 'There are several things that I am not pleased about, and I need to do some work on the training ground. I am pleased with the performance, (but) we were lucky to score at the end.'

Their final game against Vietnam was played a couple of weeks later, after it was initially called off due to rain. A few days before the team was due to fly back to Hanoi, it was announced assistant coach Tawan Sripan had quit. According to news reports, some players were upset that the BEC Tero midfielder was coaching as well as playing.

FAT president Worawi had a different take. He said he had given Tawan time off to prepare for his wedding and that he would return after tying the knot. If that was the case, then why was Tawan appointed in the first place if he was not going to be available for the Suzuki Cup, which was scheduled to start before his wedding? When the game was finally played, the Vietnamese came from behind twice to make it 2–2, but it was the Thais who lifted the trophy thanks to Patiparn's deflected effort against the Koreans.

Reid was happy to have won his first trophy for Thailand but was impressed by the Vietnamese. 'We wanted to win, but we conceded two fantastic goals, and the Vietnamese played a good counter-attacking game.'

On his appointment, Peter had talked about his players having a positive mental attitude. 'You have got to be positive in the final third and if I can give one piece of advice it is do not be afraid to miss. The top strikers are not afraid to take chances and have a go. From my point of view, when on the training ground and doing attacking sessions, it will just be positive, and do not worry about missing.'

Three weeks after the T&T Cup, it was time for the big one, the Suzuki Cup. Despite winning three of the first four editions, Thailand hadn't won the trophy since 2002, and Singapore was the pre-eminent force now in the region. With the bling of an English international at the helm, the nation was confident 2008 would be their year to end the drought.

However, while Peter and Steve were putting their players through their paces in Nakhorn Ratchasima, 160 miles north east of Bangkok, political squabbling brought thousands of people to the streets of the capital city and soon engulfed the international airport, which was closed for more than a week, shutting down international flights. For a while it looked as if the Suzuki Cup was in danger of being cancelled, but the ASEAN culture of refusing to be drawn into domestic politics ensured a compromise was found. The Thais switched the venue from Bangkok to the beach resort of Phuket, which boasted the luxury of an international airport to go with its golden sands and raunchy nightlife. Hosting Vietnam, Malaysia and Lao on the island may sound glamourous, but it caused a logistical nightmare for the visiting teams to get there. The Thais flew in a military aircraft!

As ever, expectations in the kingdom were high, and despite the political machinations bringing thousands of people on to the streets, the Thais expected their team to win. Peter was asked about the pressure, and he accepted it was just part of the job.

'When you have played football at the highest level and managed in the Premiership with Manchester City, Leeds United and Sunderland, you are going to feel pressure. But I am quite happy with pressure as it stimulates me and is something that excites me.'

It's also fair to say he would have been insulated from a lot of the media-driven hype that surrounded the team as it rarely spilled over into the English language press.

Thailand breezed through the group stage effortlessly against Vietnam, Laos and Malaysia, without conceding a goal. For the first game, Peter and Steve were introduced to a new routine where the captain stood up on the bus and led the team in a national team song. When they'd finished, Steve fished out a DVD and stuck it in the machine, and pretty soon, the players were watching a re-run of England versus Argentina from the 1986 World Cup.

'Reidy was great, real down-to-earth working-class lad. He never talked about his career or what he had seen or done. As the players watched the game, silence descended on the bus. Then the captain, Nattaporn Phanrit, walked down to the front of the bus where I was sitting. "Coach, him, him?" he whispered, pointing towards the TV and Reidy. "Yeah, yeah, that's him," I told him. He returned to the back of the bus and told the team in Thai, and they were all like "Woah, Coach, na khrap. Maladona na khrap." Until then, they didn't know who he was other than their coach. Now they knew their coach had played for England at a World Cup and not only that, played against Diego Maradona.'

Those early days were a massive learning curve for Peter. Heading to training one day, the team bus broke down. Peter was annoyed and wanted to know how the players were going to get to the training field now.

'Watch this,' Steve said. Peter stared on in amazement as the players got off and helped push the bus off the road.

'I can't believe I've seen that. They're international footballers, and they're pushing a bus!'

A semi-final against Indonesia was all that stood between the War Elephants and a final. For all his years in Southeast Asia, Steve had yet to play a game in Indonesia, home to the region's most fanatical supporters.

More than 70,000 people made their way to the Bung Karno Stadium, a cavernous bowl in the heart of downtown Jakarta, clogging the streets for miles around. The Thais weren't used to playing in such a hostile atmosphere. Their own league was little more than a genteel gathering of clubs owned by state-owned enterprises played out in near empty stadiums. But Steve had done his homework and knew the impact an early goal would have on the home support, and the fanaticism that could intimidate could also quickly turn on their own players.

The game panned out just as he planned. Midfielder Suchao Nutnum showed intent early on and was booked within five minutes. One minute later, the Thais silenced the home support. Teerathep Winothai, educated at the same school as Frank Lampard, crossed from the left-hand side and Teerasil Dangda, unmarked, rose majestically and looped his header over Indonesian goalkeeper Markus Horison and into the net.

Teerasil was the scorer, but the Thais inspiration was Teerathep Winothai who was imperious throughout the game, giving the hapless Nova Arianto such a torrid time in the first half that the Indonesian coach Benny Dollo replaced the Persib defender before the half-time whistle.

In the second half, Indonesia relentlessly attacked the Thai goal, having a good goal disallowed, a penalty appeal turned down and a flurry of corners right at the end that had Thai hearts in their mouths. It was a tough game, and the Thais worked hard for their win, but Thailand had intelligent, hard-working players like Suttee, Teerathep, Teerasil and Datsakorn, who ultimately proved too strong for the home side. But was it enough to go all the way?

Vietnam beckoned in the final with 45,000 people heading for the Rajamangala Stadium in eastern Bangkok. On the way to the ground, there was another "This is Thailand" moment. A few miles from the stadium, the bus stopped, and the players trooped off. Peter Reid sat there looking mystified, and he turned to Steve. 'What's going on? We've got a final to play. Where are they going?'

'Don't worry. They're just going to pray,' said Steve, pointing to a nearby temple.

Suttee and Teerathep went close early on as Thailand set about dominating the Vietnamese, but on the 40th minute, it was the visitors who took the lead when Nguyen Vu Phong got in front of a defender and guided the ball smartly home. Two minutes later, the home support was shocked into silence when the Thai defence struggled to deal with a high ball near the centre circle. The Vietnamese broke, and Le Cong Vinh stroked the ball home from six yards.

The second half saw the Thais pile on the pressure, and on 75 minutes they clawed one back when Ronnachai's header hit the post and somewhat tortuously bounced off the Vietnamese keeper and into the net. The Thais had the ball in the back of the net a second time, but the linesman was waving for offside. 'We looked later. The goal should have stood. The lad was two or three yards on side. The cross came in. Teerasil timed it perfect—perfect far post header. I don't think it was a bent call from the linesman. It was just incompetence. It happened so quickly. At the time I couldn't tell if it was offside, but when I saw it on TV, it was clear,' Steve recalls.

The final minutes of the game resembled a custard tsunami as the yellow-shirted Thais piled forward in search of the equaliser, but the Vietnamese defended stoutly and held on for a famous 2-1 win.

The second leg was in Hanoi, and the city was crowded as excited fans descended on My Dinh Stadium hoping to see their heroes win their first-ever trophy. For the Vietnamese, this was their Wembley 1966 or Anfield 1989, and everyone wanted to be present.

There had been a mad rush for tickets when they had gone on sale, with the ticketing website crashing under the sheer number of applicants. Touts, however, had no problems and could be found selling precious match tickets for anything up to $170, when the most expensive face value ticket was $17.

The roads approaching My Dinh were a sea of people dressed in red and the roadside face painters were doing a roaring trade. As the Thai team inched its way through the crowds to the stadium, the manager and coach did their best to play down the scenes outside where it seemed the whole country was clamouring to kiss their shirts and flags in front of the Thais.

The Thais started quickly as usual and went close on a number of occasions. Then, on 21 minutes, they silenced Vietnam's favourite player, My Dinh, when Teerasil again rose highest to nod home a free kick from seven yards out.

As they had done in Jakarta, the Thais had gone into bandit country and silenced the enemy. Now, they had 70 minutes, plus injury time, to face down the expected onslaught.

The second half was backs-to-the-wall stuff for the Thais as Vietnam piled forward in search of the goal that would see them crowned champions, but too often their final ball was wayward. Tackles flew in from both sides. It was this intensity that made the Suzuki Cup such thrilling viewing around the region, with live TV coverage being shown in Indonesia, Singapore and Malaysia, as well as Thailand and Vietnam.

The clock was running down, and it looked as if the Thais were doing enough to hold on for a famous victory. Cameras panned to the party cadres in the VIP seats, sitting miserably in their individual armchairs, impassively watching the cup slip away from them. With seven minutes remaining, it was almost game over as a header from substitute Ronnachai was cleared off the line. When Teerasil wriggled in the penalty area and got off a weak finish that was comfortably saved, a few optimistic Vietnamese fans started to believe. But as the game entered injury time, even they started to accept the inevitable. Then, in the final seconds of injury time, the Thais conceded a free kick about 30 yards out. The ball was swept in, and there was local hero Le Cong Vinh to stoop and loop the ball over Tee's despairing reach. My Dinh erupted, and the celebrations lasted long into the night as Hanoi's streets were filled by ecstatic fans.

There was frustration on the Thai bench.

'If it had gone to extra time, we'd have fancied it. We looked good. But a stupid foul on the edge of the area ... a wonderful header, but it cost us a lot of money!' More frustration followed as the team bus struggled to make his way through the rammed streets outside the ground back to the hotel.

'Reidy couldn't believe the scenes. There wasn't any trouble, but there were people on top of buses, lorries, dancing, waving flags and singing, holding posters of Ho Chi Minh aloft, and all the while there was the police battering fans, trying to clear a path for our bus. It was a long, quiet drive back to our hotel. I think it took about five hours, and they were very long hours when all you can do is think of how close you'd come to winning the cup.'

After the disappointment of losing at the final hurdle in Hanoi, the next challenge facing the Thai national team was an AFC Asian Cup tie against Jordan in Amman. Thailand had been drawn with Iran, Jordan and Singapore, and Steve knew this was not going to be an easy group. Traditionally, Southeast

Asian nations don't travel too well, especially to the Middle East.

The FAT had arranged a training camp in Qatar, but Peter had had to return to the UK, so Steve took the training before they flew on to Jordan. Peter flew to Israel and arrived in Jordan in time to sit in the dugout and see the Thais eke out a 0–0 draw in temperatures far colder than the Thai team was used to.

After another 0–0 draw, this time against Iran in the AFC Asia Cup, the Thais found themselves third in the group with just two points, while both Iran and Singapore each had four points. Unbeaten, but already the odds of heading to the finals in Qatar in two years' time were lengthening.

What followed can best be added to the "This is Thailand" folder, for it was time to hit the airport again for a friendly against Saudi Arabia in Japan. Apparently, the Saudis had an Asian Cup qualifier coming up in a cold climate on a plastic pitch in North Korea, and they wanted a practice game to prepare for the conditions.

'It was winter, and there was about two metres of snow, which of course the Thai lads had no experience of. There were no pitches to train on, so Peter Reid took the lads into a hall to do some exercises and to get rid of the travel legs.

'We did about 30 minutes of hardcore work, and I finished it off by giving the lads a tennis ball each and asking them to bowl like a cricketer. I asked Reidy to demonstrate, as he is a decent cricketer, then said to the lads, "*Have a try!*" It was like something out of a circus. The lads were all over the place, balls flying in as many directions as legs and arms, except for one player, Tee! After no practice and never having bowled before, he was soon pinging the ball down on a good line and length. If anyone thinks this is easy, try bowling with your opposite hand, and see what happens. This showed he was a great athlete. Never mind the biceps and pectoral muscles he had.'

The Saudis won the game 2–1, Teerasil scoring for the Thais in the 89th minute—and if ever Thailand was to take up cricket, they had discovered their first superstar.

In July, Steve realised another ambition when a team of his took to the field to pay Liverpool.

'Some of the Liverpool players were top class. (Jamie) Carragher, (Ryan) Babel, (Javier) Mascherano and Lucas are the ones I am talking about. Our lads matched them in technique, but we lost out in the physical challenges. Upper body strength differences were massive, and (Fernando) Torres was a bit special. We were happy he only saw 25 minutes. Peter (Reid) was really proud of the players' attitude and self-belief, and it was great to receive a good reception at the end.'

One player who wasn't overawed was Datsakorn. The tigerish midfield player positively relished his battle with Mascherano in the middle of the park, but his enthusiasm proved to be his downfall. 'He clattered into the Liverpool lad, and even from the sidelines, I winced. He was never going to be allowed to get away with that, and sure enough, the Argentinian got his own back later leaving Datsakorn in a heap on the ground.'

The 1-1 draw with Liverpool was to be the last time Steve shared the dugout with Reid. A couple of months later, rumours started circulating Reid would be returning to England, which he did, to Stoke City.

'I enjoyed it there. The players are technically very, very good. It's a great place to live in terms of the culture and the climate. But the Premier League is the greatest league in the world and I'm English through and through,' Reid said.

At the time, in 2009, the English FA was keen on working closely with FAT, not least because England was bidding to host the 2018 World Cup and Worawi Makudi was one of 24 influential voters to award the tournament.

There was a strong likelihood Reid's replacement would also be English. Part of the cooperation between the two associations was the offer made by England to send their national team to Thailand to play a friendly in 2010 with Worawi indicating to the Bangkok Post in September 2009 that a return match would happen also.

It later came to light the England FA made the offer for the return match one week before the vote was taken to choose the hosts for the World Cup in 2018 and 2022. Even though he was Chairman of the FA at the time, Geoffrey Thompson told a House of Commons inquiry into alleged corruption in the bidding process that he 'didn't think it was appropriate' to arrange a friendly between England and Thailand 'because I think it is a form of bribery'.

While this rumbled on in the background, Steve carried on working alone. His remit extended beyond the national team, and he was responsible for putting together a team for the Southeast Asian Games which were being held in Lao at the end of the year.

The Thais had won the previous eight SEA Games titles, and with the 2009 games being played in their backyard, they shared many cultural and linguistic traits with their neighbours across the Mekong River. Expectations were high they would make it nine.

But before that, he was kept busy drawing up a blueprint for Thai football, a road map he hoped would take the Thais to a first-ever World Cup. Ever since Collegiate, Steve had loved producing roadmaps. He had done one in Bahrain for an American university which controlled the Bahrain education system and worked on a couple in Australia. He was a big picture kind of guy, one reason why he felt frustrated by petty potentates and big fish who trawled small ponds with puffed-up egos. At the same time, he was fully aware long-term development in Southeast Asia was limited to a bigger win next week.

He wrote in a report for the FAT in 2009 that:

'All the elite footballing nations that regularly appear in the World Cup final have long-term development plans in action. To be successful (qualify) for the World Cup finals in 2014, 2018 and 2022, Thailand must start to put into place programs that include: Talent identification, Quality coaching, High level competition and Education programs that target nutrition, lifestyle and psychological programs.'

Steve argued that for Thailand to reach a World Cup, they would need a plan based on world's best practice.

'To give it a simplified name, Goal 22 could be a Football Thailand initiative aimed at laying down the foundations required to give our elite youth footballers the highest chance possible to succeed at the elite level as adult footballers. Goal 22 would aim to develop the next generation of footballers who will compete at the FIFA World Cup in 2018 and 2022.

'It is generally agreed in the Thailand football community that our elite players are not currently developed in an environment in which we can compete against other countries throughout the world. Whilst some truly great players have emerged, this may have been through sheer talent or luck. Also, the numbers have not been sufficient to make great teams.'

This was a harsh truth many in the corridors of power refused to acknowledge then, and still refuse to acknowledge.

Dominating Southeast Asia is one thing, but even with the players Thailand has produced, the War Elephants had made little impression beyond the narrow confines of ASEAN. Failure in the AFC Asian Cup or the FIFA World Cup was soon forgotten because, thanks to a two-year cycle, the Thais knew success was never far away in either the Suzuki Cup or the SEA Games. Considering some of the talent Steve had seen, he felt Thailand needed to be thinking big, but to do this needed forward planning and attention to detail, two characteristics local football officials were not known for.

Who cared about a ten-year plan that was being carried out under the radar, when winning the SEA Games or the Suzuki Cup guaranteed an immediate chance to muscle in on someone else's glory?

Steve knew that what he was saying wasn't rocket science. He was summarising what Japan had been doing for a few years and Germany had been doing for decades. Having seen in action and working with the likes of Kiatisuk, Suttee and Teerasil, he knew Thailand produced top-quality players, but he knew many more were going unnoticed.

'In order to deliver a quality youth development program four principles of youth development must be considered. These are:

1. *The best players: The starting point is critical to the end product, identification is key. It must not be a victim of nepotism; a poor boy must have equal rights as a rich boy.*
2. *The best coaches: Football educators not just football coaches, playing experience vital.*
3. *The best facilities: You will not develop good players on poor pitches. Maybe use artificial surfaces?*
4. *The best football curriculums: Sound education practices including Sports Sciences and strong links with universities.'*

Steve wanted Thailand to prepare for the 2022 World Cup in 2009 to identify and nurture the players who would form the nucleus of a national team 13 years away.

Steve was in England and had been contacted by Bryan Robson who was to replace Reid, ahead of Worawi Makudi announcing it to the Thai media. Robson met with Steve in a pub where they sat down and discussed the team, the players' strengths and their weaknesses. 'Robbo told me he had spoken with Reidy, and he basically said to carry on doing what we were doing.'

The players were thrilled with their new manager, if not a little in awe of him, but not for long.

'Robbo was great, very down to earth, no airs and graces. He joined in training, and even though his knee was shot, like mine, they just couldn't get near him.

'I told Datsakorn to shadow him in training. Now Ko (Datsakorn's nickname) was a good player, a very good player. I said, "Just stay close to him." Don't forget, at the time Robbo would have been 53, Ko just 26. After the session as they were coming off, I approached Ko, who was drenched in sweat, and asked how it went. "*Sorry, Coach. I couldn't get near him,*" he said. I smiled. "*He's good, isn't he?*"'

The two Englishmen spent a bit of time in the Manchester United Cafe on Sukhumvit Road, a busy road popular with tourists for its variety of restaurants, bars and market stalls. One day they were there talking about the next training session and a Thai man approached Steve.

'Excuse me. Can I have your autograph please?' he asked shyly.

Steve was a bit surprised by this. He was used to anonymity, even some verbal abuse in Malaysia, but rarely had he been asked for his autograph. 'Are you sure you've got the right guy?'

'Yes, yes, you Blian Lobson. I saw you score for England in World Cup.'

'Sorry, you've got the wrong guy. You should be asking Bryan.' Steve pointed to Robson.

'He wouldn't take no for an answer. He was convinced I was the former captain of Manchester United and England, so I gave him my autograph, and he walked away happy, thinking he had met Bryan Robson! Robbo missed the exchange, because he was on the phone to someone.'

Robson's first game in charge was against Singapore in the AFC Asian Cup qualifiers in Singapore. Given Steve's knowledge of both the Thai and the Singapore players, he told Steve just to carry on as he had with Reid. The Thais won 3–1 with two goals from Suttee and one from Therdsak. Steve had known both players well in his Home United days. It was a good result against their ASEAN neighbours and saw them climb to second in the group on five points, two points behind leaders Iran. At the heart of this victory wasn't Bryan Robson or the Singapore-based duo, but it was Teerasil. Singapore defended so well Teerasil was forced to drop deep, go wide. It was a supreme performance from the 19-year-old who was developing into a real talent.

Unfortunately, the Thais were unable to repeat the performance a week later, and it was Singapore who took the points at the Rajamangala Stadium. Qualification now hung in the balance and would involve a trip to Tehran, one of the most intimidating away games in the Asian Football Confederation.

While the national team went into hibernation for a few months, Steve turned his focus to the SEA Games and the gold medal the Thais felt was theirs by right. It may be an under-23 competition, but he knew from his time coaching the Vietnam women's team in 2001 just how important the people of Southeast Asia saw the competition and what winning it could do for his reputation.

Steve was comfortable with the pressure, being quoted by the Bangkok Post as saying, 'I have selected the team myself. I know Thai people take the SEA Games very seriously, and we have picked a good squad.'

The manager of the SEA Games party, Bangkok-based politician Samart Maluleem, concurred, saying, 'I have told our players to win the gold medal for the king.' As if royal appreciation wasn't enough, the manager said he would give the team $150,000 if it took the gold medal, and another politician offered to chip in with a further $15,000. Steve would have preferred the money be used to put his blueprint into action, but he knew that was never going to happen.

The Thais were drawn in the proverbial group of death with Vietnam, riding high on the success at the Suzuki Cup 12 months earlier, as well as an extremely promising Malaysia filled with many talented players Steve knew from his time with Perak. Cambodia was also in the group, giving Steve the opportunity to do battle with an old adversary, Scott O'Donnel, with whom he had enjoyed many a tussle in Singapore. Unfancied Timor Leste made up the group.

With the media and politicians jockeying to show their nationalism and patriotism, the coach was left in the unenviable position of not only knowing the quality of opposition, but also knowing no one cared. Gold was the constant mantra, and if he refused to join the flag waving, he knew he would be in a difficult position. He played the role of bamboo to perfection, expressing confidence, while not going too overboard by bigging up his rivals.

The first group game saw Malaysia trounce Timor Leste 11-0 with Steve an interested observer. The result and the performance confirmed Malaysia's potential. He was just sorry there were no officials from the FAT or journalists from the Thai media watching, but they were all out in force for Thailand's first game against Vietnam.

Kirati Keawsombat, better known as Pop, gave the Thais the lead on 70 minutes, and going into the closing minutes, it looked as if they would open the tournament with a win. On 89 minutes, they conceded a penalty. Just like the Suzuki Cup 12 months earlier, concentration right at the death hurt the Thais in the cruellest way imaginable.

'I felt we were robbed by the referee. They (the Vietnamese players) didn't appeal. We hadn't seen anything. I met the ref years later in India when I was with Mumbai City, and I reminded him of that penalty. He just laughed. A cynic might say he had laughed all the way to the bank, but of course, I'm no cynic!

'I don't know if he was bribed or not. I knew that in Thailand it wasn't just about a bribe. A ref didn't need to be offered a new Mercedes to make sure a team won. There were often threats. "*We win, or you don't go to work on Monday*" type of thing. When I was watching games in Thailand, you'd feel sorry for the match officials sometimes. I mean, they were often crap and deserved abuse for being crap like in the rest of the world, but when they're being threatened, or their family is being threatened, and they literally have nowhere to turn because those doing the threatening are the ones with the power.'

The team responded well by beating Cambodia 4–0 with Sompong Soleb, who had once won a training stint at Everton, scoring a hat trick. This was followed up with a comfortable defeat of Timor Leste. This put the Thais in a three-way battle with Vietnam and Malaysia. Steve's youngsters were top of the group on goal difference with seven points, along with Vietnam. Malaysia was in third place with six points, and with Vietnam, clear favourites to beat Cambodia and qualify. Everything rested on the final game when Thailand was to play the Malaysians.

Ahead of the crucial final game, Steve took time out to write a column for an English-language blogger based in Chonburi. Dale Farrington, an English teacher from Oldham, had been in Thailand since 1997, and thanks to his efforts promoting the Thai game was one of Steve's go-to people when he moved to Bangkok. Despite some bad experiences in Singapore and Malaysia with supposed football journalists, the coach made a point of sounding out journalists and bloggers who operated in areas he was interested in or could be interested in in the future. He could rely on this network of contacts outside the football bubble to offer him a different take on local situations, as well as offer advice on opponents or players.

Steve used the opportunity offered to him by Dale by penning a piece that looked beyond the usual match day and looked at the whole "football team at a tournament" experience and how teams coped with being away from home for a lengthy period of time.

'Firstly, the players have been very professional off-the-pitch. The living conditions are basic, four to a room, no TV, kettle, air-conditioning or fridge, and no hot water. However, I have not heard one complaint from a player or member of staff. They have accepted that is what the reality is and have adapted in a professional manner. The staff have the same conditions. The reality is that the athletes are the true VIPs.

'Also, in their off-field manner the players have been excellent in their physical preparation. The injured players have done exactly what the physios have ordered. The reality is that players will get 'impact' injuries and the treatment is essential as the match schedule is tight. The staff of physiotherapists have been excellent, working very long hours.'

After thanking the Thai supporters who had made the journey to Lao to support the team, he returned to his favourite subject.

'Remember some of these players will be in the 2014 World Cup qualifying squad, but the reality is the bulk of these players will also be the World Cup 2018 squad. As players peak about 28, these players will be that age in 2016 when the qualifications begin. We must start planning and thinking this far ahead. The Italians, Argentineans and Germans do. We must instil best practice and quality preparation habits into these players.'

For Steve, the message was clear; the SEA Games were just a single step on a greater journey.

The Thais took the lead through Arthit Sunthornpit early in the second half with a smartly taken kick from 25 yards, which curled around the wall but again failed to close out the game. First Nasriq Baharom on 81 minutes from close in, and it was Fakri Saarani, who repaid the trust Steve had shown in him in 2007 when he gave the teenager his debut, who ended Thai dreams of a ninth straight gold when he tapped home after fine work down the right by Norshahrul Idlan Talaha.

The players collapsed to the ground in tears. It was heartbreaking for them, but despite his obvious disappointment, the coach was in no mood to point the finger anywhere.

'We had 81 minutes in control and should have finished them off. We got chances, but we could not take them, and in the end, we lacked concentration.

'The footballing reality was that we had lost our two first choice strikers, Ronnachai and Teerasil, and they just could not be replaced. It was like Liverpool losing Mane and Salah, or Tottenham losing Kane and Son, at the same time.'

For the third time in 12 months, a Thailand team had failed to close out a game with the Bangkok Post quick to offer advice as they reported Steve had been 'temporarily' suspended. Both Steve and Robson ignored the advice.

The national team returned to Nakorn Ratchasima for the annual King's Cup where large crowds saw them beat Singapore but lose to Poland and Denmark. Robson was disappointed with how the Thais had performed against the European sides.

'We really struggled ... that was a bit disappointing that we were not a little bit more solid.'

Steve was not happy with the performances either, but he hadn't forgotten his mates at White Eagles in Tasmania and he was able to track down a Polish shirt and a program for them to display in their club house.

With AFC Asian Cup qualification beyond them, the final tie in Iran was a dead rubber. If they could have won in Tehran and Singapore and beaten Jordan, then the Thais would have gone through, but that was never going to happen. By then he was a veteran of trips to the Middle East and knew it was always wise to be prepared for the worse. 'I'd told the lads to take their boots in the carry-on luggage. Don't put them in the hold. If you lose your kit, we can get another kit, but we can't get boots.'

The night before the game, Steve received the kind of job offer you only receive once in a lifetime.

'I was sitting in Robbo's room, and there was a knock on the door. A couple of big blokes came in and politely asked to speak to Bryan. I got up to leave, but Robbo was saying, *"No, don't go,"* so I sat down again.

'It turns out they were agents for an Iranian club, and they offered both Robbo and I a large sum of money to finish the season with them. Robbo wasn't interested, didn't fancy it, so they doubled his money and doubled mine. I'm screaming inside, *"Take it, take it!"* Robbo said he'll get back to them, and they left the room. I'm sitting there saying take it, but Robbo wasn't having any of it. "I don't think I'd like it here. There's too many restrictions," he said. "There's not, there's not," I tried again. It was £1 million for Robbo and 400,000 for me just to finish the season, only a few months! I still remind him of it. I could've bought a second house!'

Iran beat Thailand 1–0 with another last-minute goal, but it was a good result for the Thais against one of the Asian powerhouses. Iran had scored six against Qatar and Singapore in recent months, so while no defeat is ever a pleasant experience, getting out of Tehran on the wrong end of a 1–0 counts as a reasonable day at the office.

After ten years in Asia, Steve had grown used to surreal experiences when travelling away. Lebanon, the Maldives, Syria, Japan and Iran—he had come away from those places with more than a postcard and a fridge magnet.

But perhaps the most surreal away day came when the Thai national team was invited to South Africa in March 2010 ahead of the 2010 World Cup. Bryan Robson had returned to England for his daughter's wedding, leaving Steve to take the team. A flight from Bangkok to Johannesburg can take anything from 13–18 hours, depending on the transit which would usually be either in the Middle East or Singapore. The Thai football team travelled via Hong Kong and Bahrain to Johannesburg and then another three or four hours on to Nelspruit where the game was to be played, and it took 36 hours!

'We stayed in a safari park, absolutely beautiful. I'd never seen anything like South Africa. There were guns everywhere, big blokes carrying big guns. We went to a shopping mall as a group—we did everything as a group there—and at the mall there were men with guns.

'One of the newspapers had sent a journalist to cover the game, and I told Robbo to be careful. I knew the guy, and he was a snake. Before the game, we were in the dressing rooms going over set pieces, telling each player what their role was. It was normal stuff, the type of thing that goes on in every dressing room around the world, but when in the news it was all about Darby taking the coaching. I also talked about Steven Pienaar's movement and how we should deal with it.

'Now in the atmosphere created by that type of media, that kind of incident can be taken in any number of ways. Robbo was lazy, I was overbearing, whatever. Those journalists thought they run Thai football, and whereas in Singapore and Malaysia there were some good lads who I could trust, I felt in Thailand there weren't any.'

The Thais lost 4–0 in front of a full house creating a vuvuzela din, and the game was later caught up in a match fixing investigation.

'It was to do with the number of free kicks. People were gambling on how many free kicks there would be, and we were also getting free kicks which should never have been given.'

Two years later, it was revealed that well-known Singapore-based match fixer, Wilson Perumal, had provided the match officials for a number of South African friendlies that year, including the Thai game. Typically, the home nation would organise the referees and linesmen, but for these games, Wilson had booked the officials. In 2016, Kirsten Nematandani, the South African Football Association President, was banned for five years by FIFA's ethics committee following charges relating to the games.

The rest of the year was spent preparing for the 2010 Suzuki Cup, with Thailand drawn in the same group as Indonesia (the hosts), Malaysia and Lao—another difficult group in a hostile atmosphere. Despite Teerasil's rapid improvement, the Thais still lacked an out-and-out goal scorer as a measly six goals in 11 games testified. Peter Reid had recognised this in 2008 and worked on building players' confidence. Robson was aware as well, but he had a different take.

'I think part of the problem during the Asia Cup qualifying was that a few of the strikers were injured … we have been a bit unfortunate … we have played a lot of decent sides, and that is why we have not got such a decent scoring record.'

Luck also played a part. The Thais had played India in New Delhi in September, winning 2–1, but had hit the crossbar five times.

To address this issue, Bryan and Steve recalled Sarayuth Chaikamdee. The 29-year-old striker was known as Joe-five-yards because that's where he did his work. Teerathep and Teerasil were comfortable anywhere, but Joe was the proverbial fox in the box that the coaching duo felt they needed to feed off any scraps in the penalty area.

It wasn't lack of goals, though, that was to hijack Thailand's attempts to win their first Suzuki Cup since 2002. No, the Thais went into the team severely handicapped by their own football authority and its singular lack of forward planning. The season had been late starting, so teams had compensated by playing more friendlies than was perhaps the norm.

Sensing an increased popularity in the local league, FAT introduced a League Cup to add to an increasingly congested fixture list. So it was, that with just days until the Suzuki Cup, the top two teams still hadn't finished their campaign. On November 28th, Muang Thong United and Chonburi met in the FA Cup final in Bangkok, 120 minutes of attrition for 12 of the players who formed the core of Robson's squad, heading to Jakarta hours later.

'We went in totally knackered,' recalls Steve.

As it was, the few thousand fans inside the stadium came close to witnessing the giant killing to end all giant killing. Thailand, the region's powerhouse for so long and now being managed by 'Captain Marvel', an English legend, was seconds away from being defeated by minnows Lao.

Lao, coached by former Barnsley and Grimsby Town defender Dave Booth, took the lead twice to have the fans back home dancing the *ramvong* in the streets. With the Thais forced into a number of changes brought on by their crippling schedule, it was Lao who had the freedom of the vast Bung Karno Stadium to play the football, knocking the ball around well and taking advantage of a weakened Thai line-up.

Football loves underdogs, and it was impossible not to feel for Booth's battling warriors when Sarayuth did what he was called into the squad to do—equalise as injury time approached. As one, the Lao players sank to the ground spent.

History books and Wikipedia record the result, but not the manner or the background to the result, and both Bryan and Steve knew they were lucky to get a draw. At the press conference, Robson made frequent reference to how little time he had with the players at the post-match press conference and that many of his core players had a tough schedule, but it is doubtful anyone in Thailand was listening.

Looking at the game dispassionately, the Thais were not that bad. With 14 goal attempts, one goal disallowed, the evergreen Therdsak Chaiman electing to go round the keeper instead of finishing when he had the chance, suggests a fine line between a convincing Thai victory and near defeat. Despite the best efforts of Booth on the training field, it is doubtful Lao could ever play that well again. As for Thailand? They suffered from an unholy fatigue, and short of important, tired players; still, they did enough to draw.

Next up was Malaysia who was thrashed 5–1 by Indonesia in the second game, but Robson wasn't reading too much into that result, and he was right to be cautious. While he made a number of changes to the Thai starting line-up, his opposite number, K Rajagobal, had been working away quietly under the radar on his team's discipline.

Malaysia was a much tougher proposition to the one which had lined up against Indonesia on match day one, and Thailand struggled to break them down. Suchao thought he had a penalty when he went down in the box, but the Myanmar referee didn't agree, and right at the death Teerasil, so often Thailand's saviour, went close with a couple of efforts. However, it was not to be their night, and the game ended 0–0. With Indonesia beating Lao 6–1, the hosts topped the group, while the Thais came second with two points, and Malaysia third with just a single point. The maths was easy. Thailand had to beat a resurgent Indonesia in their last game or hope Lao could better their performance in the opening game and beat Malaysia.

The Thai team would have been aware of the apocalyptic reaction their results had created back home, but as ever while on the road, they were isolated from the travelling media pack as much as possible. It wasn't that Steve wanted to control messages from the camp; he just didn't want an inadvertent slip from a player to give reporters more ammunition to attack the team.

Therefore, when the *Jakarta Casual* blog, known for its irreverent look at football in the region, posted a light-hearted story of Thai players enjoying a night out in Jakarta, Steve saw red. He knew how the Thai press would deal with that story if they picked up on it, and he fired off an email telling the blogger, in no uncertain terms, how the post would pan out if they did. It says much about the relationships Steve had developed with people both in football and in its fringes, that the blogger nipped out of the office at the first opportunity he had, turned on his analogue desktop, kissed his newborn baby on the head and deleted the post before returning to work.

Thailand had Sarayuth, Suchao and Therdsak on the bench, while Teerathep and Sutee weren't even involved. Despite the changes, it was Thailand who took the lead against Indonesia, silencing the 65,000 people in the crowd when Suree Sukha drove home on 68 minutes. Not for the first time, the War Elephants couldn't hold on to a lead in a crucial game as local hero Bambang Pamungkas, on as a second-half substitute, scored twice from the penalty spot in the last nine minutes to send the Thais packing in the group stage for only the second time in the history of the competition. Malaysia overcame their poor start by going on to win the trophy for the first time in the team's history.

Despite the outrage in Thailand following their failure in the Suzuki Cup, Worawi stuck by his English duo, but in June 2011, Robson stepped down due to a diagnosis of throat cancer. Steve also knew it was time to leave.

'I met Worawi, and he said there was no way I would get the national team. Had we won the SEA Games, I may have stood a chance. I appreciated his honesty. Like I said, I never had a problem with him, and we still chat on WhatsApp! But I had been in Thailand nearly three years which is quite a good spell by local standards, and I got to work with two great coaches.'

10. Kelantan

Was there ever a worse fit than Steve Darby and Kelantan?

The one had enjoyed lengthy spells with Johor FA, Home United, Perak and Thailand, and the other, a coaching graveyard in the north-east of Malaysia which had gone through 11 coaches in 11 years. The club was a synonym for mismanagement which was a shame for Malaysian football because they were potentially massive but a perennial underachiever.

With previous Coach Hodak leaving at the end of the 2013 season, with an FA Cup triumph and a Malaysia Cup runner-up added to their honour roll, hopes would have been high in the north-east that the experienced English coach would have built on the club's recent success.

Club advisor, former club president, Tan Sri Datuk Seri Panglima Haji Annuar Musa (frequently known by the acronym TSAM), announced on his Facebook page Steve would be taking over from Hodak, just hours after the team had lost to Pahang in the Malaysia Cup final.

TSAM was a colourful character who had his own way of doing things, and at first glance, it was hard to see how Steve, who was never backwards in criticising the way football clubs were run, was going to get along with his new boss. That Kelantan was in the AFC Cup could have been a factor in him taking the job as it offered him another chance of the prize that seemed to forever elude him. Or there was the opportunity to come up against two of his big mates, Ron Smith, who was with Pahang, and Robert Alberts at Sarawak. More prosaically, there was a mortgage and school fees that needed paying.

Whatever the reason, Steve was happy to be back in Malaysia and had soon sensed some changes, both positive and negative.

In the south of Malaysia, changes were taking place which would alter domestic football. Royal patronage rebranded Johor FC as Johor Darul Ta'zim, ironically with Bojan Hodak freshly installed as coach, and they started their journey to domestic domination. Yes, money was at the heart of the southern revolution, but the Ringgit wasn't just being thrown at players and agents. The crown prince of the state wanted JDT to be a professional football club in the European sense, and this was a massive culture shock to Malaysian football where most clubs were state-owned football associations with little financial acumen or companies with no tradition or knowledge of football.

'The biggest change to me was the size of the crowds and the intensity of the passion. Kelantan, Johor and Pahang all had full stadiums with Ultras ... it's great for players ... real football atmosphere. The game is also being marketed far better now by the clubs, with magazines, promotions and the massive use of social media. But pitches sadly have not improved, and you will not get good football on hard bumpy pitches. Most teams haven't got proper training facilities and the pitches are council owned and can be hired out by anybody. The league has made fitness coaches compulsory. The next step is groundsmen.'

Unfortunately for Steve, if JDT was the digital revolution using cutting-edge technology, Kelantan, for all its potential, was positively analogue, and unfortunately for Malaysian football, the gap is growing bigger.

Steve looked forward to helping the Red Warriors capture more silverware, and he was pleased to see some familiar names in his backroom staff, including assistant Hashim Mustapha who had signed for Johor 15 years earlier. Another valuable member of the team behind the team was Pak Harun, one of those unsung institutions even the biggest clubs in the world have. If Pak Harun had a job title, it was kitman, but he also provided a thread of continuity to a football club where incessant change was in its DNA.

'He was just a lovely bloke. All the players loved him. Nothing was too much effort for him. No matter what went on behind the scenes, and a lot did, the players could always rely on Pak Harun to be there, smiling, having a laugh, doing his best for them.'

The new coach set about rebuilding the squad ahead of the 2014 campaign with an eye to the AFC Cup. A number of players were allowed to leave after the Malaysia Cup final loss, including a couple of players familiar to Steve, S Subramaniam, Keita Mandjou, K Nathakumar and Indraputra, all of whom had been offered big money to move south.

Steve told local media that it was a massive turnover '... but I knew the situation before I took up the job. I can't blame the players for leaving. It won't be easy after losing the core players, but we aim to win all our home games. Nowadays, teams need to get as many points as possible from away matches, too. I am glad 'Piya' (Badhri Radzi) is around as he is a real local hero.'

Another familiar face who stuck around was Fakri Saarani, who was less culinary minded, but who hadn't really kicked on since his eye-catching debut with Perak as a 17-year-old. He had been shunted around a number of different clubs, including a short spell in Portugal with Atletico Sport Clube Reguengos. Steve had high hopes that Fakri, only 24, still had a lot to offer.

Steve turned to another familiar face when it came to assessing his striking options. Lebanese forward Mohammed Ghaddar had impressed when Steve's Home United had faced Al Nejmeh in the AFC Cup, and his name had been filed away in his mental D-drive.

'He was one of the best one-versus-one players you will ever see, but sadly he turned out to be injury prone.' The 29-year-old Ghaddar, who also played for Egyptian giants Al Ahly, had come to Malaysia in 2012 when Kelantan had first signed him. After a season in the north-east, he moved to Felda before returning to Kota Bahru for a second time. With his proven track record in front of goal and Malaysian experience, it looked to be a good signing.

To complete the new look front line, Kelantan signed 27-year-old Francis Forkey Doe, a Liberian international who had previously played for teams in the US and Ghaddar's old club Al Ahly before heading to Malaysia in 2012.

One other signing completed a hat trick of Al Ahly alumni. Mohamed Shawky was an experienced Egyptian international who played just in front of the defence. 'Shawky was one of the best professionals I had worked with. He had played in the EPL with Middlesbrough, where he played under Gareth Southgate and a Confederations Cup semi-final against Brazil when he scored. He was a humble, hard-working player who put the team first, but again, genuine injuries impinged on his season. He also found it difficult to accept some of the unprofessional things that were going on.'

In the goal was the finest keeper in the country at the time, Khairul Fahmie. A locally born lad, Khairul had been with Kelantan since 2009 and had won both the AFF Suzuki Cup and the SEA Games with Malaysia before he was 22.

On paper it looked a good combination.

As he prepared for the new season, he settled into his new surroundings. Kelantan's religiously conservative state implemented an Islamic weekend, meaning businesses shut down on Fridays and Saturdays. One Thursday, Steve was out with one of his players and saw a traffic jam heading north. Pointing to the cars, he asked where they were all going. 'They're going to Thailand,' was the somewhat subdued response. Just across the border was the Thai town of Sungai Golok, which offered the kind of nightlife that couldn't be found in Kota Bahru. Sensing the possibly uncomfortable direction this conversation was heading, Steve changed the subject back to the team.

The opening league game of the season was against Sime Darby, a multinational conglomerate which branched out into football for a few years. Steve opted for Francis Doe and Fakri upfront from the start, leaving Ghaddar and Shakri Ali on the bench, and he was banking on the home support to do their bit. Ever since his first visit with Johor, he knew what an intimidating place Kota Bahru could be to play.

'Kelantan have a reputation like Turkish club Galatasaray (huge fan base) ... always full house at home. I want teams to hate coming here,' he told the media ahead of the game.

But his plans were thrown into disarray when Shawky went off on 25 minutes with Sime Darby already leading 1–0. Ghaddar was thrown on as Steve sought to regain the momentum, but it wasn't until the hour mark that the 25,000-person crowd could breathe a bit easier when Ghaddar equalised. Shakir Ali was thrown on as the Red Warriors went for the three points, and at times like this, Kelantan came into its own turning the Sultan Muhammad IV Stadium into a cauldron of noise. They were rewarded with just nine minutes remaining when Kelantan was given a penalty and up-stepped Ghaddar to make it 2–1. The points were Kelantan's, but they'd had to work hard for it.

A week later, Kelantan was top of the table thanks to Francis Doe's 90th minute winner from an excellent cross from Ghaddar away to Sarawak, against Steve's mate Robert Alberts, but again the Red Warriors had made hard work of it, and Steve knew the luck wouldn't last forever.

Relations with TSAM were cordial in the beginning, and as Steve had learnt about the wisdom of "managing upwards" from his time in Australia, he took 3.00 a.m. phone calls in his stride.

'He rang after one game and started discussing the team for next week. I actually found him okay, especially when it was just me and him. It could change, though, when there was an audience! He's the boss, he pays my salary, so I'm not going to tell him to do one. That doesn't work in Asia. He told me who should play and gave me the line-up. I'm knackered, I need my sleep, but I also need to stay on his good books, so I said, "Good team that. We'll definitely win the game if we use that team."'

The club president seemed pleased at his coach's reaction but wanted to know how he could be so sure of victory. 'Well, you've gone for a 4-4-3 formation, so we'll have more players than them for a start!'

Unfortunately, the good start didn't last long as Kelantan lost 2-1 at home to unfancied PKNS and 2-1 in Ipoh when Steve made his first return to Perak since leaving in 2008. There was no rest as two days after the Perak game, Kelantan was in FA Cup action against PKNS at home, and already, four league games into the season, there were grumblings among the home support. Kelantan narrowly won 3-2 and finished the job a week later, drawing 3-3 in a nervy game.

Happy to be in the next round, Steve addressed the issue of unhappy fans with the media. 'The team have been abused for perceived poor form, but we have won five out of eight matches,' he said. 'That should say something about us. It was a great match for both teams ... the neutrals would have loved the action-packed game. We scored late goals, and I know my team are capable of scoring goals. We are in the semi-finals of the competition now. How could I not be happy with the team's performance? If people are expecting beautiful stuff, they should watch ballet instead ... We will take the win, no matter if the football is beautiful or not.'

In the league, the team had dropped to sixth, and their home game, a north-east derby against T Team, sandwiched between the PKNS FA Cup ties, pulled in just 15,000 people as supporters voted with their feet after two losses. Shawky, Badhri Razli and Ghaddar gave the loyal supporters something to cheer about as Kelantan won 3-0 and climbed up to second.

The team didn't have time to think about how the supporters were feeling. They were fully focused on their first AFC Cup tie against Yangon United in Myanmar, and the coach was not looking forward to the game as Kelantan travelled with a number of key players missing through injuries. The Myanmar side was 3-0 to the good at half-time, but Kelentan's cause wasn't helped when Shakir Ali was sent off. The Red Warriors were much better second half, but the damage was already done, and they returned home licking their hooves after a 5-3 loss and their coach bemoaning the lack of depth in the squad.

After Yangon, the team was packing passports one more time, this time for a league game against LionsXII. The Singapore side had joined the Malaysian Super League in 2012. They hadn't started the 2014 season well, with only a last-minute winner against Selangor earning their solitary win after five games. Inspired by Amri and Shafiq Ghani, Kelantan started the brighter of the two. When Amri scored after 26 minutes, it was no more than they deserved. Early in the second half, a statuesque LionsXII defence allowed Fakri to nip in between two defenders and roll the ball past the on-rushing keeper. As if the lesson wasn't learned, another through ball split the defence, and Forkey Doe should have done better when one-on-one with the keeper. It was third time lucky when Forkey Doe nipped past the non-existent defence, and this time he rounded the keeper and finished well.

'It feels nice to be back on top of the Super League, but the problem is to ensure that we stay there despite our tough schedule. The players were exhausted and while other teams will play nine matches in the next 41 days, we have 14 matches because of the AFC Cup commitments. It will not be a problem for a team like JDT (Johor Darul Ta'zim), who have 25 internationals and two coaches. But I am operating with just 19 players in my squad. It will be physically challenging for Kelantan. And because we're always looking to our finances, we had to travel the cheapest way possible, often having to wake at 5.00 a.m. to take advantage of the cheapest flights,' Steve told media.

The win in Singapore was the day Kelantan clicked. The team had defended well and broken with pace and power. Sadly for Steve and the players, it wasn't a home game, so the Kelantan supporters were not able to witness what their team was capable of. Despite their team being top of the league, the supporters had made up their mind and were in no mood for changing their opinion.

When Hong Kong's South China rolled into town for the AFC Cup just a few days later, less than 5,000 supporters made the effort to see the league leaders win 2–0, and if that paltry attendance can be explained away by apathy towards the AFC Cup, just 13,000 turned up for the next home game, a 2–2 draw against Pahang. It was the lowest crowd of the season.

There followed a run of two wins in nine games as Kelantan's season imploded. Vietnamese side Ninh Binh came to an apathetic Kota Bahru with just 1,500 fans who made the effort to be there. The visitors left with a 3–2 win on a nightmare evening. Kelantan's cause wasn't helped when the two strikers were sent off, Shakir Ali and Khairul Izuan Rosli, either side of half-time. It was Kelantan's 14th game in 41 days, a crippling schedule by any measure and especially in Malaysia where financial insecurity forced clubs to operate with pared back squads, meaning a couple of injuries would soon decimate squads. Back-to-back defeats in the league followed against Selangor and JDT as Kelantan slipped down to the middle of the tale. Further humiliation came in the North-east Derby when Kelantan earned a draw at Terengganu, only to find they had played an illegible player, and the game was awarded 3–0 to Terengganu.

'This summed up the club. They wanted professional results, but the administration was often in the hands of amateurs.'

At the beginning of April, Kelantan's and Steve's AFC Cup dreams ended on the Red River Delta as Ninh Binh swatted Kelantan aside in the return match, winning 4–0. The good news was he had all four foreigners available to him. The bad news was he had to travel without Badhri Radzi (back injury), midfielder Amar Rohidan (ankle), striker Ahmad Fakri Saarani (knee), as well as suspended strikers Khairul Izuan and Shakir Ali.

The coach could have been forgiven for thinking *Sod it, I'm going home to Hanoi,* where he was based but he stuck with his players and returned home to a crescendo of jeers from supporters who had stopped going to games, but still made their voices known online. Mathematically, there was still a chance to go through in the AFC Cup, but there was little belief in the squad or the state in the science of numbers.

After back-to-back league wins, Steve was sacked in the middle of April following a 4–0 thrashing at Sime Darby. In keeping with the manner of his appointment, when the axe came, it was via the social media account of the advisor Tan Sri Datuk Seri Panglima Haji Annuar Musa.

There were the makings of a good team, but Kelantan was already going to be the wrong club at the wrong time for Steve as it had been for so many coaches. FIFA has yet to devise a coaching course which can help coaches with the vicissitudes of luck and injuries and supporters who were used to success. For Steve, there was still one more battle ahead.

Steve and Kelantan had signed a two-year contract. When he was sacked after just six months, the coach wanted compensation as he was entitled to. The club saw things differently, so in July 2016 the FAM stepped in with an ultimatum—pay their former coach within 14 days, or they will take action. Kelantan continued to do nothing, so the FAM announced they should now pay Steve RM636,000 and not the RM240,000 he initially sought. Kelantan played the victim card and threatened to withdraw from the Super League.

When Steve was eventually paid, he received only RM165,000.

The sorry saga left a bitter taste in the mouth of the coach. He loved working in Malaysia, but this had been the second time he had been left waiting for monies he was owed. When it was revealed Kelantan had been signing new players even though he and some players had wages outstanding, he was livid.

'It would appear unethical to allow clubs to buy new players and staff if they still owe money to their ex-staff. My case took over two years to be settled. If FAM had a quick process of appeal, and an embargo was put on new registrations, it would make the situation fairer. No need to punish fans and current players with points deductions or fines. It would speed up the legal process and ensure ethical procedures are followed.'

Steve remains phlegmatic about his time in Kelantan.

'The reality was that we didn't do too bad. When I was sacked, we were in the semi-final of the cup, fourth in the league, but were battered by the travel schedule of the AFC Cup. We received no help from the FA. The only worry I had was that there were times when I thought some of the players were making "strange" mistakes. One of the players had come to me to say he felt there was fixing going on. I reported it to the team manager, but he took it nowhere. He was also a manager who, one game when I made a sub, told the sub to play in a different position. He didn't realise I understood the language. He was the classic interfering Malaysian manager who backed his favourite players, including when I was going to fine a foreigner for being drunk. He just thought it was funny! The game versus Ninh Binh where we had two sent off was officially declared fixed by AFC and Ninh Binh suspended, but the AFC never interviewed any of my players, and neither did the FAM. I personally rang AFC to offer assistance, but they never responded.'

Some of his happiest moments in Kota Bahru came when he fronted up at his favourite food stall run by Marzita Mahmood. There he tried to fathom the inner workings of football in the state, planned how to get to away games, or sometimes just absorbed Marzita's calming influence while dipping *roti canai* in a bowl of curry. '(She) used to keep me sane with her cultural wisdom and fitness salads ... I used to try and understand the battering we were getting in social media and later would find out much of it was being engineered from within the club.'

Despite the disappointing end to his time in Kelantan, Steve still looks back fondly on his time in Malaysia.

'I had six and a half seasons there, and I loved every minute of most of them!

I love the country, I love the people, and I love the food. Good things are happening football-wise there, as well, with Johor Darul Ta'zim and the national team winning the SEA Games and the AFF Suzuki Cup. Really, Malaysia should be looking to go to the next level, doing better in the qualifying rounds of the AFC Asian Cup for one. JDT are too big for Malaysia, and they are thinking big, which is right, but they can't do it alone. There needs to be a stronger league, and they need to have clubs challenging them for the MSL on a regular basis.

'Malaysia has the players, and it has some very good coaches. It needs better administrators, smart young university graduates who love football but who are savvy enough to see what other clubs and countries are doing and how they can apply those lessons in Malaysia. There is no need for politicians to be anywhere near a football club. You need people who can identify markets, who can develop grass roots programs, and attract sponsors, but too many officials don't have those skills. They are excellent at snagging free overseas trips but less good at working out how to provide good training facilities or developing a scouting network, but these are more important for the sake of Malaysian football than a shopping trip to Japan at someone else's expense, which is probably why I'll never get to coach the Malaysian national team! I'd love to do that. After all my years there and the lasting friendships I made, I would be so proud, but it will never happen.'

A return to Malaysia hasn't been ruled out at some time in the future. If he does, despite the deep Liverpool roots, it would feel like a homecoming for the proud scouser.

Part IV: The Indian Summer
11. Mohun Bagan

A city appears, enormous and sprawling around a wide, brown river which has shaped itself in a dog-leg and which has ships hanging at anchor. Silver oil tanks sparkle in the piercing light but there is a haze of smoke over the city which renders a range of high dockside cranes as an indistinct thicket of industry and a vast row of factory roofs as a rusty sheet of corrugated iron. It could almost be Liverpool on a sensational summer's day—Calcutta, by Geoffrey Moorhouse.

Oh Calcutta! A city synonymous with poverty, Mother Theresa, and the black hole of British colonial lore, yet there was another side to this city on the banks of the Hooghly River that Steve knew little about even after his decade and a half coaching in Asia.

While India is best known for its cricketing prowess, Calcutta, now known as Kolkata, is home to a passionate footballing culture and one of the biggest rivalries east of Tehran. In Mohun Bagan, it boasts the oldest professional football club not just in India, but in Asia, and their games with East Bengal regularly attract crowds of 50,000 people or more to the Salt Lake City Stadium. In 1997, 131,000 people were at the game.

In some respects, the Kolkata Derby is on a par with the Old Firm of Rangers and Celtic in Glasgow. One city, two teams, proud of their origins and roots. East Bengal has traditionally drawn on the migrants from the eastern part of the province of Bengal, a province that was split asunder at the time of Indian independence, while Mohun Bagan, as the original Kolkata club, has been the club of choice for people from western Bengal, including Kolkata.

The phone call from an Indian-based agent, Anuj Kichlu, asking if he was interested in coaching Mohun Bagan was unsolicited. Despite his successes with Johor FA, Home United, Perak, and the Thai national team, it seemed the agent only knew about Steve through his punditry work for ESPN which, at the time, was also being shown in India. Steve had never worked with an agent. He had found his jobs through word of mouth or his own contacts in the game. He knew nothing about Indian football beyond what Bhaichung Bhutia (a former Indian international who had played for both Kolkata giants, as well as Perak in Malaysia and Bury in England) had told him. He was intrigued, though a little perturbed, when the agent advised him to get a lump sum sign-on payment upfront.

There was a striking parallel between Steve's appointment in Kolkata and his first foray into Asian football years earlier. Whereas in Johor he had an old mucker, Ron Smith, coaching his city rivals Johor FC in India, he would be coming up against Trevor Morgan, a former Bournemouth and Bristol Rovers striker who had coached in Australia and Singapore, and Steve was looking forward to crossing swords with the East Londoner.

A job interview over Skype, where Steve was being asked questions by a number of different people, followed before terms were agreed and contract signed.

Now aged 56, he embarked on another journey into the unknown, and he was looking forward to the ride. After 15 years in Southeast Asia, he thought he had seen it all but, at a time of life when many people are thinking about retirement and putting their feet up, the Liverpool-born coach was embarking on his very own Indian summer.

For much of his Asian experience, Steve had the fortune of working alongside a manager who had both supported him in his efforts team building and provided that degree of separation from the dreaded committees who felt their football knowledge, or personal ego, should trump all else. At Mohun Bagan, Steve soon realised he would have no such barrier. In Kolkata, the committee members wanted to be seen and heard, or else what was their role to be?

Steve was met at the international airport in Dum Dum to the north of the city and taken to his apartment. Looking around, he noticed a few drinks and snacks had been brought in for his arrival, and he was halfway to appreciating the thoughtful gesture when the driver held out his hand. Knowing nothing about the local currency, rupees or the value of items, Steve just held out a handful of rupees and told the driver to help himself. It was perhaps the most expensive packet of biscuits you're every likely to get outside of Harrods!

At a press conference, he was introduced to the local media saying, 'It really made sense to come here. From FIFA to the AFC, all eyes are now on Indian football, which is on a rise. The whole world wants Indian football to succeed with the population and passion for sport. I think it's an intelligent move for me.'

Later, he was taken to the club's training facility which also doubled as a home ground at times, on the Maidan, a large green expanse in the heart of Kolkata.

'We are the Manchester United of Asia,' said one committee member as they gazed at a large pile of cow shit on the pitch.

'I don't think they have that at Carrington (Manchester United's training ground),' suggested Steve.

Immediately, a lad was beckoned and told to scoop up the poop. Here, in the shadow of the jaw-dropping Eden Park cricket ground, one of India's biggest football clubs was having someone clean shit off the pitch. Inwardly, Steve groaned. The Manchester United of Asia? The Old Firm Derby of Asia? This was going to be fun!

It wasn't long after arriving that Steve realised his appointment had not been a popular one.

'I found out later it was the sponsor who wanted me. They knew my reputation as being honest, and they wanted me to come in and clean the club up, much as I had done at Perak. The committee, however, felt differently. They had wanted a local coach because, sadly, the impression was a local coach would do as he was told.

'I also made a mistake by being the last in. Normally, a coach gets to have at least some input on the players he would like to sign or the positions he needed filling, but here I had neither. I was given the squad and told to get on with it. If we failed, it was my responsibility. I don't mind that if it's my team, my squad, but not like this.'

From day one, Steve had sensed an unusual atmosphere, and it took him a while to put his finger on it. 'I had never been anywhere like it before, but it seemed like there was a culture of fear hanging over the club and the players. There was lots of whispering going on, but people wouldn't speak up.' It was a far cry from the camaraderie that Steve liked to develop in his teams. "There was no strong figure in the dressing room. Don't get me wrong. They were good lads, but the atmosphere around the club wasn't conducive to building a team spirit.

'Players came and went as they pleased. Someone had to go here; another had to go there. When our star import came in on the first day, I thought he was

Billy Bunter. He was three stone overweight! He just did what he wanted. Nice guy, but as a professional footballer earning a high salary, it wasn't what you wanted. There were some good pros, but no one was allowed to be a strong presence. The club committee weren't keen on having leaders in the dressing room for some reason.'

Alongside the sense of fear was an overriding feeling of neglect. The club offices had locked cupboards. No one knew what was in them. They had been locked for years. The dressing room had just two showers and a slow-moving ceiling fan creaking under the accumulation of years of dust. A gym was packed with the latest equipment, so someone had obviously identified a need for players to work out and gone to a lot of expense getting in good gear. 'I went into the gym. It was covered in six inches of water. There were lads in there doing weights—in six inches of water! And in the corner was a ghetto blaster! I couldn't believe my eyes. "You can't go plugging that in with all this water!"' he told them.

Despite the lack of facilities and professionalism, the players were keen to learn and threw themselves wholeheartedly into the training sessions. At the end of one such session, one of the goalkeepers approached Steve.

'Coach, can we go and do some skipping exercises?' Impressed by the positive attitude, the coach replied, 'Of course you can, lads,' and off they trooped to one corner of the pitch.

'I watched them skipping on their own, so I went down to offer them support and say well done lads ... they had no skipping ropes! They were skipping without ropes! They were doing everything right, changing their hands, changing their feet, one bloke counting, one bloke leading. They were doing everything correctly, except they had no ropes. The club wouldn't buy skipping ropes!'

The club also wouldn't buy a washing machine or dryer. 'In Kolkata, it rains a lot. They guy who washed the clothes, a lovely lad always smiling, would scrub the kit then hang it out to dry on a clothesline. We're talking one of the biggest football clubs in Asia, and they're hanging clothes out to dry! Of course, the clothes would often get drenched in the regular downpours, so the kit would never dry.'

When Steve suggested that the club buy a washing machine and dryer, the committee refused stating that the washerman wouldn't be able to operate them. It seemed to Steve the committee wasn't interested. He also realised that they such a low opinion of the poor washerman (*dhobi wallah*) and his ability to learn to handle new technology, that he was witnessing India's caste system being played out in front of him at the football club. The Dhobis are what is known as a scheduled caste, formerly known as untouchable, and it is their role to wash clothes. Pressing a few buttons on a machine didn't count as washing clothes in the eyes of higher caste committee members.

It wasn't the last time Steve was to fall foul of the caste system. While it was normal in England to have apprentices, and later kitmen, to clean players' boots, this was less common in South East Asia.

In Mohun Bagan, Steve had a boot man, and at the end of his first month, he gave the lad a tip. The committee found out and went wild. 'Why are you giving him money? He already gets paid.' Steve was a bit put out by this admonishment. 'Why not? He does a good job.'

'No, don't do that. He'll expect others now to give him a tip every month.'

'You mean no one else gives him a tip? Right, I'll make sure they all do from now on!'

What Steve hadn't realised before handing over his tip was how much the boot man had actually earned, so when he had handed over his rupees, he was totally unaware that what was, for him, a small amount was, for the boot man, almost a month's salary.

'I was struggling to understand how the caste system worked but was starting to get a handle on it, and it was explaining things. I mean, no one sat me down and said, "This is how it works," but among the players, there were some of the higher Brahmin caste who were treated a little deferentially. To be fair, the players weren't an issue. Once I knew what the telltale signs were, I became aware, but it wasn't something that affected team spirit. The only people who seemed bothered by it were the committee members who jealously guarded their positions and privileges.'

Every day of that preseason was like a surreal journey into *Alice in Wonderland*. One day, Steve found boxes full of Reebok gear just gathering dust, possibly the fruits of a long-forgotten sponsorship deal. Another day, he learned the Manchester United of Asia had no official kit supplier so had just commissioned some local guy who was probably known to a committee member to knock up a few shirts. However, despite boasting such a large fan base, Mohun Bagan had no club shop, no way of cashing in on their popularity.

Early on, Steve fell to a pair of afflictions common to many visitors to the subcontinent. At a players' dinner one night, he made a point of mingling with the players, trying to get to know them as people as he had done elsewhere. It was much easier in Kolkata, of course, where the standard of English was much higher, which was a relief to him. After enthusiastically making the effort to learn Arabic and Malay in his younger days, now he couldn't be bothered to try and learn a new language, in this case Bengali.

Like everything he did, Steve threw himself wholeheartedly into the meal and the chat without thinking how the food had been prepared. "Delhi Belly" is a real ailment. Its medical term is travellers' diarrhoea, and it is well-named as people who get caught out do suffer from a dire rear. It's actually a stomach and intestinal infection which may be accompanied by abdominal cramps, nausea and fever.

'One night, I slept in the bathroom. I had the pillow and the blanket in there. I just couldn't risk sleeping in my own bed and being caught short. I was shitting on the hour, every hour. I was curled up in agony. I thought the night would never end.'

The next morning, feeling somewhat the worse for wear, he staggered into the office and asked how often the players got sick like this. 'Oh, all the time,' was the cheery response. Steve insisted on some basic hygiene in the preparation and service of food, so the servers had to wear hats, gloves and basic outer clothing.

One week into his time in Kolkata, Steve came out 'in the biggest rash I had ever seen in my life. It was all over me.'

He went to see the club doctor, and together they went to a local, crowded, public hospital. Again, that quote of "Manchester United in Asia" sprang to mind.

'I walked to the front of a queue of about 200 people and into a room where a doctor was seeing patients. There were people all over the place who had been evidently queuing a long time, if what was outside was anything to go by. I felt awful. Had my socialism been trumped by a petty rash? What right had I to just march in and almost demand to have my illness treated before those who had been queuing longer? I later realised this was one of the "perks" of being at Mohun Bagan, but that didn't make me feel any better.'

With an audience looking on with keen interest at this strange white apparition in their midst, Steve was given a check-up and the doctor announced he had bedbugs. Within hours, people were round his apartment with a paraffin spray to consign the little critters to the afterlife, and the club consented to buying him a couple of new mattresses.

As well as these daily battles just to get basic facilities, Steve had to prepare the team for the upcoming Federation Cup. Mohun Bagan had a special affinity for the trophy, having won it eight times up until 2011, but their last triumph had been in 2008, and the year before had seen them lose to bitter rivals East Bengal in the final in a campaign derided as 'pathetic' in the local media. Triumph in the Federation Cup would continue his happy little knack of winning a trophy early in his career at a new club.

A friendly against Kalighat MS was Steve's first chance to see how well his players had bought into his ideas. A 5–1 victory suggested good times ahead, but the new coach wasn't so enthusiastic.

Nigerian striker Odafe Okolie was seen as a superstar in India after hitting over 100 goals for Churchill Brothers during his six years in Goa, prompting Mohun Bagan to bust the bank for him, reportedly paying $600,000 a year to tempt him. The new signing was looking forward to playing alongside Jose Ramirez Barreto, telling the press, 'He is great player. I'll be really happy to play with him. He wears number ten, and I will wear number 101!' There was an immediate return as Odafe scored two, had a hand in the other three goals, and went close on numerous other occasions.

A few days later, Steve announced his squad for the Federation Cup. A forward line comprising Chhetri, Barreto and Odafe suggested an attacking style of play, while the appropriately named Shilton Paul was in goal and Aussie defender Simon Storey, who was also a qualified physio, was expected to provide guile and experience at the back. Defender Rahim Nabi, midfielder Jewell Raja and striker Ashim Biswas had all scored against Kalighat MS and were rewarded with places in the travelling party.

Mohun Bagan entered the competition at the second stage, or the group round. A total of 16 clubs had been drawn into four groups of four, with each group based either in Kolkata or Pune. It was Steve's misfortune to be drawn in Pune, while East Bengal got to stay on home turf. Joining Mohun Bagan in Pune were Shillong Lajong, Royal Wahingdoh (both from the north-eastern state of Megalahya) and Churchill Brothers from Goa on the west coast.

Their first game was against Royal Wahingdoh, and the same supporters who were so optimistic after the friendly victory were now incandescent with rage. The target for their anger was goalkeeper-coach Hemanta Dora. Having declared

Mohun Bagan to be among the favourites to win the Cup, they were now sure they wouldn't even qualify from the group stage.

A 3-1 loss to Churchill Brothers followed and the rage increased as the fan site called for the new coach to answer some serious questions about where he saw the team going. For the supporters, it was simple. There was a 'lack of leadership in defence, lack of leadership in midfield and poor show by the costly forward line.' In a series of questions, they asked, 'When will Darby be able to get his defenders to concentrate for an entire match?'

Such was the frustration felt by the fans. One supporter, described as a 'heartbroken' fan, was moved to write a letter to the committee that was full of the angst of a football fan and the unrequited relationship they have with their club, an angst that remains dormant when results go their way, but quickly erupts after a string of poor results.

Mohun Bagan returned to Kolkata with their tails between their legs to face the ire of their supporters. To make matters worse, East Bengal had reached the final, and their fans were enjoying their rival's humiliation in the offices, restaurants and street stalls around the city.

The final between East Bengal and Salgaocar (from Goa) was played at Salt Lake City Stadium in front of an estimated 85,000 people, and Steve could only look on as a frustrated spectator. He was disappointed not to have done better in the group stage, but his focus was the I-League, India's premier league at the time.

The intensity of three games in quick succession, plus the travelling involved crossing India, took a toll on the players' bodies but Steve was prepared for this. He knew from Bhaichung how committees would pressure players to recover from injuries quickly, so he had brought in a young English physio who was looking to get into the game and was prepared to work cheaply. 'Coach, these lads are dead. They're not being allowed to recover properly. They need rest.'

Rest, however, is not a commodity looked on favourably by committees, and anyway, Steve now knew he was fighting to save his job even before the I-League started. The club was rumoured to be lining up former coach Subrata Bhattacharya as a replacement should they decide to axe their English coach.

The decision not to enter the Durand Cup, another preseason competition, also came under criticism. Steve told the committee he needed friendlies against top-quality opposition, but none were available as they all entered the Durand. Mohun refused to compete in the Durand for political reasons!

Confidence in the squad was low after Pune and the coach felt the players needed more playing time to improve their self-belief. Despite the fine words of Swapan Sadhan Bose earlier, his position was still under threat as the I-League season drew ever closer. Fans weren't happy, and Steve was growing weary with the constant petty arguments and the lack of movement from the committee. The atmosphere within the club, never particularly positive, worsened as players grew wary of who they were talking to and what they were saying, for fear of being seen as troublemakers. Steve longed for an aide or an ahamad in the dressing room to sort things out!

It was a matter of if, not when, someone would make the first move.

Steve was grateful to his agent for insisting on getting some money upfront. He got three months, and that soon morphed into a fixed date from his viewpoint. The final straw came when the club appointed a three-man committee to oversee team affairs. There was no way Steve was going to live with that.

'Coaches get sacked all the time. We accept it as part of the job. But if I'm going to get the sack, it's going to be because of the decisions I made, not some committee forcing decisions upon me. I just refused to work with a technical committee, one of whom was after my job.'

A bitter war of words followed with the normally circumspect Steve slamming the 'stone age' administration at Mohun Bagan in a statement, a slight, that the president wasn't going to let go unanswered.

'I was repeatedly told Bagan was a big club, a powerhouse in Asia. But I remember on the first day, cleaning cow waste off the pitch. Trying to scrape the mould and rust off the gym equipment in a flooded gymnasium.'

He called upon the club sponsors to get more involved in the day-to-day running of the football club, saying, 'At the moment there is no press officer or a marketing manager and no club shop. UB are a top-class professional organisation. They have the ability to take the club to the next level and indeed make it a big club.'

Swapan responded by accusing Steve of being a politician. 'Why did Darby not have the guts to point out these things while he was here in Kolkata? This proves that he is not a football coach but actually a politician,' Bose said, himself a politician.

It was an unseemly end to a job that Steve had perhaps taken on 15 or 20 years too late. Arguably, a younger Steve would have made more of an effort to learn the language and may have chosen his battles more carefully, but now, he was set in his ways, ways which, after all, had brought him success in a number of countries.

He worked best when he was allowed to focus on the football and had a strong middleman who protected him from the arcane politics of football clubs run by committees of suits who thought they were Sir Alex Ferguson or Arsene Wenger.

The city of Kolkata beyond football made a big impression on Steve who couldn't help but contrast the conditions many of the population lived in with the opulence found elsewhere in the city.

'It was terrible seeing the abject poverty and the massive wealth in the same place. Seeing the appalling public hospitals with great doctors doing a fantastic job in such difficult circumstances and comparing that with the sense of entitlement and ostentatious wealth of the richer types. You could weep, but I knew I could change none of it. I used to be driven around the city and look out at the wretchedness of everyday life, and I'd remember the advice Haji Ahamad had given me when I first arrived in Malaysia. *"You're not going to change the way things are done, so don't even think about it. The best thing you can do to help is to set up the team, so they win and know that will bring happiness to thousands and thousands of people for a short while at least."* Oh, how I could have done with a Haji Ahamad or a David Conceicao! It confirmed my view that the quality of administration dictates the culture of a club.'

12. Manipur

After his adventures in Kolkata, one could forgive Steve for blocking any incoming numbers from the agent who had lined him up with the Mohun Bagan job, but Anuj Kichlu had impressed him with his honesty and the small matter of insisting on getting three months money upfront. So, when Anuj did call again, Steve was all ears.

It had been a couple of years since his ill-fated stay in Kolkata, and although he still shivered at the mere mention of Mohun Bagan, Steve had enjoyed working with the players and kept in touch with events in Indian football through a couple of pals, Dave Booth and Trevor Morgan, both former English professionals who had managed to handle the stresses and strains somewhat better than the Liverpool-born coach.

India is a massive country, and its two hotbeds of passionate support are Kolkata in the east and Kerala in the south-west. This role was in Manipur in the north-east which is known as a goldmine of aspiring footballers. The region is made up of eight states: Arunchal Pradesh, Assam, Manipur, Meghalaya, Mizoram, Nagaland, Sikkim and Tripura, and shares extensive land borders with Tibet, Myanmar, Bangladesh, Nepal and Bhutan, covering an area larger than the United Kingdom. It is connected to the rest of the country by the narrow Siliguri Corridor, a sliver of land about 14 miles wide, bordered by Nepal to the north and Bangladesh to the south. Veteran football writer Novy Kapadia describes it as a place where 'neither Bollywood nor cricket has reached'.

Steve was first made aware of the richness of football potential in the northeast by Bhaichung Bhutia, the legendary forward who was born in Sikkim and would later play in England for Bury, as well as Perak in Malaysia. Other well-known players from the region include Jeje Lalpekhlua (striker born in

Mizoram), Jackichand Singh (winger from Manipur), the promising young goalkeeper Dheeraj Singh Moirangthem (Manipur) and midfielder Udanta Singh (Manipur).

'This is different,' his agent Anuj told him. 'This is working for the state government, coaching young players how to be professional footballers. No games, no matches. Just coaching.'

Steve was hooked. Coaches love coaching, and while setting up a team to win a game is rewarding enough, it doesn't beat the work done on and off a training ground to develop a promising young player.

His visa sorted, Steve made the roundabout journey from Hanoi, where he was based, via Kolkata to Imphal, the state capital of Manipur and scene of a major battle during World War Two. The program was organised by the All Manipur Football Association that held initial trials for 100 players before whittling that number down to 30 lads, and Steve was ably assisted by local Manipur coaches Nandakukar Singh, L Choaba Devi and G Dhanakumar Sharma.

'I couldn't have worked in a better place, and the support from the AMFA was top class. When I was in transit in Kolkata, I was met by someone from AMFA who had flown down to meet me. Lovely bloke.'

When he got to the hotel in Imphal, he was told he shouldn't go out after 6.00 p.m. because Maoist insurgents were causing trouble.

The next morning, the driver arrived on time—another culture shock for Steve. After 15 years in Asia, he had almost forgotten the concepts of time and punctuality. They set off from the hotel and pretty soon were driving through pot-holed lanes with donkeys roaming free, not showing any concern for other road users. They eventually pulled up into a swampy car park, and Steve made his way gingerly through the puddles, wondering how he was going to handle the next couple of months.

The pending gloom and despondency soon gave way though. 'It was the best artificial pitch I have ever seen. They had a FIFA grant, and they had used that money wisely. Other places I've been and heard about, FIFA grants are seen as perks of the job for officials, but here in Imphal, they had used that money as it was intended. When I asked for portable goals, next day they had portable goals! When I thought about Mohun Bagan players pretending to skip because the club were too mean to buy skipping ropes, I could have cried! Everything AMFA did was for the players.'

Steve was expected to further pare down the numbers, but soon after arriving, he knew this was a task he didn't want to do. He was so feeding off their players' enthusiasm, he didn't want to end their dreams before they had even started. Unfortunately, it was a decision that had to be taken. The lads were staying in dormitory accommodation, and there weren't enough beds to go around, so the coach set up some physical tests based on those conducted by Everton in more salubrious surroundings, and those who failed were, reluctantly, sent on their way.

'The top 30 were taken into hostel accommodation and given excellent food for this period. I was initially going to undertake a number of physical tests and compare them with results for EPL Academies and professional teams in Asia, but when I went to do the body fat test, I saw that my diet and nutrition lecture was going to be changed to just three words, "EAT MORE FOOD." The lads were in great physical shape, lean with good aerobic ability, obviously based on the lifestyle in the state, especially the mountain areas.'

For once Steve found himself in the position of managing down. Ever since he had moved to Asia, so much of his time was spent managing upwards, dealing with unrealistic expectations of committee members with no knowledge of the game. In Imphal, he had players from the villages of Manipur asking for two sessions a day instead of one. 'I had to tell them they couldn't go from two sessions a week to two a day. Their bodies couldn't take it. So instead of a second training session, I started taking them to a local gym to build them up. Their attitude was top class.'

There had never been an issue with English in Mohun Bagan, where nearly everyone was familiar with it, and many people were bilingual or even multilingual, but things were different in Manipur where a number of different languages were used. 'I gave each player photographs of Thailand national team players doing core work exercises as an example. The reason? A few spoke English, most spoke Manipuri (not Hindi), and a few spoke tribal dialects. So verbal translation was an unusual process, and I relied on the excellent assistant coaches I had to be football translators.'

At the end of the first week, Steve allowed the players Sunday off, so they could spend time with their families. Remembering the issues Bhaichung had had at Mohun Bagan trying to get a ladies' toilet, Steve was surprised to see quite a few women around the training ground, as well as one of his coaches, Choaba. He had been introduced to the boxer, Mary Kom, who had won a bronze medal at the London Olympics the previous year. Choaba approached him and asked if he could take a session with the girls, and he was only too delighted to help out. 'Most of them were in the national team. They were great girls, so every Sunday while I was there, I took a session with the girls. One of them, Ngangom Bala Devi, who was a policewoman in her day job, signed for Glasgow Rangers in 2020! She was one of the lucky ones, though. Many of them, once they get married, that's it. That's their careers over.'

While Steve was basing much of the training on traditional course material, he knew he had to adapt to local conditions once he had an idea of what standard the players were.

'I had watched the players play, and what I felt was that they were technically excellent, derived from many hours of playing in unorganised games, but in many ways football naive. For example, they were great dribblers of the ball, but often in the wrong part of the pitch, so the aim was not to lose this skill but show where it was best used. I explained to the local coaches, as part of the program was also coach education, that as a kid I had played 60 games a season—school, boys club and Sunday League. Playing this number of games gives you a game education and helps eliminate things such as ball watching. Also, playing with older men soon gets you out of bad habits, such as not chasing a ball you lost! These kids were only playing about 10-15 games a season due to distance, facilities and organisational problems.'

With his coaching team, Steve started by emphasising how important the dull things are and produced a sheet which he had printed off in English and Manipuri.

DO THE BORING THINGS WELL

DEFENDING

Close the man with the ball down
Make the player pass backwards (you can't stop that)
Track your player, do not ball watch
Organise at set pieces, take responsibility
No stupid fouls
Keep ball out of our penalty box (90% goals scored in the box)
Block crosses

ATTACKING

Get the ball into the penalty box as soon as you can
Get as many players in the penalty box as we can
Receive the ball when you can see the opponent's goal (side on)
Keep the ball moving, passing or dribbling
Quality delivery at all set pieces
Keep ball at throw ins, throw down line, never square
Shoot at every opportunity, "hit the target"
Watch the ball hit your foot, don't look at the goal

Every day the players would have these basic tenets of the game drilled into them, and in the evening, they would watch DVDs where the coaches would highlight where world-class players were putting "the boring things" into action. By the end of the month, they were having a go at each other when they weren't closing down or blocking crosses!

Another sheet Steve distributed to players and coaches was one prepared when he was coaching trainees at Sheffield Wednesday.

'One of the realities of football in Asia is that the EPL coverage on TV is killing the local game, and whilst these young players all knew Gerrard, Suarez, Rooney (and of course Messi, Ronaldo and Beckham), they struggled to name Indian national team players. This is happening all over Asia and is a growing problem for Asian Leagues, Malaysia being a great example where Malaysian money is sponsoring EPL teams, and local teams are bankrupt.

'To help this problem, a copy of the "Perfect Player" was given to each player to both let them see that no player is perfect, and that they always could strive to be better. We asked them to try to illustrate the idea with Indian players who were similar to the big names mentioned.'

One thing that struck Steve was how humble even the big names in Indian football were and how willing they were to do their bit for aspiring young players. 'Players like Gourmangi and Renedy, who were local internationals, were added. These two players, despite becoming internationals, still returned to help out with the game on a local level. They were top class role models.'

On a rare day off, Steve was looking forward to reading up some notes when he was called down to the hotel reception where a couple of officials were waiting for him.

'Come with us. We want to show you something.' A short drive later, they pulled up in a slum and walked through a gateway in front of an immaculately manicured lawn and invited their coach to enter.

'It was the Commonwealth Graves Commission graveyard in Imphal. I'd never heard of it, but it was here where the allied soldiers stood and defeated the Japanese during World War Two. I had a quiet walk around, taking in the names and the ages of those who had died serving their country all those years ago. I'd never heard of any of this stuff, and it was fascinating and humbling at the same time. Thing is, I'd have been happy staying at the hotel preparing for the next day's training, but these guys thought it would be a good idea to show me a little bit of history, and I'm glad they did. It's just another example of how people in Manipur went out of their way to make me feel comfortable and welcome.'

The guidebooks like to describe India as an assault on the senses, and Steve was finding the truth in that every day. He knew he shouldn't compare his two experiences in India, but he couldn't help it. It was the generosity shown by people giving up their day off to show him around, compared with the arrogance of assuming someone could not operate a washing machine because they thought it would be too difficult for him to operate.

'I used to go to this little hole in the wall store next to the hotel to buy snacks and drinks. It was run by a charming little old lady who had grown up in British India, seen the Japanese try to invade, and now lived in an independent country. Every time I went there, she would give me this big toothless grin. I don't know what language she spoke. If I had picked up any Bengali, she wouldn't have understood me. One day, I bought all these biscuits for the players as we were going on a long drive. She put them in a plastic bag, and I handed her a large denomination bank note. I would have walked away there and then, she could keep the change, but she signaled me to wait, and she started rummaging around in a drawer, eventually pulling out all these crumpled bank notes and coins which she counted out for me.'

At the end of the stay, Steve recommended a handful of players to the All India Football Federation Academies instructor, who just happened to be his old sparring partner, Scott O'Donnel, the players he felt had the potential to go on and play for India one day—M Dhanajoy Singh, K Omesh, S Prikanta, Vencent Pauchungnung and Gopi Singh.

'The northeast people love the game. They understand the social value of the game as well and treat the female players equally. I also conducted a number of clinics for the female players, and they showed great football intelligence. Someone is doing a great job producing female players in Manipur. The potential here is massive.'

It was only two months, but Steve enjoyed Manipur in a way he hadn't enjoyed coaching for a long time. He was in his element, working with people who wanted to learn on a daily basis and not having to worry about what was going on behind his back. It may not have been the most glamorous of postings, but he was glad he had kept Anuj's number on his phone.

'That was Manipur. Football-wise, it was fantastic. People-wise it was fantastic. People doing things for football for the right reasons, spending money in the right way.'

As he flew out of Imphal for the last time, Steve thought he was bidding farewell to India. He was 58 now, and his thoughts were turning increasingly to retirement and even a return to England. However, he was to get one more chance at coaching an elite team, and this time he would be ringing a pal offering a job.

13. Mumbai City

Bombay, you will be told, is the only city India has, in the sense that the word city is understood in the West. Other Indian metropolises like Calcutta, Madras and Delhi are like oversized villages. It is true that Bombay has many more high-rise buildings than any other Indian city: when you approach it by the sea it looks like a miniature New York. It has other things to justify its city status: it is congested, it has traffic jams at all hours of the day, it is highly polluted and many parts of it stink—Khushwant Singh, *Truth, Love and a Little Malice.*

It is difficult to write about India without succumbing to cliché, but its football is so unknown beyond its borders, the task becomes a little easier. Enough has been written of the land of Gandhi, Tagore and the Moghuls to fill any number of libraries, but the story of football in Goa, the fanatical supporters of Kerala and the historic derby of Kolkata remain a mystery to football lovers around the world.

The average visitor is fed scenes of spice-filled markets and lads enthusiastically playing cricket in the shadow of India Gate, and spends so much of their stay in awe of the dreamy serenity of the Taj Mahal at dawn or the immense scale of the hillside forts in Jaipur, they can be forgiven for thinking the game of football has passed the country by.

The I-League has never really caught the public's imagination since it was created in 2007/08, with ten teams from New Delhi, the Punjab, Kerala, Goa, Kolkata and Mumbai, and it has made headlines more for stories of monumental mismanagement, rather than its quality of football. Clubs rose and fell at the whim of owners and sponsors, with large swathes of the country unrepresented, and it wasn't until 2013/14 that a club arrived on the scene that had pretensions of professionalism with the founding of Bengaluru. Coached by former Manchester United trainee Ashley Westwood, they won the I-League twice in their first three seasons as they attempted to rewrite Indian football.

At the same time Bengaluru was taking its first tentative steps to becoming a major player, talks were underway between private companies and a TV broadcaster to set up a separate league known as the Indian Super League. Franchises in nine regions (Bengaluru, Chennai, Delhi, Goa, Guwahati, Kochi, Kolkata, Mumbai and Pune) were up for offer with the nobility of 21st-century India, cricketers and Bollywood stars among the bidders.

Each successful bid was to be tightly regulated, a sharp contrast to the laissez-faire in the I-League, with successful franchise winners committing to investing in grass roots as well as marquee players. In the past, it has been seen clubs spend huge amounts of money annually on player salaries, but a very little part of it is spent on developing the sport. Therefore, one of the main eligibility norms in the ISL is development of football in the city the club represents. Each team was to have a squad of 22 from different age groups, 14 domestic players and eight internationals or former internationals.

The eight successful bids set about building their teams—Atletico de Kolkata, Pune City, Mumbai City, North East United, Chennaiyin, Kerala Blasters, Delhi Dynamos and Goa—with owners that read like an edition of *Forbes* magazine. The organiser's intention was that the boardroom bling would succeed where traditional football mismanagement had failed and generate interest in football. Guaranteed media attention, the new clubs set about building their squads for the season that would begin in October 2014.

'I was in Vietnam doing not much when I got this phone call from India, a different agent, Arunva Chaudhuri, a well-known German-Indian who knew his football. He asked if I was aware of the ISL, this new project, and would I be interested in getting involved for three months. I said yes, of course, no problem. He then said I would need to come in with another coach as the organisers only wanted coaches who have worked at the highest levels. He asked me could I find someone. I asked how much and when he told me, I thought I should be able to find someone.'

Steve was now in the position of calling his former boss in Thailand, Peter Reid, and asking him if he would like to work in India for three months. Reid was quick to accept the offer.

Mumbai City was owned by Bollywood actor Ranbir Kapoor, a scion of the influential Kapoor family, and one of the leading actors of his generation. He had also been named the "Sexiest Man Alive" in 2009 and the "Sexiest Man in Asia" a year later. His mere presence at the football club guaranteed it would be in the limelight.

'A dream has come true for our city today,' he said at the launching of the team. 'As the Mumbai City Football Club comes to life on this day, I would like to share one thought you should always remember: the fact that this team belongs to not just me but 20 million Mumbaikars whose hearts beat here and who call the city home. This is our team, Mumbai. It is one which will celebrate our unwavering spirit and, like the city, fulfill the dreams of players and football fans.

'I could never have asked to get more than the Mumbai franchise. It is the city I've grown up in and a city I love. We have many plans for the future, and I hope we can make all of them come true.'

As a foreigner living in Asia, there is always a disconnect between the privileged life they lead and the life lived by the vast majority of the population, and India magnified the disparities.

Steve and Peter were put up in the swanky six-star Palladium Hotel, and from the rooftop bar and swimming pool, they could look down upon the carriage workshop at the nearby Lower Parel Railway Station, one of the busiest in the city, and marvel at the infamous Mumbai commute. To the west was the Mahalaxmi Racecourse, and beyond, the waters of the Arabian Sea. The hotel had fine dining and up-market boutiques, but outside, beyond the lavishly uniformed hotel porters and air-conditioning, was another world. Neither coach had grown up in Liverpool with a silver spoon for their porridge, but Mumbai was a different level, especially the juxtaposition of ostentatious wealth and down-at-heel poverty coexisting side by side.

'I can't change these people's wretched lives, but maybe if their football team can win a match, I can at least spread some short-lived joy,' Steve would think as he sat in the back of an air-conditioned car being driven around the city.

Reid wrote in this book: 'There was a girl with one tooth selling coconuts to try and make ends meet, so I would make sure I passed her whenever I was out, and I would buy one for 100 rupees (£1), which isn't a great deal of money,' but on the streets of Mumbai, it would have been a small fortune for the girl.

One-time Liverpool legend Ian Rush was in town making a short film, and one day the three of them went for a walk in the area around the hotel. 'I had been for an early morning walk one day and found this slum only a short walk from the hotel. When Rushie came to make a documentary, he wanted to see the "real India" so the three of us went to this place and ended up paying cricket on a concrete pitch that really took spin. All three of us love cricket, but the kids were far better players than we were. Plus, the kids had never heard of any of us!'

Steve was used to the poverty, though such familiarity didn't make it any easier to accept. He was there to do a job and, unlike at Mohun Bagan, here in Mumbai, there was an infrastructure in place off the field to support the coaches' efforts.

'There was a good administration guy, top class, an excellent doctor, three physios. Everything was done by the book, and everything was top class. The club owner, Ranbir Kapoor, was a lovely fella. The lads all knew him from the movies, but when they met him, I was falling over their tongues! My goalkeeper who was quite happy shouting and bawling at the defenders in training, he went all starstruck and couldn't speak. Bollywood stars are everywhere, on TV, at the cinemas, in the tabloids, on TV, painted on giant billboards, and now all of a sudden, one of them was taking the players out for a meal, and he was up there dancing with the players. I got dragged on to stage as well and had a dance. Later I would tell people I had danced with Ranbir Kapoor, and they couldn't believe it. Nor could I. A few days earlier, I had never heard of him!'

Peter and Steve were similarly starstruck when they were introduced to Sachin Tendulkar, the legendary cricketer who had invested in Kerala Blasters.

'We were invited to this party at an apartment block and had to go through two sets of security guards. We were looking for the apartment, but they told us no, the host owns the whole block. They brought us some champagne, and I thought, *Hey, this isn't bad*. I Googled it later. Each bottle cost 250 quid ... and there were bottles everywhere! We were talking to one guy there about cricket, and Reidy asks if he'd ever been to Lords. "Yes, I have. I got my first century there," and then we realised who we were talking to!'

Mumbai City's first game of the season took Steve back to Kolkata for the first time since his time with Mohun Bagan, and this experience was to be very different to what he had experienced with them.

Ahead of the game, Steve praised the team spirit in the squad. 'Everyone in our squad is trying his best to ensure that it's a happy, settled outfit. Indians like Nabi, Subrata Paul and Rohit Mirza take the initiative to approach foreign players and forge a friendship with them. They also serve as a bridge for the other younger Indian players ... That gives us a settled environment within the team.' It was also revealed the former Borussia Dortmund and Germany defender, Manuel Friedrich, was learning Hindi!

'I hadn't heard of Friedrich,' recalled Steve, 'so I Googled him, and the first thing I see is a picture of him marking Ronaldo in the Champions League. I would watch him in training and wonder what he brought to the team. It certainly wasn't pace! But nobody got past him, and he always passed the ball to a teammate, so that's good enough for starters! He played every game that season, and not many of the foreign players managed that across the whole league.

'One night, Reid arranged a quiz for the lads to take their minds off the interminable travelling they were doing, just to go training. "All right, listen up. Which player has played in the North London Derby, the Manchester Derby and the Liverpool Derby?" And the lads are looking around, wondering who it was. Nic Anelka looks up, and Reidy sees him and says, "Not you. It's Paul Stewart." The lads fell about, and Nic looks at Reidy and says, "Yeah, but I scored in them all!" and when everyone stopped laughing and was drying their tears, he asked almost innocently, "Does the El Classico count as well?" But it was the way he said it. He wasn't boasting; he wasn't being the big "I am"; he was almost self-deprecating in a way, and you realised what a top bloke he was.

'He played in one game when perhaps he shouldn't have done, but he begged and pleaded. Anyway, Reidy hooked him off after about an hour, but instead of going down the tunnel or sitting somewhere by himself, he put his bib on and sat with us in the dugout. He was shouting and cheering the lads on. He was like a supporter, a really positive influence. At the end of the game, he jumped up and banged his head on the roof of the dugout!

'Not all the foreign players had the same class. A couple, by rights, shouldn't have been there. They just weren't good enough. Nice lads, but not good enough. But when the recruiting had been going on, word had got around the agents there was big money swilling in this new league, and they wanted their slice of pizza, and they made a few quid out of it.'

A large, expectant crowd filled Salt Lake Stadium, creating a festive atmosphere inside the arena with plenty of Mexican waves rippling around, and face painters kept busy by youthful fans, many of whom were attending their first football match live. Given the football history in Kolkata, any new franchise was going to have to tread carefully to avoid upsetting the local giants and their large fan bases, so ATK did its best to appeal to fans of both Mohun Bagan and East Bengal while developing their own identity, which was largely based on Spanish side Atletico Madrid's colours and branding.

For all its talk of grassroots and football development, at its heart the Indian Super League was a TV program which happened to be centered on a football match, and viewers watching at home could enjoy regular sightings of their Bollywood idols talking with their friends, who happened to be other celebrities, or standing up to join in with the waves that never seemed to stop.

The actual game itself was almost incidental to the viewers, but Mumbai City was without two of its big-name foreigners, with Nicolas Anelka serving a FIFA suspension of three games and Freddie Ljungberg injured. Despite that, Reid was still able to field a starting 11 with six foreigners, but his team still lost 3-0, and the large crowd went home happy.

The downside of the new league soon became apparent. Mumbai to Kolkata was a six-hour flight, and the 30-hour train journey wasn't considered an option for elite athletes, so once the team had returned home after the game and had some down time, they were straight out to training for their next game, this time at home to near neighbours Pune City. A lack of training facilities in the city meant the squad was spending three hours a day sat in traffic, going to and from a pitch in the suburbs. Given the state of overcrowding in downtown Mumbai and the real estate prices, the lack of a football pitch is hardly surprising, but it was an inconvenience as well as a strain on the finely tuned athletes.

Mumbai's game against Pune City was played at the DY Patil Stadium, about an hour's drive east of the city over the Vashi Bridge, and despite having defender Peter Costa booked, after three minutes Andre Moritz's hat trick set the groundwork for a convincing 5-0 win with Manipur-born Subhash Singh and Frenchman Johan Letzelter also getting on the score sheet.

Steve was delighted. 'You're delighted with the whole result, but it's pleasing for the player. He came on last week after about 60 minutes and did well, and this week he really showed his worth. The team also showed their potential and quality tonight. Great team effort, all in all.' He was also pleased to see Singh get on the score sheet. 'It was great Subhash (Singh) scored because we ended up with seven Indians on the pitch. So it's great to know that they have taken the chances we have given them, because we've still got Nicolas (Anelka) and (Syed Rahim) Nabi to come. That thought is a bit scary!'

It was the perfect response after the disappointment of the previous week, but any hopes the win would kick start their season ended a week later when they lost 2–0 at home to North East United, ending the game with ten men after Pavel Czmos was red-carded with 15 minutes remaining. Former Arsenal winger Freddie Ljungberg managed to get his first run out of the season, coming on as a second-half substitute, but he failed to provide the inspiration his coaches were looking for. As for Reid, 'That was the first time I'd had people singing my name after losing a game!'

Nicolas Anelka was available for the next game and the trip to Chennai. Peter and Steve had had no input on signings. They had arrived and been told these were their players.

'Nicolas Anelka joined us, and to be honest, I was wary as I had read so much negative stuff about him. However, off the pitch, the man was not the image! He was humble, almost shy, and a dedicated family man. He had the immediate respect of all the Indian boys. It showed that and I should have known a lot of the media is producing garbage. It also confirmed to me that the best players work hard.'

The French striker started in Mumbai's next game away to Chennai, but for all his positivity off the field, he wasn't able to influence on it as Mumbai was roundly thrashed 5–1. Back in Mumbai, the coaching team set about sorting its porous defence out with immediate results. Anelka scored his first goal as they edged Kerala Blasters in their next game, and they followed that with a similar score line against Delhi Dynamos.

While Anelka was working his way back into the first team, Steve kept bumping into lads he had worked with at Mohun Bagan. 'I had 35 lads there, and now they were sprinkled throughout the ISL and earning good money. I was happy for them finally playing in a professional set-up and being treated as professionals.'

Soon after the North East United loss, a Malaysian film crew led by Michelle Lee came to Mumbai to do a feature on the city's football club. While Steve had managed to upset more than a few officials with his outspoken views and knack for calling out incompetencies in the way the game was run, there were sections of the media who loved him, and he had been happy to keep in touch with them, so when he was approached to help make a documentary, he was more than willing.

The crew turned up for a training session, sang a few songs with the supporters who turned up, and managed to persuade Peter Reid to play charades before going out on a tour with Steve. Once again, he chose to take visitors to a slum area. 'It puts in perspective how some of the footballers live. I try to bring my foreign players down here to stop them moaning ... they complain about the pool being too cold or the air conditioning in the dressing room not being cold enough. I say, "Come down here, lads, and see the real world." And this isn't considered one of the bad places.'

Mumbai took to the road for its next two games, Goa and Kerala, and picked up a couple of points and clean sheets for their efforts. Steve was unapologetic about his team's supposed dour approach and instead claimed the league was getting better.

The game at Jawaharlal International Stadium in Kochi against Kerala Blasters was memorable because of an appearance by cricket legend Sachin Tendulkar who owed the club. Before kickoff, he was driven around the perimeter and given a rousing reception by the adoring legions in the stands. It was Beatlemania to a factor of ten. Even the two Liverpool-born coaches, both big cricket fans, felt a shiver down their spines at seeing the great man and the applause he was receiving.

Back on home turf, Mumbai was held to another scoreless draw, this time by Goa. It was the fifth clean sheet in the row after the debacle at Chennai, but the tactical tweaking the coaching team had done to their defence wasn't appreciated by supporters who had grown used to the excitement. Steve was asked about a strike force that had scored just three times in their last six games. 'We would love to score more, believe me. Sometimes, you get lucky when you score, to be honest. We haven't scored in the last two games, but we haven't been lucky. There were decent performances by all the sides we played, and our performance was good as well.'

Unfortunately for Peter and Steve, they were unable to turn things around and Mumbai's season faded away. Three defeats in ten days, including 2–0 away at Pune City, the one away game they didn't fly to, ended any hopes they may have had of going into the play-offs. When a win did finally come against ATK in their penultimate game of the season, it was too little, too late. They finished the season drawing 1–1 away to North East United.

There can be no denying the season was one of disappointment. Andre Moritz failed to score again after his hat trick earlier in the season. Ljungberg only started one game, but both coaches agree about Anelka. 'I loved him,' wrote Reid in his book. 'He liked to keep himself to himself, which I was aware of before I worked with him, but he got really involved in training and did everything he could to help the Indian kids, which reflected well on him ... I found him brilliant to work with.'

After three months, Steve's third Indian adventure was over. He was to return as a TV pundit in 2016 and was pleased to note clubs were now taking responsibility for their own player recruitment, rather than what he called 'the false auction system, in ISL-1 which had many poor foreigners in it.' Joining him was Steve Coppell, a Liverpool lad who went on to play for Manchester United and England. He had played against a few times back in the 1960s. Now, here in India, they would sit together talking about an ISL game before retiring to a cafe somewhere and reminiscing over their old battles on the muddy fields of Liverpool, a Mersey-themed memory lane with a Mumbai postcode.

Part V: The Lao Years

14. World Cup Campaign

There was still time for one final hurrah. While Steve would not have been averse to returning to the Indian Super League, the chance of coaching in the World Cup qualifiers was one he was never going to refuse. His old mate, Dave Booth, had been coaching the Lao national team, but he really wanted to focus on the SEA Games team.

Dave and Steve went back a long way and had shared many a conversation about football in Southeast Asia over the years, so the former Grimsby Town and Barnsley defender had no hesitation in recommending his old mate from Liverpool. He explained his preference to the Lao Football Federation, and they suggested bringing in a technical director, so Dave rang Steve, and after declaring they didn't know what a TD was, agreed Steve would coach the national team for their upcoming World Cup qualifying campaign which was to start in June 2015. With everything agreed, Steve boarded a plane for the short hop to Vientiane, knowing he was taking on perhaps the least pressurised job in world football, but he didn't care. This was World Cup qualifying, and that was pressure enough.

Land-locked Lao isn't known for its football prowess, and no one seriously expected they would be able to overcome South Korea, Lebanon, Kuwait and Myanmar, but optimism burns eternal.

There wasn't long to prepare for the first games, home ties against Myanmar and Lebanon, so Steve had to lean heavily on Dave for selecting his first squad and his assistant coach, Kanlaya Syomsvang, another familiar face. Kanlaya had been part of the Lao SEA Games squad in 2010, which had reached the semi-finals for the first and only time in their history. As is the nature of football Kanlaya had scored a screamer for Laos against Thailand!

Steve didn't have much time. He needed to fly from Vietnam to Vientiane, meet the players, arrange some training, and prepare for his first games at home to Myanmar and Lebanon. To give him an idea of what he was working with, he managed to arrange a couple of friendlies.

First up was Buriram United, the best team in Thailand. Backed by the deep pockets of a local, politically influential family, Buriram United, much like Johor Darul Ta'zim in Malaysia, was a club with no history, only coming into being in 2012 after a merger between two existing clubs. Flushed with cash, they set about hoovering up the best Thai players, as well as signing talented foreigners and building a football infrastructure in the north-east of Thailand that left many in Bangkok looking enviously on. They had won the Thai Premier League in two of the three previous seasons and were rapidly becoming a force to be reckoned with, both in Thailand and also overseas. Steve learned that the monthly wage for one foreign player was greater than the wage bill for the whole Lao squad. Lao's World Cup squad travelled down for the game on an overnight bus.

Steve knew what he was letting his players in for of course. He had given winger Anawin Jujeen his debut at the SEA Games in 2009 for one. It just wasn't fair to compare the Thai players with their Lao counterparts, on any level. When the game reached the 20-minute mark, and it was still 0-0, the coach may have allowed himself a momentary sense of relief, but he knew it was only the calm before the storm. Once Korean midfielder Go Seul-ki had opened the scoring, it was only a matter of how many. Buriram United went on to win 6-0. The last 20 minutes the Laos lads were really struggling.

If the Lao Football Federation was expecting results anytime soon, the new coach quickly moved to dampen that particular ardour. 'There is no short cut to fitness. Long-term weight training programs have to be implemented at LPL level and National Youth teams (Young Elephants).'

Steve couldn't fault the players' effort and tried to follow instructions, especially at set pieces, but pointed out several goals came from individual errors and when opponents speed and power could not be matched.

Immediately after the game, Steve was asking searching questions of his bosses. Why were some players not available? Were players injured? Were they not allowed time off work? He was calling for greater transparency from the federation even though he knew it was pointless, but he was only articulating what he knew was a cause of frustration within the players.

He concluded his report to the LFF with an indirect attack on the team manager, Bounlap. He was not happy about some of the comments the manager had made on social media after the game, which had been pointed out to him by some of his players, but he had been kicking around Asia long enough to know any criticism he made must be couched in such nebulous terms to avoid any loss of face. 'I am happy to take all criticism for result. Unfair if Bounlap gets any blame as he was not involved in the preparation and selection. However, it is important that he shows loyalty to the group publicly and privately. Players are not stupid. They are already talking about his Facebook comments.'

It was classic Steve Darby. He knew what lessons were there to be learned from the defeat. That's his job after all, but he was supporting his players to the hilt, and he expected the federation to provide him with the support he needed to do his job.

Nine days later, Laos hosted Afghanistan in Vientiane in a game Steve described as 'excellent preparation' against a nation ranked 45 places above them. This time there were no key players missing, and Steve was happy to praise the team spirit in the camp. The Afghans, who could draw upon a number of players who were playing overseas in Germany and the Netherlands, won 2–0, and although the Lao players could match them in speed and endurance, the visitors were stronger physically.

'The preparation was good, and the only problem would be that two of our starting 11 (Boo and Lay) came straight from work. We have to try to ensure they get at least two days off before the Myanmar game. All our sessions are based on practices from world-level teams.'

There was time for one last friendly before the real business of qualifying for the World Cup began, and that was away to Cambodia. This time the team was able to fly to the Cambodian capital Phnom Penh for the game, which helped ease the aches and pains associated by bus travel. After a couple of ough workouts against strong opposition, Steve was pleased to see the team had made some progress as they drew 1–1 on a rain-sodden pitch in front of a hostile 40,000-person crowd, with striker Sangvone Phimmasen stooping to head home from a free kick and level the score, only his second goal for his country.

After the game, and when the crowds had cleared, the Lao team went out in search of local delicacies, eventually finding a roadside stall selling crispy cockroaches.

With the opening World Cup qualifier just over a week away, Lao would be focusing on working the back four as a unit—set pieces and shadow play. The strikers would also be made to think about technique; against Cambodia, they too often opted for a pile-driver from distance, which ended up in Row Z of the cavernous Olympic Stadium, rather than taking a touch or a moment when there were better options available closer to goal. And, with an eye to the future, the national team would play against younger age group national teams, which allowed them to work on set pieces and patterns of play, as well as allowing the youngsters good experience.

No one really expected Lao to qualify from their group, though the Lao Football Federation was offering eye-watering bonuses if they could beat South Korea or Lebanon, tasks everyone knew were beyond the gallant Lao players. In fact, Steve was soon to learn these bonuses were the only financial incentive on the table for the players; in effect, they were playing for the love of the game and the experience and not getting any money for their efforts. Little wonder coaches like Steve and Dave were left fretting over which players would be granted the time off necessary to prepare for and play important football matches. The contrast with Mumbai City couldn't have been starker!

It was also little wonder there was match fixing going on, though Steve was assured it only affected away friendlies and not qualifiers.

'They told me they were going to lose anyway, and as they weren't getting paid, they might as well make some money somehow. How can you argue with that? I had players who would finish work, jump on their motorcycle, pick up a teammate, and come to training, knowing they wouldn't be picking up any money at the end of the month. How can I apply a Western morality to that? It's so easy to preach from the pulpit of privilege, but unless you have walked in their shoes, or unless there is a structure in place where professional footballers are treated professionally, all the pontificating won't change a thing on the ground. I felt sorry for them; I really did, but also immensely proud at how they put all the nonsense behind them when it came to training and playing.

'I was lucky I had full support from President Viphet, the General Secretary Keo, and other officials like Khamphay and Somsanouk. This block of administrators did a sterling job keeping a lot of corrupt influencers at bay.'

The first game was against Myanmar in Vientiane, and after a disappointing first half when Myanmar trooped in with a 1–0 lead when Zaw Min Tun nodded home just before half-time, Steve, with the help of his coaching staff and translator, set about making some changes. He wasn't happy with the marking at the free kick that led to the goal but felt if his team could get behind the Myanmar defence, they stood a chance. 'We were outplayed in the first half. There seemed a fear, lack of belief, that I had not seen before from the players. This changed in second half, and it looked mentally a different team. We appeared slow in midfield, but this was due to us being outnumbered. In the second half, when we changed to hitting long diagonal balls which bypassed midfield, we had more success. We realised at half-time their back four was slow, so we tried to hit beyond, and we had many chances from this.'

Khampeng Sayavutthi equalised on 81 minutes with a penalty, and when he made it 2–1 two minutes later, it looked as if Lao was heading for its first win in the World Cup since 2001. Sadly, Kyaw Zayar Win made it 2–2 two minutes later, leaving the Lao players distraught and their coach wondering what might have been. Certainly, a win would have been a significant morale booster, but Steve was fully aware, five days later, they would have to face Lebanon, and he was more than familiar with some of their players.

Steve knew the only real advantage players from the Middle East had over Southeast Asians was body strength, and it is noticeable that one of the understated reasons behind the success of Thai players overseas in recent years is down to more attention being given to building up body strength. Goalkeeper Kawin Thamsatchanan, for example, turned his back on rice early in his career and started eating more pasta as he felt that would improve his chances of playing in Europe, which it did. But Kawin had been a professional footballer from a young age. Lao players often had to juggle training and playing commitments with full-time jobs.

Lebanon won the game 2–0 with Ghaddar opening the scoring within five minutes, and, unsurprisingly, it came about because of an opponent's greater physical strength.

There was now a lull of two and a half months before the next round of qualifiers, which allowed time for Steve to take stock of what he had inherited. He rated his goalkeeper Seng but bemoaned the fact there was little competition.

However, he was a confident lad, good in the dressing room, and had good English, so Steve had to overlook the occasional slip which had led to a goal. He was impressed by Khampeng, felt he was the team's best player, and he possessed an excellent attitude, but recognised his best days were past him. He wasn't winning balls in the air and, as seen against Lebanon, lacked the physical strength to impose himself on opponents. One other player Steve liked was Saynakhonevieng Phomimapanya out wide. He wasn't the best player technically, but he was intelligent with a good engine and combined well down the flank with the fullback.

Lao's next qualifier was to be against South Korea in Seoul, and ahead of that game, the LFF arranged a couple of friendlies to help prepare the team. The first game was in the north-east of Thailand, so again the players were forced onto a night bus as a cost-cutting measure, this time to Nakhorn Ratchasima where they lost. Another overnight road trip led them to play Cambodia in Bangkok, winning 2-1, with the players celebrating by having an early night before heading to Seoul, a journey which took 24 hours door to door!

No disrespect to Lebanon, Myanmar or Kuwait but as far as Steve was concerned, this was the biggie. South Korea had long been a power in Asian football. Was this the pinnacle of his career? He had led teams out in front of crowds of 80,000 at finals before, he had worked with two bona fide legends in Thailand, and he'd met cricketing nobility, but not everyone got to coach in World Cup qualifiers.

Steve felt an immense pride as he watched his players warming up on the playing surface at the Hwaeseong Stadium and felt he had prepared them well. Coaches often talk about managing the occasion, and Steve had told his players not to be overawed by their surroundings, but he knew he was only doing it because it was expected of him. Son earnt more in a week than his team would in several years. He knew it, and the players knew it.

He had prepared a special game plan to take care of the mercurial Son. 'I told my players to kick him on the halfway line. I thought if we could keep snapping at his ankles, he might not want to play anymore. I had a plan B as well. I asked (Korean manager) Uli Stielike not to pick Son and one or two others.'

The German coach, who had won treble titles in Germany with Borussia Monchengladbach and in Spain with Real Madrid, listened to the advice and politely turned it down. 'He told me he was under lots of pressure to win this game and win big. Son played the whole game, and my lads couldn't get near him to tackle.'

South Korea won 8-0, and the next day Steve and the dejected travelling party started their journey back to Vientiane at 6.30 a.m., utilising the cheapest flights along the way, though there was some relief when they got to Bangkok and found out they would be flying the last leg to Lao, not boarding an overnight bus again.

They arrived home to mass apathy and the news that their next opponent, Kuwait, had already arrived, checked in and done some sightseeing. Backed by a football association flush with money, the Kuwaiti team and officials had their own private jet waiting for them on the runway in Qatar, and once they had beaten Myanmar 9–0, they travelled at their own convenience.

Lao lost the game 2–0 to leave them rooted at the bottom of their group. They returned to Bangkok the following month. This time they flew to face Myanmar who had been forced to play their home games outside of Yangon following crowd trouble at an earlier game. Khampeng gave the Laotians an early lead, but they weren't able to hold on to it, and they went down 3–1.

Steve was disappointed that while countries like Singapore, Thailand and Indonesia had been going down the path of calling up players who had become citizens of their country, or were brought up overseas in mixed marriages, Lao stubbornly refused to consider their diaspora for the national team.

'There were a number of players in the French league who wanted to play for Lao, but the government insisted they would have had to give up their French passports, and that was never going to happen.'

Steve, though, will be forever grateful to the country for giving him the opportunity to coach in the World Cup. The record books do show Lao won a game, but that was purely an administrative result. Kuwait had been banned by FIFA, and although the results of games played stood, remaining ties were awarded 3–0 to their opponents. His last game came at home to South Korea, and while his players were making the journey in style and comfort, Steve had to write letters to employers asking for his players, like Souliyavong, who worked for a government department, to be released from work at lunchtime on match day, so they could play in a World Cup qualifier. The Koreans were 4–0 up at half-time, and although they took the foot off the gas in the second half, went on to win 5–0.

'Lao was a pleasure to work with. There were some excellent administrators trying to professionalise the game and keep the corruption away, and players who gave everything despite all the handicaps that were thrown in their way. I would recommend any coach to work in Lao if given the opportunity. It can only progress.'

Part VI: Epilogue
from Steve Darby

I remember standing in the tunnel at Anfield, waiting to play my first-ever game on this pitch, waiting to touch the 'This is Anfield' sign.

I felt a strange tightening feeling in my stomach and found it hard to breathe. It disappeared. I played only the once on Anfield, but I can say I never let a goal in! We, Tuebrook Boys, beat Norris Green 2–0. I once mentioned this when I was talking to the former Newcastle player John Beresford, whilst working with him on ESPN Asia. He laughed and said it happened 'because it matters'.

Yes, football does matter, and to paraphrase JB Priestley, to say football is a game 'is merely to say that a violin is wood and catgut, that Hamlet is so much paper and ink'. Football matters to people all over the world.

I've been lucky I have spent over 40 years getting paid to do what I love and, as this book shows, travelled to over 50 countries, met kings, presidents, sultans, mafia and a hitman (who was a lovely bloke!).

Antony has done an incredible amount of research, finding things I have said in the media which I had forgotten about or, in the case of the Indian media, never said anyway! He has interviewed people who have helped and influenced me and has been very thorough in his approach, exposing the defeats as well as the wins. He has also questioned many things I did and was prepared to be objective. He wrote it in his own inimitable style.

I have tried to name the people who have helped me in my career as I have, indeed, met many tremendous people in this time and made lifelong friends. The very few people I have disliked I haven't named. Football people will know who they are. If I have missed anybody out, I apologise. Space also meant many people were edited out.

And that's it. Looking back, it's not been a bad career—certainly not bad for a lad growing up taking tin baths in the kitchen. Antony reckons I grew up with a strong sense of identity, a yearning for learning, and a strong need to know. Why does something work, but not something else? What is in that book? Why do some players score more than others?

Mentors have been important to me from my days at Collegiate, with its Victorian traditions, through Merv Beck, Jack Mansell, all the way to Vic Tuting and a score more. They taught me loads without even knowing they were doing it, but I was a sponge. I never knew everything, but I knew I wanted to know more from those days watching the Cologne school kids batter us.

As a lifelong socialist, I've never been one for titles. This proved kind of awkward at times, especially in Asia where those who adorned themselves with various ranks and honours never realised how sad they looked to those of us who preferred a more level playing field. And yes, it was disappointing and frustrating to know these people could hold the fate of the football club, or, more importantly, me in their hands.

Over the years, I got loads of advice, some of it good, much of it bad. Some I followed; some I ignored, even when it was useful. When John Constantine told me to be more politically savvy, I understood he was trying to help me keep my head above water in the tank of sharks, and I appreciated that, but it was impossible. I was never going to keep quiet. I saw my old man coming home from the docks giving both barrels to people with self-inflated egos, and my experiences soon taught me he was right to do so.

Some people handled the politics side of football superbly—Bryan Robson and Peter Reid, for example. You should have seen how they handled the status-conscious Thai elite. People who had locals bowing and scraping treated those two football royalty as landed royalty. In fact, they were both down-to-earth blokes, happy to have a laugh and a joke with the lads. The media likes to build superstars, but those I've come across at the top of the game are thoroughly decent people. The only problems I've had with football people, and there have only been a handful, have been with people whose careers never quite took them where they felt they deserved to go, but they still put themselves on a pedestal.

The best advice I ever got was soon after arriving in Malaysia when Haji Ahamad taught me all about bamboo. That, and John Constantine talking about choosing your battles, stayed with me, and this particular stalk of Liverpool bamboo was not for bending too far!

Just as I looked to mentors as I was setting out on my coaching journey, now

I appear to have become a mentor. I don't push myself out there, but if someone approaches me and asks for advice, I am only too happy to give it. But honestly, if you're coaching under-12s in a local district school league, I don't think clubs in Japan or South Korea will be looking at your resume with any great desire. I try to answer every email, as I remember when I wrote to people and they took the time to reply, people such as Worthington, Houllier and Souness.

Would a 21st-century Steve Darby go overseas as readily as the one born in the 1950s? I would hope so, but cannot say for sure.

I look at my teenage daughter and her friends; their lives, their environments are so different. She quite happily goes on the train to Sheffield to play basketball with her friends, while I remember what a big deal it was for me and my dad to go to the FA Cup semi-final there in the 1960s and how excited I felt in the days building up to it! I grew up in Anfield Road, and for years I never had any need to leave the postcode. My daughter has grown up taking flights from Hanoi to Singapore, Kuala Lumpur and Bangkok as naturally as I used to carry my milk crate through Stanley Park to Goodison.

But for those who ask if they should, I always say yes, go for it. Look at Simon McMenemy, for example. He was floating around the English non-league. Then something told him he needed to apply for the position as coach of the Philippines, a country with no great footballing pedigree. He took them to the semi-final of the AFF Suzuki Cup first time of asking, playing in front of crowds pushing 100,000. Later, he coached an unfancied team to the title in Indonesia.

One thing that does concern me is how coaches who do go overseas are treated when they return home. It can be very difficult to have your achievements recognised. Look how long it took Roy Hodgson to earn recognition in England, despite having been a very successful coach in Europe for many years. Instead, probably because of Jose Mourinho, clubs seem to want a Portuguese coach!

That's why I'm interested to see how well Graham Potter does at Brighton. No one had heard of him until he took Ostersunds to Arsenal in the Europa League and won.

After I finished coaching, I rang Australia and checked on the status of my licences, and some disinterested voice thousands of miles away said I would probably have to do some of them again. 'What was your last coaching job?' she asked. 'A World Cup qualifier versus South Korea ...' If I wanted her to be impressed, I was going to be disappointed. According to the rules and regulations, I would have to do some badges again! She wanted me to travel to Australia for a weekend course given by a coach who I had passed on his licences! I strongly believe in updating and accreditation, but the future has to be online.

After I'd finished in Lao, I knew it was time to go home. My mother is getting on, and my daughter needed a stable education. In 37 years of coaching, I'd never employed an agent; jobs had found me by word of mouth, but back in England, it was difficult to make an impression. 'Coached in the World Cup qualifiers? Wow. Lao? Oh ...' You could sense the rejection that came with the final syllable.

But that's the way it is. I was happy enough teaching, so I started teaching special needs classes, and that was more my thing. I don't know. Maybe because I was an only child, I've always had to do things for myself, and I've always appreciated people who went that extra mile or people who were seen as different. Khalid Jamlus at Perak. I was told not to sign him because he was trouble, but he never gave me any trouble. There may be no "I" in team, but each member of a team is an individual and responds in different ways.

In Australia, I genuinely enjoyed my time at the jail or working at the young offenders' centre. Society had said they were "bad" people, and yes, there were a few naughty people there, but nearly all of them had had family issues growing up. I came along, treated them with respect, and got a real buzz out of seeing them want to work. It's the same at the special needs school. They want to study, and they appreciate the effort we're putting in for them.

I still do some online stuff, but if I got the right offer, would I go back into coaching full-time? It would have to be local. I'm a Liverpool lad, remember, but until now, Liverpool hasn't been looking to replace Jurgen Klopp.

I am delighted to see that Australia, along with New Zealand, will host the FIFA Women's World Cup in 2023. It's all a far cry from the late 1980s when we struggled to raise the money to play a few qualifiers in our own backyard. I am especially happy for players such as Anissa Tann, Moya Dodd, Tracey Wheeler and Alison Foreman who I had the great pleasure to work with. That team was in many ways a pioneer, blazing a trail for what was to come, and I hope they feel a sense of pride. Australia will be hosting the world's best in 2023.

Okay, now for the fantasy football. Who would I select in my all-time best players I've coached? It's a cliché I know, but this is never easy. With four decades of preparing teams, there are so many players to choose from, but I can only pick 11 plus a subs bench! All have sheer natural talent and are hard-working pros. All played for the team, not themselves. All had character!

Hamood Sultan (Bahrain)
Best natural keeper I've worked with. Made impossible saves. Nothing worried him.
Subramani (Home Utd), **Frierdrich** (Mumbai City), **Aide Iskander** (Home Utd)
Subramani (Singapore) and Aide Iskander (Singapore): Both 100 caps.
Defended first and were great leaders on and off the pitch.
Frierdrich (Germany): You don't get caps for Germany by being average!
Never got his shorts dirty and read the game so well.
Mark Leszcinsky (White Eagles), **Mohamed Shawky** (Kelantan), **Ned Zelic** (AIS), **Ahmad Sharul** (Perak) **Sutee Suksomkit** (Home United and Thailand)
Mark Leszcinsky (Tasmania): The only non-international, but he should have been. If he had been born in Sydney, he would have been.
Every game, every training session, gave everything, never injured!
Mohamed Shawky (Egypt): 70 caps for Egypt, scored versus Brazil in Confed Cup. Played EPL. Underrated. Did the work of three players at Kelantan. Fully professional.
Ned Zelic (Australia): Sheer talent! Played EPL, Bundesliga, League Une. Could play anywhere.
Ahamad Sharul (Malaysia): Great box to box. Leader on and off the pitch.
Sutee Suksomkit (Thailand): Pace, power, left foot to die for. But most of all, lit up training sessions and dressing rooms.
Nicolas Anelka (Mumbai City), **Teerasil Dangda** (Thailand)
Nicolas Anelka (France): Just the best player I've worked with and a great bloke off the pitch. Image not the reality.
Teersasil Dangda (Thailand): Could have been a European star. Just loved playing football, but hated training!
Subs: Peres (Home United), **Rizal Sukiman** (Johor), **Darren Stewart** (Johor) and **Milan Blagojevic** (Johor) **Mario Berros** (Perak)

THE DREAM TEAM

Gordon Banks
Trent Alexander, Sergio van Dijk, Franco Baresi, Paolo Maldini
Johan Cruyff, Bryan Robson, George Best
Lionel Messi, Diego Maradona, Alfredo Di Stefano

Nothing would get past Van Dijk or Baresi, and if it did, Banks would have saved it. Robson's job? Win the ball and give it to the front five. I think they would have scored!

The greatest I have seen? Has to be Diego Maradona. I would have loved to have been him or Banks for just a season!

I would love to have coached this team. But I will bow to the ultimate hero doing the job, Bill Shankly. He started the dream, and hopefully it's not over yet.

Coaching Record
Coaching Experience and Honours

Laos Football Federation   2015/16
     National Coach for 2018 World Cup
     First World Cup points
     Highest FIFA Rankings
     15 A FIFA International games

Mumbai City FC (Indian Super League)   2014
     Inaugural ISL
     Team included Anelka Ljunberg, Friedriche, Moritz

Kelantan FA   2013/14
Manipur Football Education Program Indian Govt   2013
Everton FC Coaching Consultant in Asia (China)   2012
Mohun Bagan FC India   2011
Thailand FA Mens National Coach   2008/11
     (Peter Reid and Bryan Robson Managers)
     Asian Cup Qualifiers
     Suzuki Cup Finalists
     T and T Cup Winners
     SEA Games/Olympic Team Coach
     Kata Cup Winners
     Thailand FA Technical Director   2009
     Coached in 55 International games

Perak FA Malaysian Super League   2005/8
   Super Cup Winners
   3rd place Super League
   Malaysia Cup Semi-finals
   (Keita Manjou) Golden Boot
      Dato Mhd Zahid PFA Cup   2006/7
   Malaysian Super League Runner-Up
   Malaysia Cup Runner-Up
   (Keita Manjou) Golden Boot
   Malaysian Golden Boot (Khalid Jamlus)
   Player of Year (K Nanthakumar)
   Coach of the Year finalist
   AFC Cup Qualification
   President Cup (U21) National Champions
   AFC Cup Quarter Finals   2008

Home United Singapore   2002/05
   S Lge Runner-Up
   AFC Champions League Knockout Stage   2002
   S Lge Winner
   Singapore FA Cup Winner   2003
   FAS Player of Year and leading Goalscorer (Peres D'Oliveira)   2003
   FAS Coach of the Year Finalist   2003
   S Lge Runner-Up,
   Singapore FA Cup Final   2004
   AFC Cup semi-final   2004
   FAS Player of year and Leading Goalscorer (Surachai and Gonzales)
   AFC Finalist for Team of the Year   2004
   FAM/FAS Cup Winners Cup Champions   2005
   Singapore FA Cup Winner   2005

Coach **Sheffield Wednesday FC** Youth Team   2001/02
   EPL Youth Play-Offs   2002

SEA Games Football Gold Medal **Vietnam FA**   2001
SEA Games Player of Tournament (Ngoc Mai)   2001

Coach **Johor FA** 1998/2000

Malaysian FA Cup Winners *1998*
Malaysian Charity Shield Finalist *1999*
Malaysian Premier League Champions *1999*
Malaysia Cup Quarter Finals *2000*

Fiji FA National Teams *1997*

Manager/Coach **Sydney Olympic**, Australian League. 1995/97
Technical Staff FIFA World Youth Cup (1993)
Staff Coach for FIFA/Oceania Coaching Courses
    (Fiji, Oceania Level 3)
Staff Coach, Australian Soccer Federation Senior Coaching Courses (1981/95)
    C Licence Coaching Courses Conducted 34
    B Licence Coaching Courses Conducted 11
    A Licence Coaching Courses Conducted 9
    Goalkeeping Coaching Courses Conducted 5
    Instructor Courses Conducted and Organised 3
Australia Schoolboys National Team Coach (1989)
Australia Women's National Team Coach FIFA World Cup (1991)
Australia Women's Technical Director Women's FIFA World Cup (1995)

East Rifaa Football Club Bahrain
Assistant National Coach Bahrain (1978/79)

HONOURS

Tasmanian Coach of the Year
ACT Coach of the Year
AFC Coach of the Year Finalist
Vietnam Order of Labour
Les Rosbifs International Coach of the Year
World Soccer Player of the Year Selector
FIFA/Ballon D'Or Selector
House of Lords select committee on child slavery via football.

Acknowledgements

In a way, Steve's and my careers have been running along parallel lines. We were in Australia at the same time, we've both worked in Thailand and India, and we're both football daft. That's where the similarities end, though.

From an early age, Steve had the drive and determination to make a successful career out of the beautiful game by keeping to his principles, which he imbibed in the shadow of the Kop in the late 1960s.

I first came across Steve when he was a frequent contributor to football newspapers in Australia, his grainy black-and-white mulleted image staring up from the pages of tabloids I religiously bought week in, week out. A decade later, he was providing expert punditry on both local and English football from a studio in Singapore being beamed around the region.

When I started the *Jakarta Casual* blog, with a daily readership charging like a high-speed express train towards double figures, Steve was one of the first people from within the game to contact me, and that gave me a massive boost. That a professional football coach had not only noticed my primitive ramblings, but had also taken the time to reach out to me, had me buzzing.

The more people I got to meet within the game, the more positive vibes I got about him. Not just from the European players and coaches, but from the local lads. It's a cliché, but in all my football chats with people in the region, there was never a bad word spoken. Of course, I stayed away from officials and assorted suits. I'm sure they may have had differing opinions, but football people, those who knew the game as a sport and not an ego trip, were all of one voice.

It wasn't until he got the Thai job that we finally met, and soon after, he was in Jakarta for an AFF Suzuki Cup tie. Being a romantic at heart, I'd taken my wife to the game, and she sat with a couple of her friends while I sat among various police officers and journalists in the press box. Second half, and Steve made his way into the stand for a different perspective of the game, and my wife yelled out, 'Oi, Steve!' The assistant coach of a national team saw my wife and climbed over a few rows of seats to sit with her, and they spent most of the second half nattering about I know not what!

A germ of an idea was forming. If I ever managed to make the leap from blogger to writer, I would love to write his story, and when, almost a decade later, I got the chance, I grabbed it with both hands. I made a couple of trips to Liverpool to meet him, and those visits were essential in getting to know the person and his background.

As an Arsenal fan with a strong London accent, going to Merseyside was never fun. But Steve showed me round his city with a large amount of pride, and I began to see Liverpool in a different light. We walked the terraced streets where he grew up, walked through the park where he carried his milk crate, and peered through the fence at the school playground where he scuffed his knees more than once or twice.

In the Malay-speaking areas of South East Asia, they talk about the *kampung* kid and how you can take the kid from the *kampung*, but you can't take the *kampung* from the kid, I soon realised how quickly Steve had been able to adapt to Malaysia and Singapore.

For all his travels overseas, for all his royal appointments and football medals, at heart Steve remained the *kampung* kid who had grown up in L4, and it was this shared upbringing which allowed him to empathise with the players he later came into contact with. It gave him a sense of humanity that towered over a basic job description and offered him a holistic view of his chosen profession that was not always shared by the people he worked for.

This is that bit where the writer sits down and breathes a huge sigh of relief as he bids farewell to a project that has been such a huge part of his life for the last few years. It's also the bit where he tries to recall everyone who has been a help and contributed to the narrative in whatever way and no doubt omits a crucial name or two.

So, and sincere apologies if any names are missing, with a deep breath and a heartfelt word of gratitude, take a bow Merv Best for his Carnegie memories, Walter Pless for leading me down into a rabbit hole of Tasmanian football, Matthew Rhodes, Nick di Martino, Andrew Howe for being perhaps the best statto in the southern hemisphere, Mark Boric and Greg Stock for their unstinting efforts in archiving an almost forgotten era in Australian football,

Robert Lattanzi, Peter Brine, Ron Smith, Aide Iskandar, Shamir Osman, Haji Ahamad, Haresh Deol, Dez Corkhill, Dave Roberts, Dale Farrington and his voluminous archives, R Sasikumar, Ko Po Hui, Subramani Shunmugham, Bonita Mersiades, Debanjan Banerjee, Jason Dasey, John Dykes, and last, but by no means least, May and Dominic Sutton for their patience and understanding of a family member who keeps jetting off to weird and wonderful football matches in Southeast Asia.

Antony Sutton

About the Author

Antony doesn't remember a time when football wasn't part of his life, but he also isn't entirely sure how it all started.

His earliest memories are of being given Arsenal books and programmes in the early 1970s, listening to the BBC World Service commentary from his home in Belgium on a Saturday afternoon, whilst mentally kicking every ball as he was doing so.

Antony attended his first football match in 1973 and travelled on a double-decker Southdown bus to watch Brighton play Plymouth Argyle with his father and older brother—just a few weeks after returning to England to live. This was the Brighton of Brian Clough though, a fact he was unaware of at the time. Antony says his abiding memory was not of being able to get a programme. Though it took more than 20 years to finally track one down, he understood that football was about memories.

From supporting his passion—Arsenal, and his home side—Aldershot, from a young age, the next logical step for Antony was to watch some football overseas, a past-time that began in 1984 in continental Europe, one that continued for more than 30 years starting with Australia , where he adopted St George as his team—to Asia where he lived for a while in Thailand, then a brief return to England and Germany before settling in the Indonesian capital, Jakarta, where he started the popular blog, *Jakarta Casual* in 2006.

The Itinerant Coach – the Life and Footballing Times of Steve Darby is Antony's second book.

His first book, *Support Your Local League: A South East Asian Football Odyssey* was published by Fair Play Publishing in 2018.

Really good football books

Code War$
The Battle for Fans,
Dollars and Survival
by Dr Hunter Fujak

The Australian Youth
Footballer Regulatory Guide
by Peter Paleologos
(Popcorn Press)

The Away Game
by Matthew Hall

Achieving the Impossible
– the Remarkable Story
of How Greece Won
EURO 2004
by George Tsitsonis

Whatever It Takes – The
Inside Story of the FIFA
Way by Bonita Mersiades
(Powderhouse Press)

Surfing for England
Our Lost Socceroos
by Jason Goldsmith

Encyclopedia of Matildas
Revised and Updated
by Andrew Howe
and Greg Werner

Encyclopedia of Socceroos
by Andrew Howe

'If I Started to Cry,
I Wouldn't Stop'
by Matthew Hall

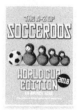

The A-Z of Socceroos –
World Cup Edition 2018
by Andrew Howe (with Ray
Gatt and Bonita Mersiades)

Playing for Australia
The First Socceroos,
Asia and the World Game
by Trevor Thompson

The World Cup Chronicles
31 Days that Rocked Brazil
by Jorge Knijnik

Chronicles of Soccer
in Australia – The
Foundation Years 1859 to
1949 by Peter Kunz

Support Your Local League,
A South-East Asian
Football Odyssey by
Antony Sutton

The Aboriginal Soccer Tribe
by John Maynard

Introducing
Jarrod Black
by Texi Smith
(Popcorn Press)

Jarrod Black
Hospital Pass
by Texi Smith
(Popcorn Press)

Jarrod Black
Guilty Party
by Texi Smith
(Popcorn Press)

Anna Black
This Girl can Play
by Texi Smith
(Popcorn Press)

The Time of
My Football Life
by David Picken

www.fairplaypublishing.com.au/shop

FAIRPLAY

PUBLISHING